:LL

NORTHWEST AREA DIRECTOR, PRISON FELLOWSHIP

WHEN
MOUNTAINS
DON'T MOVE
A TRUE STORY OF FAITH UNDER FIRE

DIANA
WEINBERGER

WHEN
MOUNTAINS
DON'T MOVE

A TRUE STORY OF FAITH UNDER FIRE

DIANA
WEINBERGER

FSP
FIRST STEPS
PUBLISHING

WHEN **MOUNTAINS** DON'T MOVE
A TRUE STORY of FAITH UNDER FIRE

by DIANA **WEINBERGER**

Second Printing © March 2018

Published by
First Steps Publishing
PO Box 571
Gleneden Beach, OR 97388
541-961-7641

Interior photos, cover image © Diana Weinberger
Cover photo "Mountain Road" by Pawel Nolbert / Unsplash.com
Cover photo "Woman in Handcuffs" by Lacie Figueiredo
Cover design, interior layout by Suzanne Fyhrie Parrott

ISBN - 978-1-937333-51-5 (pbk)
ISBN - 978-1-937333-52-2 (ebk)

10 9 8 7 6 5 4 3 2

PRAISE FOR

WHEN **MOUNTAINS** DON'T MOVE
A TRUE STORY OF FAITH UNDER FIRE

An intriguing and riveting real-life account of Diana's roller coaster journey through a nightmare of circumstances and choices. Diana's ability to paint a picture of her experience in prison had me feeling as though I were right there with her, in the jail cell. Her recorded thoughts are raw and transparent. It left me amazed at God's faithfulness and power to change the human heart and bring His children through unbelievable trials.

—Michael Hendricks
PASTOR, THE LIFE CHURCH, HAILEY, IDAHO

This book was hard to put down. It made me cry sometimes and laugh other times. I don't remember another book that ever affected me like that. Diana has a gift with words. I could feel her feelings. I would highly recommend this book!

—Shirley Alonzo,
LEGAL SECRETARY

Amazing story and an amazing woman! This book takes you from tears to laughter and back to tears again. Diana's story is gut-wrenching and very personal. Things you rarely even share with a best friend, Diana shares with the world. It's a reminder that God is always there for us even in our darkest hours. I will pass it on to my daughter and then read it again like I do all my favorite books.

—Doree Elam

What a triumphant story of redemption and God's intervention. I am deeply touched by the way Diana reveals God's character in so many facets, His mercy, His tenderness, His ability to answer prayer and to know your every need even before you ask. I believe that people who read this book will find themselves touched and challenged to walk with God in their own lives, and perhaps to remember Hebrews 13:3, "Remember those in prison, as if you were there yourself..."

—Fay Williams
CURRENTLY WITH YOUTH WITH A MISSION
FORMER M/V ANASTASIS LEADER
DIANA'S DISCIPLESHIP TRAINING SCHOOL
LEADER ABOARD THE ANASTASIS IN 1981

Diana writes with candid honesty about her journey through life—the good, the bad, and the ugly. This is a story of grace, of how someone can turn their life around by being real, by persevering, and by taking the time to listen, obey, and walk in humility with God. Diana demonstrates both the courage to do what is right, and the willingness to count the cost. This is a great read that I'm sure will be a blessing in your life. I know that it has blessed and challenged mine!

—Marie Tylander Perez
FORMER ACTIVITIES DEPARTMENT HEAD
M/V ANASTASIS

Hang on to your hat!! Diana shares a heart wrenching, vulnerable, and inspiring personal story sprinkled with humor and God's profound Word and strength. The transparency with which she writes is captivating. Thank you for sharing your journey of faith, forgiveness, redemption, and love!

—Julie Brown

I loved this book! I am a fellow court reporter, so I can relate to that part of the story. I am also a fellow Christian. I loved Diana's honesty about her troubled marriage and how, through praying and listening to God, she was able to forgive her husband and move forward through a very difficult time. She reveals how her husband, with God's help, was able to change his life. I was moved by the reminder that we must pray for people who have hurt us. It makes such a difference in our lives and in theirs. Wonderful book!

—Denise Schloder

I could hardly put the book down, and when I finished I couldn't wait to share it with others. Life can be full of hard choices and moments that take your breath away. I'm so glad Diana wrote her story for people to read and consider in their own lives. I'd recommend this to all my friends. A GREAT read!

—Teresa Lubovich

Thank you, Larry, Dana, and Bethany,
for believing in me and giving me the
freedom to write our story as it happened.

Amy, thank you for keeping me on track!
This book is complete because you were
with me throughout the journey.

Thank you, Dad, for giving my story a five-star review.

And to all the rest of my family with love.

Diana Weinberger

NOTE TO THE **READER**

This book is based on my recollections and pertinent sources. If others recall things differently, I apologize. This is my story as I remember it, with accounts of others as I understand them.

Songs played a vital role in my story, and so I have included some of them along the way. I have named the title and the artists for three of them: Keith Green (*When I hear the Praises Start*); Jason Crabb (*Let Mercy Hold You*); and my daughter Amy (*This is the Beginning*).

Apart from those songs, all song titles and lyrics in this book are the creation of this author. I have attempted to stay true to what the Lord was teaching me, even while honoring copyright laws. I've changed the words, but the *when* and the *where*, as well as the sentiments expressed, came to me just as I have written.

Within these pages, I quote Bible passages from the Amplified Bible (AMP), the New International Version (NIV), the New Living Translation (NLT), the New King James Version (NKJV), and The Message (MSG). Although I only had access to the Amplified Bible when I was in my cell, I have occasionally substituted different versions for ease of reading.

Finally, it is my hope that readers will find within these pages a story of *redemption*, rather than of *instruction*. Every person is unique; every circumstance is different. What was right for me may be completely wrong for another. Only God knows the road each should take.

The Good News is when we listen to Him, He is with us every step of the way.

That said, enjoy!
Diana Weinberger

CONTENTS

FOREWORD

Those words, written nearly 400 years ago, sound as though they were written for us today.

We live in a culture where many walk in a fog, trying to find their way through competing and conflicting worldviews. What really matters? Is there such a thing as truth? What values should determine our responses to life's challenges?

Life is not easy.

Even in the most ordered of worlds, unexpected circumstances take us places we never expected to go. We find ourselves facing situations we never anticipated; making choices we never imagined.

What happens when you make a decision that you immediately regret — one that stands in contradiction to all you have believed and stood for?

How do you move beyond that choice?

Where do you turn when life becomes surreal and there are no good or easy answers?

When Mountains Don't Move is a fascinating story told with stark transparency. In its pages, Diana Weinberger introduces us to dilemmas which at first seem improbable, yet were overwhelmingly real! Her life was turned upside down. Yet, in the midst of incredible pain and confusion, she had to make choices and take a stand. These choices ended up having devastating consequences.

Our worldview shapes our values, and our values shape our behavior. As Diana realized what was of paramount importance in her life, she also had to come to grips with what would be required to live out what she believed. Would she have the courage and tenacity to stand against the adversity she was facing?

A court reporter from a small Idaho community, Diana is very much like most of us: she is not rich, powerful, or famous. That is why this story is so profound; she's a real person who was confronted with extraordinary challenges.

Books like this are of great worth; they compel us to examine our own lives, values, and resolve, and ask us to consider how we would respond in similar circumstances. As we read, we identify attitudes and actions to avoid as well as attributes that we admire and want to manifest in our own lives.

This is a book that will challenge and inspire. It offers views into places and situations most of us never see and tells a story that is not easily forgotten.

I invite you to turn the page, and begin the journey . . .

—Mark Hubbell

NORTHWEST AREA DIRECTOR
PRISON FELLOWSHIP

PART **ONE**

THE CELL

They confronted me in the day of my calamity,

but the Lord was my strong support.

(Psalm 18:18 AMP)

CHAPTER **ONE**

COURT, DAY ONE: 10:45 A.M.

Handcuffs.

I hadn't imagined handcuffs.

I staggered a little, fear making my legs wobbly as I was told to stand up and face the wall. The bailiff pulled my arms behind me and clamped steely cold rings tightly around my wrists. Ouch! Could they do this? How could this be legal?

As I was led into the jury deliberation room and told to sit down, I found that my hands, bound behind me, prevented me from sitting properly. If I tried to move my elbows up, so I could sit without jamming my fingers into the seat, the cuffs dug in harder. My shoulders and wrists, now tweaked at impossible angles, stiffened miserably.

Pain.

I hadn't imagined pain, either.

I stared around the room, heart pounding. I was familiar with much of the courthouse, but having never been on a jury, this room was new. I wondered vaguely where was the bathroom. Didn't they have to provide a bathroom for jurors? I didn't really care, of course. For me, this room was merely the first stop; a way station *en route* to hell. (Okay, maybe that is an exaggeration. But it feels good to say it.)

Alone in that jury room, awaiting transport to the jail, I was overcome by a black, oppressive fear as I contemplated my future.

15

How would this end? When would I see my family again? And the more immediate concern: what would the next day hold? The next hour?

I'd barely slept the night before. I had far too many unknowns flying around in my head. This morning my husband Larry and I rose early, preparing ourselves for events that I had spent serious energy trying to avoid. All the months of loss, threats, and hard decisions – months also of forgiveness, strength, and hope – had brought us to this implausible state. Forced into this nightmare, I was unable to see where fear would end. Yet, I had arrived on my own two feet, quaking on the inside, but determined to stick to my plan.

This morning Larry had made me my favorite breakfast of scrambled egg whites and gluten-free toast. I had read my Bible, prayed, and committed this day to God. Our very future hung in the balance. Larry had patted my knee frequently throughout our drive to the courthouse, silently reassuring me.

Once inside, I had taken a seat in the front row of the audience section, while Larry made his way to the defense table. With my attorney at my side I had listened to the testimony of Sergeant Shybar, cringing as he recounted, in painful detail, the events of the evening of November 1, 2012. I'd felt queasy as the officer finished his testimony and left the witness stand. I had jumped a little when my attorney whispered into my ear, "We're on."

Handcuffs bit into me as I studied the empty chairs in the jury room and wondered, *Was that really only 15 minutes ago?*

I gazed about me and drew in a deep breath to steady myself. *I am not alone,* I told myself. *Jesus, You are here with me.* I tried to think of well-loved scriptures to recite to myself, but was too rattled to recall anything but Psalm 23, that first Psalm we learn as kids in Sunday School. In truth, it was probably more relevant for me now than it had ever been. I began to whisper it softly, closing my eyes and speaking from my heart to the Lord:

The Lord is my Shepherd, I shall not want.
He makes me to lie down in green pastures;
He leads me beside the still waters...
Yea, though I walk through the valley of the
shadow of death,
I will fear no evil; for You are with me.
(Ps. 23:1-4 NKJV)

My eyes flew open at the sound of a voice behind me. "Brave girl." Unable to turn around, I had no idea who would be saying that to me until my attorney came and sat on the table in front of me. He had warned me that this might happen, though he had thought it unlikely. He did have a plan in mind, however, in case the improbable became a reality. I knew he disagreed with the Court's decision, but he smiled slightly, trying to encourage me. Promising to visit me tomorrow, he left. Alone again, my thoughts swirled.

How had this happened?

I was a lifelong Christian. Not perfect by any stretch, mind you. I'd made a lot of mistakes. Whoppers. Having spent 13 years on the mission field with Youth With A Mission (YWAM), I had sidelined my relationship with the Lord when I returned home. It wasn't long before I gave up on a floundering marriage, and divorced.

Ever faithful, God had sought me out and drawn me back into a relationship with Him. I was now almost fifteen years into a second marriage; I had a wonderful church home and was a student at the church's Bible school; I was committed to honest living and hard work; I was the adoring mother of two grown daughters; and the fanatical, picture-waving, Skype-addicted grandmother of two young grandsons.

Now, after years of trying to obey the Lord in all things, and do right even when it hurt, I was going to jail.

But even if you suffer for doing what is right,
God will reward you for it. So don't worry or
be afraid of their threats.
(1 Peter 3:14 NLT)

CHAPTER **TWO**

I knew three men who, years before, had faced incarceration for the sake of doing right. One was Don Stephens, founder of Mercy Ships. Before it became known as Mercy Ships, it was a ministry of Youth With A Mission, fondly called YWAM (Why-Wam) by those involved with it. Another was Alan Williams, a man near and dear to many. He helped lead the work and the crew of YWAM's ship, which was purchased in 1978 and was undergoing repairs in Greece. The third was a wonderful Greek man named Costas Macris, who was of invaluable help and friendship to the ship ministry.

In his book, *Trial By Trial*, Don Stephens recounts the story of how, in 1984, a Greek court found himself, Alan and Costas guilty of proselytism. In plain English, they were charged with converting a young Greek man to Christianity. How could this be? Greece was a cradle of Christianity. The New Testament had, in fact, been written in Greek.

The truth was that there remained on the books a single law that dated from an earlier dictatorship in Greece. The mother of the young convert, disliking the changes in her son, extracted that one law from the archives and used it to charge the men. They were found guilty and sentenced to three and a half years in a Greek prison.

They appealed and were allowed to remain free while their appeal made its way through to the higher court. Years later, the appellate court overturned the convictions. This wonderful outcome cannot, however, downplay the personal battle each man had walked through as he faced imprisonment for the sake of the Gospel.

As I faced my own incarceration, I couldn't help but remember back to that story and those men who had given their lives into God's hands, even as they knew they might be called upon to suffer for doing what was right.

Now I was in a similar situation, only, for me, it had gone the other way, and I was heading to a jail cell. My small story does not compare in magnitude to the larger one I have just recounted, but from my perspective it was pretty serious.

In 1984, when those men faced not only a public trial but also a trial of their faith, I was twenty-two years old. You might ask how I knew about these Greek proceedings, half a world away from my hometown in Southern California.

Well...

* * *

January 1981. I'd graduated from high school six months earlier, celebrated my 18th birthday in August, cast my first vote in a presidential election in November 1980, and was now on my way to Greece. My friends and family in Southern California had had only a few weeks to adjust to my decision to quit my job, sell my car, and head to a little port outside of Athens with my sister Dana, bound for a ship that was anchored in Eleusis (E-lef-sis) Bay.

The vessel was the M/V (Motor Vessel) *Anastasis*, a retired Italian passenger/cargo ship. She was unique in that she could house hundreds of people, yet she also boasted four huge cargo holds, not the norm in modern cruise lines. Such holds could contain food, equipment, medical and building supplies, anything useful in bringing aid to areas where it was needed.

The *Anastasis* (Greek for Resurrection) had been purchased at a scrap price in Italy, and then towed to where it was now being refurbished, top to bottom, by an all-volunteer crew. The crew was comprised of approximately two hundred people who lived aboard full time, and the name of the game was *work*. The ship was a mess when YWAM had first acquired it, and a great deal of work was already underway to make it habitable and seaworthy, but there was a long way yet to go.

In addition to willing laborers, the ship was staffed with licensed and vastly experienced seamen, including Captain Ben Applegate and Chief Engineer John Brignall. The immediate goal was to clean, repair and ready the ship to begin its ministry of providing many kinds of relief to people in need all around the world. It was also to have a fully functional hospital on board.

The fact that I was traveling to the ship with my older sister was a miracle in itself, as she was my lifelong tormenter-in-chief. My young life had been shaped under Dana's domination and criticism, and I carried a lot of fear and a dreadful self-image with me as I approached adulthood. I couldn't know then how my ingrained responses to heavy-handedness would impact some of the most important relationships in my life.

By the time we were traveling to Greece, Dana had been with YWAM for about eight months. When she came home for a brief visit, she was a *changed* person, which really caught my attention. Her new persona was barely recognizable. She was humble, thoughtful, kind. Whatever had happened to her, during her stint with YWAM, had utterly transformed her. She had even written me a letter of apology months earlier, asking my forgiveness for all she had put me through as we were growing up. When I saw her in person, I knew I was seeing God's transforming power at work. And I knew I wanted what she had.

Dana and I flew to Athens with Eric, a young man from church. Our route took us from Southern California to New York, where we had a very lengthy layover. We entertained ourselves by pretending we had New York accents and trying to mimic all the intercom announcements. Everything was new and exciting, especially for me, as I had not traveled much.

After New York, we had a nine-hour flight to Rome, and from there it was two more hours to Athens International Airport, where the ship's van was awaiting our arrival.

We were delayed when Customs wouldn't allow Eric's drum set into the country. It was a valuable drum set, its arrival highly anticipated by the *Anastasis* crew. I wasn't included in the negotiations, but after an hour or two, the officials agreed to release the drums, provided they went straight to the ship and nowhere else.

By the time we departed it was early evening, and the outside air was chilly. I burrowed deeply into my coat even as a brisk wind seemed to blow frigid air right through me. We were all thankful to load our stuff into the van and head off. As it was already getting dark, I was unable to make out very much on that first ride from Athens to little Eleusis. What I *could* see was all very foreign to me, and I marveled as our driver wended his way with effortless familiarity through the streets, avoiding pedestrians, mule-drawn carts and other drivers who didn't heed a single lane line.

It was when we got to Eleusis that the adventure really began, though. The brisk wind was closer to a full-blown squall near the sea, even in the protected bay. The ship was anchored out in the middle of the bay, and the only way to get there was by launch: a boat designed to carry people and their belongings out to ships and neighboring islands.

Once our luggage was stowed safely away in the launch's cabin, we stepped onto the boat as it rocked and bumped up against the dock pilings. The poor weather couldn't dampen my enthusiasm, but even so, Dana told me to go on inside the cabin, where it would be warmer. The cabin was enclosed on three sides, with the aft end open to the elements. As I sank down onto one of the bench seats, I could see the captain throw the ropes ashore and climb into the wheelhouse that dominated most of the stern. From my enclosed position, I would not be able to see much of the journey.

As we left the security of the harbor, the weather hit us head on, and the launch charged through the whitecaps, pitching violently as she powered ahead. Dana, who was with me in the cabin, occasionally rose to peer through the small, steamy windows, and after about 15 minutes she told me to join her. In spite of the storm tossing us about, I managed to lean on the cabin's bulkhead and squint into the darkness outside. We were approaching some lights, but that was all I could make out.

"There she is!" said Dana excitedly. "But we're not gonna be able to use the A Deck entrance in this weather."

I didn't know what she meant, but it sounded a trifle ominous.

Our launch captain was a salty Greek sailor if ever there was one, with his seaman's cap cocked to one side, a three-day stubble on his face, and a pipe dangling from one side of his mouth. He hadn't said much yet, but now he was directing us to come up out of the cabin and prepare to board the ship. He spoke no English, and we spoke no Greek, but he got his message across.

When I stepped out of the cabin's protective interior, the storm and the spray from the boat's bow hit me full in the face. But now I could see her!!! I'd been dreaming of this moment, and there she was, the *Anastasis!*

She was immense!

But wait! She was moving in the storm, too, her 522-foot vastness heaving away from us even as the captain reversed the launch's engine to slow our approach.

And Dana was right. The ship's gangway was not our destination. In this weather, the launch could easily smack against the platform, damaging both it and the smaller boat. As the white ship loomed large above me, I could see people in an open entryway, awaiting our arrival. While this entrance was lower on the ship, and thus nearer to the water than the A Deck opening, it didn't have a gangway. Instead, it had a cargo net made from thick rope, which had been secured inside and draped out of the door so that it hung flush with the ship's hull. I soon learned that we were meant to climb it, up and into the ship.

You've got to be kidding me! was all I could think. *This is impossible!* The cargo net was far too high to reach from the deck of the launch. But, wait! When a large swell raised the launch up, the latticed ropes were, just for a moment, within reach.

Dana told me to go first. She wanted to be sure I made it before boarding herself. The guys just inside the ship's doorway were shouting instructions to me. "Hold on tight, and wait until we say 'go.' And when we say 'go,' GO! Reach out and grab the net, and don't hesitate!"

The ship's white hull heaved away again, rolling to expose the green paint that normally hid below the water line. Unperturbed, our launch captain edged close to the ship once more, and he motioned for me to get ready. We waited as the swells buffeted us about, and at last a huge wave rolled beneath the launch and lifted us up higher than ever. They all cried, "GO!"

I lunged wildly for the cargo net, grabbing hold with my hands and feet even as the launch's deck fell away again. The captain maneuvered back from the ship so that another large wave wouldn't crush my legs between her hull and the ship's side.

I tried scrambling up the vertical incline, and it was then that I remembered: I had no upper body strength! My eighteen-year-old, one-hundred-ten-pound self should have done more push-ups! The wind was blowing my hair into my face, and the rain beat into me as I clung to the ropes like a drowned spider. Effort!! Move a foot up and use that to push yourself up a little until you can get a higher handhold. Okay, now do it again.

I was absolutely exhausted, with no idea how far I had yet to go, when two strong pairs of hands reached under my arms and hauled me the rest of the way up and into B Deck Reception.

I didn't know it then, but I'd arrived aboard what was to be my home for the next ten years.

CHAPTER **THREE**

JURY ROOM, DAY ONE: 11:00 A.M.

My reveries were interrupted when the bailiff entered the jury room and motioned for me to follow him. Upper body strength wouldn't help me now. There were no friendly crewmen at the ready to help me out. I was alone.

The outside air shocked me. It was a warm day for March in my small Idaho town, edging up to an expected high of 61 degrees. I looked around in bewilderment as the bailiff ordered me to wait while he secured the door from which we'd just exited the courthouse. The *back* door. Cars drove past. I could see people across the street, walking along, going about their business. Ordinary citizens casually enjoying their freedom, drawn outside by the mild, near-spring temperature. People with errands to run, destinations to gain and lives to manage. People who were not headed to *jail*.

As we left the courthouse building, the bailiff pointed to his cruiser, parked only a few feet away, while speaking on his walkie-talkie to some unseen person who was walking him through the routine of bringing someone *in*. How could that someone be *me*?

For what seemed like the millionth time, I asked myself, *How can they compel me to testify against my husband? What about spousal privilege?* My attorney had tried to explain to me that there was a loophole in the law, but at this moment I couldn't make sense of it.

Terror rose up within me like a suffocating force that originated in my chest, squeezing the breath out of me, and initiating a thrumming *boom, boom, boom* in my head.

The bailiff opened the cruiser's back passenger door and instructed me to watch my head. I looked at the seat I was to occupy. Had I not been in my current state of near panic, my first thought might have been, *Seriously?* A hardened panel separated the front seat from the back leaving barely any leg room for back seat occupants. There were only a few inches between the board and the rear seat cushion.

There is no dignity in arrest. I looked at the cramped space and realized my hope of entering the car with some remnant of poise was a pipe dream. I am five-foot-nine, and remember, my hands were cuffed behind me. Sticking a leg in the car, following with my body and gracefully pulling in the other leg wasn't going to happen. I decided there was nothing left but to turn my back to the car and sit down, ducking my head as best I could. Then after lifting one foot and then the other into the car, and now I was sideways on the seat with my knees sticking out the door at least half a foot. There was no way to shut the door. What now?

They make it look so easy on TV. A cop arrests a person, tells him to watch his head and places a hand on said noggin, just to prevent bumps. The person seats him or herself in the car, unhappy, but not squashed in half. I couldn't guess what my next move was supposed to be, but the bailiff was waiting, so in desperation I brought my knees up to my chest and rolled my entire self around toward the center of the car, further brutalizing my steel-clad wrists against the seat belt buckle beneath me. My left leg remained bent upon the seat, but I managed to squeeze my right foot down onto the floor.

There are seat belt laws in Idaho, and the Sheriff's department does its best to ensure the safety of persons being transported. I thought surely we'd waive this small detail since the buckle was under me and I could do nothing to assist in its retrieval. To my astonishment, however, the bailiff was now leaning in, reaching around my tangle of arms, legs and torso, determined that I would be belted. He found said buckle, retrieving it from its embarrassing location, straightened up and closed the door.

Needless to say, the ride to the jail was dreadful. The Sheriff's cruiser was silent but for the bailiff and his communications with the afore-mentioned faceless person. "Transporting one adult female," he spoke into his walkie-talkie, and the voice spoke back to him, confirming that he was transporting one adult female and informing him that he would receive further instructions upon our arrival at the facility. This was all business as usual for them, while I sat in the back, ordering myself not to hyperventilate, pass out, or throw up.

Get a grip, Diana. Calm your breathing.

The location of our county lock-up was well known to me, not because I'd ever been arrested, but because for the last year and a half I'd been visiting the place every Sunday afternoon, along with my friend and ministry partner, Patty. We'd been granted permission to hold church services every week, and we brought worship and Bible messages to the ladies there. This jail houses both short-term and long-term inmates, some locals, others "holds" from other counties, and even some awaiting a prison bunk to become available. We loved these inmates and sometimes managed to get over there during the week to visit and try to bolster their spirits.

The guards were bound to recognize me.

Our town is small, the jail only about five-minutes from the courthouse. I had been hoping for a delay before being escorted inside as a prisoner, but when the bailiff was advised to wait in the car outside the back door, my nerves frayed even more. Maybe they were booking some other unfortunate soul. Maybe the guards were on a break or doing rounds.

As the minutes ticked by, questions roared through my head:

Where would they put me? I knew parts of the jail's interior, but I'd never been to the blocks.

Maybe in a little while I'd be among people I knew. Maybe they'd put me in the block that housed five or six of my current church attendees. Maybe I'd be placed among strangers. Maybe, maybe, maybe…One thing was for sure: I would soon encounter people who would be surprised to see me on this side of the wall.

As we waited, my musings took me down the road of remembering how all of this had started. My second marriage had had its share of problems, but no one could have foreseen trouble of this magnitude on our horizon. Events had snowballed into an avalanche of consequences: a personal confession, the barrel of a gun, arrest, separation, impending divorce. Surely our experience of forgiveness, redemption, and restoration should have saved us, but instead we faced fear, flight, a courtroom and my subsequent arrest.

I asked myself, was there a single event about which we could say, *But for this or that, things would be different?* Probably not. Nothing is so cut and dried. I did wonder, though, what life would have looked like if I'd never gone to that motorcycle lesson…

CHAPTER **FOUR**

By the time I was on my way to jail, my husband and I had been married for almost fifteen years, and while not all of it was great, not all of it was bad, either. We had survived a huge move of ourselves and our business to a new state, where we had bought a house and settled in to earn a living, pay bills, and have a good time when and where we could find it.

My husband bought a Harley.

Larry really loved that bike, but soon learned that to ride it legally in Idaho he would have to go to motorcycle school and get certified. I don't know why, but I found myself offering to take the course with him.

This was not my typical style. If ever anyone looked like a meek, indoorsy-librarian type, it was me. A super-conservative court reporter, I was far more comfortable with my steno machine than with outdoor pursuits like motorcycle riding.

Scariest thing ever, that course. They brought out these tall bikes that could go either street or dirt, and they were impossible for me to master. I didn't know Thing One about motorcycles. I understood shifting gears manually, but I'd only ever done that in cars. I knew if I stalled a motorcycle I could end up on the ground. Those tall, jumpy bikes could have stopped my weekend before it got started.

Fortunately, we weren't graded on anything that first afternoon. We just waddled the bikes around, getting used to the friction zone between throttle and clutch, starting and stopping.

Then we were required to get on the beasts and do figure eights around the parking lot, being sure to Turn Our Heads and look in the direction we wanted the bikes to go. We learned a lot about Turning Our Heads. On a motorcycle, the bike follows your eyes. What you're looking at is what your bike is aiming for. It's no good leaning and steering and hoping you'll make a turn. You will succeed only if you Turn Your Head and Fix Your Eyes on your intended destination.

I was doing okay, Turning My Head and minding my business, when a guy, who apparently hadn't Turned His Head at all, plowed into me. The instructors adamantly blamed the other guy as they scraped me off the ground, but that nearly ended my motorcycle-riding career right there. If someone's going to knock you off your bike in a class setting, what on earth would it be like in real life?

The instructors were eager for me, their one female student, to succeed, so they encouraged and pleaded and cajoled and said if I would "only get back on the bike for a couple of minutes" the day would be over and I would be allowed to return the next day. Apparently, you needed to finish Day One before you could experience Day Two. Falling and refusing to "get back on the horse" wasn't considered completing Day One. So I pulled myself together, got back on the bike, made sure the Non-Head-Turning rider was nowhere nearby and finished out the day.

Next day, the instructors had a surprise for me. They told me that they did have this one other bike, a little thing that looked like a baby Harley, no tall dirt bike component to it at all. A little 125 something-or-other. Did I want to try it?

Where on earth was this thing yesterday? It was my new best friend. I rode that motorcycle around that parking lot all day, through cones, through sudden swerves-and-stops. I managed to lock up the rear wheel and skid when told to, and I achieved the dubious honor of being the only student to make it through our wide, accelerating turn without reducing or adjusting speed once. I Turned My Head.

By Sunday afternoon I had passed my motorcycle course and was cleared to get the appropriate endorsement on my license. I was officially allowed to take my new prowess out on the highways and byways of our fair state. And I'd never even gotten out of second gear.

I went on from that scholarly success to purchase my very own Harley. It was a pretty blue Sportster 1200. We lowered it, got an Easy Clutch and did some of the custom things that every bike owner will tell you are fundamental. Since I did not have powerfully strong hands, the Easy Clutch made it possible for me to shift gears.

What I couldn't do, however, was start, stop, turn, lean, or otherwise control the thing well at all.

In spite of this, I managed not to fall off. I missed a turn once while we were practicing; instead of turning left onto our quiet practice street, I headed straight across the street and into high desert brush. I learned that I could use my fear of falling to advantage as I turned the bike, sliding dangerously in the loose dirt, and willing my way back onto the paved surface. Now heading in the right direction, and worried that adrenalin would make me drop the bike if I stopped, I puttered home without further incident.

Later that evening, Larry said he knew why I had ended up off the road, in the sagebrush and sand, and why I'd nearly torn myself and my new bike to pieces. "You didn't Turn Your Head," he observed dryly.

Jail Journal Entry:

I turned my head now, and saw that the bay door had opened at last, and the Sheriff's cruiser was pulling neatly inside. A ball like hot lead dropped to the bottom of my stomach as the bay door rolled down behind us, sealing us in.

CHAPTER **FIVE**

COUNTY JAIL, DAY ONE: 11:10 A.M.

A sergeant named Grizz approached the car, and the bailiff got out and handed him my paperwork. Grizz was a big guy, scary looking when not smiling, and he never smiled at work. I'd had limited contact with him on a prior occasion when Patty and I brought a box full of Bibles to the jail library. At the time, I had thought he was a good man, doing a tough job where a stern countenance was required and where his height and obvious strength were no doubt advantageous.

Right now Grizz was examining my paperwork with a frown, and I thought I heard him saying, "Are you kidding me?" As he read the paper further, I was able to catch a few more words as he murmured incredulously: "...hereby remanded...contempt of court..."

When he finished reading, he spoke into his walkie-talkie, summoning help from somewhere within the facility. This time I was sure I heard him clearly as he said into the speaker, "We're going to be handling this one a little differently."

The bailiff leaned once more into the car, reaching around the mess that was me and then, unfastening the buckle, slid the shoulder strap back into place. Getting out of the car was slightly easier because now I knew the knees-to-chest maneuver that would be required to bring my legs doorward. I set my feet on the smooth concrete of the jail's back bay floor. I didn't think I'd be able to bring myself to a stand from this low and awkward position, being unable to use my hands. But the bailiff took my arm and helped raise me up.

Here I was at last. My heart started thudding anew.

I had never experienced anything like this before. I had tried to live my life in such a manner that I would never find myself in the custody of law enforcement. I not only had never robbed a bank, but I'd never so much as hugged a controversial tree. I couldn't know what to expect, nor did I know what "handling this one a little differently" could possibly mean. I never did find out.

Grizz directed me to a painted square near a wall and told me to wait. Soon a female guard arrived and made me place my hands on the wall so she could search me.

Have you ever been searched? If you have, you'll understand how degrading it is. If you have not, trust me, you do not want the experience. I had no pockets to empty, but she patted me down thoroughly and shook my bra to make sure I wasn't smuggling anything in. Yes, I was wearing the bra as she did this.

She told me to lean over, shake my head and run my fingers through my hair, proving there was nothing lurking beneath the locks. So much for my hairdo. I'd been so hoping to look my best for my mugshot.

At least they had removed the handcuffs.

I was wearing a long green sweater shell over a slim black turtleneck and yoga-like black stretch pants. I was horrified when they took my sweater away from me. I try to dress modestly, and I instantly became a 50-year-old woman in a black Jack LaLanne outfit. I felt indecent, exposed.

They also took my glasses, though I told them I needed them. Now I was more frightened than ever. I had been counting on being able to read, at least.

I was then taken to the main booking area and handed a large, lidded tote.

"There are sheets in there," commented the female guard, gesturing to the tote. She then led me to a cell and said, "In here." My tote and I entered the cell.

A pastor friend of mine, who was arrested when he was young, once told me, "There's just something terrible that goes up your spine when they shut that cell door behind you."

I couldn't have said it better myself. When the door slammed shut, that terrible thing crawled up my spine and even made my teeth hurt.

My cell was roughly eight feet by eight feet; one side housed metal bunk beds and the other dominated by a small metal sink and toilet. No toilet seat. Along the back wall stood a solid concrete bench, built in seamlessly with no cracks or crannies in which to hide anything. All the surfaces were smooth, rounded, and…cold.

The cell door was made of heavy steel, with a small, toughened glass window in the upper half, and no bars. I was entirely enclosed.

Trembling, I stood in the center of the cell. Nothing can prepare a human being for such an experience. Many people *have* experienced it, but nothing prepares you.

This morning I had awoken in my own home. I had showered and dressed in privacy, eaten a nice breakfast, read my Bible, and readied myself for the day in relative comfort and freedom. Was that only a few hours ago? I knew it was around 11:00 a.m. when we'd left the courthouse. What did that make it now? Eleven-thirty? I looked around to see. No clock. *No clock???*

Undiluted panic welled up within me. No clock! How long would I be here? Weeks? Months? And never knowing the time?

I stepped toward the rear wall, set my tote on the concrete bench and myself beside the tote. The bench was ice cold. My yoga-like pants did nothing to stop the penetrating chill. I started shivering as I sat there, waiting.

Suddenly I was aware of a camera, up in the corner of my cell, observing my every move.

Terror! I was shut away from the rest of the world, utterly alone except for those who, by virtue of their job, would view me as a last name at best, a number at worst. The people who cared about me were out of reach.

What was Larry doing now? Had anyone brought my Bible? Would this go on for months? When would I be moved to one of the blocks?

I'd love to say I prayed as I waited, bravely facing whatever might come while quoting Scripture and exerting great faith. But the truth is I was frightened, claustrophobic. I just sat on that freezing bench and stared in disbelief at my surroundings until my teeth started chattering and my muscles began tensing up from shock and chill. I have no idea how long I sat there: an hour, two?

Larry had told me that when he'd been arrested they had given him a sweatshirt. What wouldn't I give for a sweatshirt. Why hadn't I already been issued one?

At last I realized I should do more than sit. I needed to begin taking stock, see what was what. I noticed an intercom button near the door. I was familiar with these buttons from my church visits to this facility, and I knew if I hit the button I'd probably speak to a person. But should I? Did I have any right to make a request? I felt so isolated and forgotten that I feared even speaking, for fear I'd be rebuked and told to sit back down.

Come on, Diana! What has God been telling you for the past three years? I reminded myself of what I had written in my journal, time and again, fully believing the Holy Spirit was instructing me:

BE STRONG AND COURAGEOUS!

I quoted Joshua 1:9 to myself: "Be strong and courageous! Do not be afraid or discouraged. For the Lord your God is with you wherever you go."

Why be afraid of pushing a little button? I gathered my courage, went to the intercom, pushed the button and waited. A voice responded, "Control."

"Uh…I'm wondering if I could have my glasses and a sweat-shirt?"

The voice responded, "I'll pass your request on."

I thanked the voice and turned to face my cell. Suddenly I noticed my tote, sitting on the concrete bench. I removed the lid and discovered that all this time I'd been sitting next to wealth! Right there on top was a blanket. I pulled it out and wrapped myself in it. I sat down on the bench and let my head drop, closing my eyes and reveling in the warmth it afforded. Then, curious, I glanced inside the tote again. Another blanket, and the aforementioned sheets.

At that moment my cell door opened and there stood Grizz, holding a sweatshirt. I eagerly approached and he handed it to me, along with my glasses. I thanked him, and as he was about to leave, I again gathered my courage. "Someone is bringing me a Bible. Am I allowed to have it?"

He seemed to reflect and then nodded.

Thank You, Lord. I prayed inwardly.

Once more finding my voice, I asked, "Is this where I'm stay-ing?"

Another nod and he shut the door. I was alone once more.

Staying here? Inconceivable. Who could stay in such a place? And why did I have to stay alone? I had thought maybe I could bear this situation if I could be around other women. But stay alone in this awful cell? With no clock and nothing at all to do?

The shock of my predicament left me breathless.

I slumped down onto one of the metal bunks, but popped right back up again. A thin foam mat did nothing to soften the hard metal beneath it. And where was the pillow? Only a little lump, oh-so-slightly higher than the rest of the mat, represented this luxury. It hurt just to sit on this torture rack. Who could sleep here?

I'd certainly faced stark living conditions before. On more than one occasion my quarters had been cramped, encased in cinder block, metal and cement. While serving overseas with YWAM, I had endured tiny, cold spaces, and unusual places where I couldn't speak the language and didn't get enough to eat. None of that had seemed a hardship because I had chosen to serve, and was free to come and go as I liked.

That had been twenty-four years before...

CHAPTER **SIX**

While my first husband Bill and I were living aboard the M/V Anastasis, we were privileged to help lead two of the Discipleship Training Schools that were held on the ship. YWAM refers to its Discipleship Training School as a DTS, and no one is allowed to join YWAM long term unless he or she first attends one. A DTS will typically include a lecture phase of three months, and an outreach phase of two months.

We were in our outreach phase and had taken our students, 90 percent of whom were women, to a campground in the Dominican Republic, which was where the ship was currently docked. Our outreach consisted primarily of drama, with our students performing skits in market places and wherever else we were allowed to bring them. We followed the skits with testimony and invitations to speak with people. The ship was nearby, with staff performing medical and dental procedures, teaching safe agricultural practices, providing practical help in many ways to the local population.

Our group was housed for this outreach in a small campground comprised of several buildings, one of which housed the team leaders. Bill and I, along with our two daughters, six-year-old Amy and four-year-old Bethany, were, therefore, housemates with another couple named Phil and Debbi, as well as another wonderful woman, my friend Donna.

It was a tiny little place, with a "front room," if you will, just inside the entryway. A few steps through that room lead you to two doors, one on the left and one on the right, each leading to respective sleeping quarters on opposite sides of the house. Take the door to the left and you find the two bedrooms and bathroom that became my family's temporary home. The room on the right held another bathroom, Donna's bedroom, and, a little further, the small room that Phil and Debbi shared.

The front room had a cement floor and walls of cinder block. Its furnishings consisted of a card table and three folding chairs, nothing else. It was on one of these folding chairs that I sat in the wee hours of one morning, waiting for my mug of water to heat with my heating coil. It was early enough that it was still dark outside. My Bible and journal were lying on the table, and once I had added some instant coffee to my boiled mug of water, I settled in for my morning time with the Lord.

The weather had been sweltering, but with the window louvers open, and considering the early hour of the morning, I found it quite pleasant as I sipped my coffee, opened my Bible and began to read.

It wasn't long before a scratching noise coming from the window disturbed me. Curious, I looked up just in time to see the nose of a huge rat poking through a hole in the window screen. He squeezed himself between the open louvers and plopped down onto the floor. He seemed surprised to see me. Not alarmed, but definitely surprised. I had never seen anything like him, menacing and evil of countenance, as large as a cat.

My hand and coffee cup had frozen in mid-air. I carefully set the mug on the table and laid my Bible beside it. Clearly, this rat had been here before. He no doubt had a plan that included roaming through the sleeping quarters of my family and friends. I couldn't let that happen. Keeping both eyes fixed on him, I stood and slowly sidled over to first one hallway door and then the other, closing both doors. I was now alone in the room with a huge island rodent.

I could have escaped by the front door, exiting into the still-dark morning, but if I did, he would have the run of the house. Glancing around, I saw a broom leaning in the corner by the entryway. Never taking my eyes off my unexpected intruder, I moved steadily toward my weapon, reaching for the broom handle. Got it!

I pulled the door open and stepped aside, hoping he'd want to make a quick get-away. But this rat had established the run of this campground long before our arrival, and he was fearless. He moved away from the windows, which were directly beside the front entrance, and scurried rapidly to each of the doors leading to the hallway. Unable to push either one open, he ran under the card table, turning his beady eyes toward me. The table didn't afford much protection for him, and I could see him calculating. Wielding my broom, I moved away from the front door, determined that the only one who would be out the door and into the dark would be the intruder under the table.

I stomped my foot, trying to unsettle the beast and get him moving. We were eye-to-eye, thin house broom against sharp teeth and claws. Twitching his whiskers, we squared off.

I have no idea how the house slept through what ensued. Mr. Rat did not intend to go quietly, and with every charge he made, whether toward the hall, a corner or back under the table, I parried with my broomstick. I batted him silly with the bristled end, scooting him one way and then the other, trying mightily to gain enough purchase on his flank so I could sail him through the air and out the door. But he was cunning, wriggly and fast, and I began sweating in earnest as our dance continued.

I'm happy to report that, in the end, the victory was mine, as with one last blast of effort I shoved him out the door and shut it firmly behind him.

Whew! Overheated, I stood still for a few moments, relishing the cooler outside air as it flowed in through the windows. *The windows!!!* They were still open, and every one of them had a large hole in the screen. He'd be back!

Replacing the broom in the corner, I focussed my attention on the windows, turning the crank on each, closing all of the louvers. The room instantly boiled over with heat; far better than rats running rampant.

My coffee wasn't cold due to the overall warm temperature of the room, but it wasn't hot either. Nonetheless, I picked it up and sat still, trying to calm myself. I waited and waited for a scratching sound and wondered if the metal louvers would be strong enough to keep him at bay. Thankfully, he'd had enough for this time and didn't return.

* * *

My wee hour adventure with the rat initiated what has become a memorable saga in camp life on that outreach. My husband Bill dubbed him Alfredo Garcia, and could frequently be heard proclaiming, in a mock accent, "I want the head of Alfredo Garcia!" He had no doubt seen the 1974 movie of a similar title, and it had stuck with him. Bill was determined to kill Alfredo, not only because he was terrorizing our camp, but because Bill had seen some runny droppings and believed the rat to be diseased.

There were various sightings, followed by screams, but Alfredo successfully eluded Bill's grasp. We all sweltered in our concrete and cinder block houses and dorms, unwilling to leave windows open. Everything came to a hilarious head when, as we were all seated at long tables in the dining hall, our co-leader, Phil, cried out, "Ladies! Lift your legs!" We didn't know the reason, but we all lifted our feet off the ground. Except for one poor woman. She wore an ankle brace on one leg and couldn't raise that leg up. As Alfredo scurried beneath us, all she could do was sit in wide-eyed disbelief as he scampered up and over her immobilized ankle.

A day or so later Bill's rat trap yielded one dead rat, and everyone celebrated, making a show of throwing some palm leaves and the rat on a small barbeque. We took a picture and opened our windows again.

Weeks later, when it was time to clean up and leave the campground, we found out that, while Alfredo may well have been diseased, whatever plague he carried probably wasn't the cause of his runny excrement. Checking to make sure all the rooms were empty of our belongings, I discovered, under one of the beds, a half-eaten bar of chocolate-flavored Ex-Lax.

CHAPTER **SEVEN**

COUNTY JAIL, DAY ONE:
APPROXIMATELY 1:30 P.M.

Dragging my mind back to the present, I realized that, as grim as my circumstances are, at least there were no rats. My cell was clean, and for that I was grateful.

What would my YWAM friends think if they could see me now? I snaked my arms into my sweatshirt, pulling the hood out of the way as I poked my head through. I was glad Grizz had brought a nice big one for me. Once I had it on, it fell halfway to my knees. I felt decent again.

I'd forgotten my tote exploration when Grizz came to the door. It seemed unlikely that I'd find much of a pillow there, but I decided to investigate anyway, just in case. Nope. In addition to the second blanket and the sheets, I found a cup and a spork, an odd little plastic utensil shaped like a spoon but having four tiny prongs on the end to serve as a fork. I also discovered a baggie containing two tubes of some clear substances, a small comb, and a toothbrush…well, sort of a toothbrush. Maybe two inches long, a disproportionate section contained the bristles. I understood the precaution here. Anyone who has watched *The Shawshank Redemption* knows that a real toothbrush can be made into a lethal weapon.

Since I now had my glasses, I could see that one of the tubes claimed to be shampoo. One of the girls in our jail church service had said she avoided this stuff. There was no conditioner. That may sound like a luxury, but with my head of hair, had I washed it with harsh shampoo without anything to soften it back up, it would turn into an unbrushable Brillo pad.

The other tube read Toothpaste—that I would certainly make use of.

The small plastic cup had its obvious purpose, but I was at a loss as I held up the small comb. I had hair clips bigger and toothier than that comb. What on earth was I going to do with that?

But what is this? I pulled out a small composition notebook. Holding my breath, I moved aside the blanket and smile at the small, rubbery pen.

To my non-writing friends, it might be difficult to properly explain what that notebook and pen meant to me. They were wealth unimaginable. The notebook was paperback and the pen was small and floppy, but it didn't matter. I could *write!* I had been sitting right next to this treasure trove for *hours,* and hadn't known it existed. My main priority in digging through my tote was that I was cold, and hoped to find help within it contents. I never dreamed I would actually be provided pen and paper.

When I write, I am not alone. I've filled numerous journals throughout my lifetime, and their pages contain what I can only call my conversations with God. I write to Him, and He makes His Word come alive to me, and then I write down the portion that speaks to me at any given moment. Writing helps me to express my relationship with my Lord. Knowing I would be able to pen my side of the conversation brought comfort to my terrified soul and frozen body in a way nothing else could have, with the exception of my Bible. No sign of that, yet.

Well, there could be no thought of writing while sitting on this oh-so-cold concrete bench. I eyed the lower bunk again. What if I took the mat from the upper bunk and made a double mat down below? Couldn't hurt. I later found out that was a no-

no, but hey, I was new. I didn't know the rules. So I doubled the mattresses and set about making up the bed. Lower sheet, upper sheet, one blanket, the first blanket still being wrapped firmly around my chilled self.

I tucked the blanket in all around, folded the top sheet neatly over the top three inches of the blanket, and stood back to survey my handiwork. Homey it was not, but the cell was slightly less stark with a made-up bed. I returned all the other items to the tote, withdrew the pen and paper, grabbed the big flat tote lid, tucked my blanket more securely around myself and sat down on the lower bunk, pulling my head in carefully and propping myself against the wall behind it. I placed the lid on my lap to form a perfect writing desk. I felt better as I began to write, describing my circumstances and whereabouts.

I hadn't finished even one page when the cell door opened and there stood Grizz, holding out my Bible. I scrambled up spouting numerous Thank Yous, as I clutched the large, delicious paperback like the life preserver I knew it to be. Riches! Christmas! A treasure chest, right here in my hands. I had purchased this very Bible just in case...

People thought I was crazy to have bought this paperback Bible in case of incarceration. "Overly dramatic." I'd heard it again and again: "No one is going to put you in jail, Diana." But I knew unspeakable comfort as I held that Bible in my hands, and I knew it had to have been the Lord Himself Who had encouraged me to go ahead and buy it, have it ready. It had been the Lord Who had softened the hearts of my jailers so that they allowed me to have it. The sergeant in charge, Grizz, had discretion in such matters, but jail policy, at that time, prohibited inmates from receiving books delivered to them from someone on the outside. My Bible was a miracle.

The version I chose for such a time as this was Joyce Meyer's *Everyday Life Bible*. This particular Bible hadn't long been in print as a paperback, and I was very thankful to have found it. If you are familiar with the *Everyday Life Bible*, you know it is the Amplified version, and it is filled throughout with Joyce Meyer's teachings, nuggets of truth and helpful insights. It was the best possible choice for me because I felt less alone, what with this wonderful woman of God speaking to me right from the pages in her down-to-earth, no-nonsense style.

Jail Journal Entry:

Grizz just handed me my Bible!!! I am so happy to have it! I have pen, paper, and my Bible filled with teaching by Joyce Meyer. The Lord is good. Lord, You are good! Help me, Lord, to not get sick in here. If ever You wanted me alone with you, here I am.

CHAPTER **EIGHT**

COUNTY JAIL, DAY ONE: 3:10 P.M.

At 3:10 p.m., the jail nurse came to perform her routine inmate intake evaluation. I know it was 3:10 because she wore a watch and I peeked. I'd been here about four hours. My blood pressure was up, which got her attention, and she asked me, "What's wrong with you?"

Um, *Really??* I looked at her to see if she was joking, but no, she was all business. I started to explain that my doctors were searching for answers to some apparent heart troubles I was having, but she wasn't really listening. I looked fine from the outside.

She then moved on to her regular questions: Was there anything she needed to know about allergies, addictions, depression? A fleeting thought of my intolerance to gluten swam through my head, but I told it to just keep swimming. Why complicate matters? She asked if I was suicidal. I said no.

Her eyes bored into mine. "Would you tell me if you were?"

I didn't blink. "No."

I wasn't suicidal, but I felt like my thoughts were my business. I'd barely arrived, and I was already trying to hang on to some privacy.

She stared at me a bit longer, assessing. She then explained that my thyroid medication had been delivered to the jail, and told me I would receive it at 6:00 a.m., when meds were handed out.

Her name was Molly, and she was a nice enough woman, but the situation was surreal and my mind wandered some as she carried on with her questions and explanations. I found myself wondering, *Why is she allowed to have a real pen?* I'd never brought a real pen when I'd come for church services. All the times I'd wanted to write down an inmate's name so I could remember it and come for a visit, I'd had no pen. And here she was, waving it blithely around like it was the most acceptable thing in the world.

My other thought was, *Please don't leave. I've been in here alone for hours. Surely there must be more to discuss in order to prolong this visit. Please don't leave.*

But leave she did. She finished her check-up and out she went, with a guard clanging the door closed behind her. Fear rose up afresh within me and I felt dizzy as the solitude closed in again. *I'm stuck in here and can't get out, can't get warm, can't see a clock, can't use the toilet except on camera. How long, Lord???*

CHAPTER **NINE**

COUNTY JAIL, DAY ONE: 3:20 P.M.

When the nurse left, I sat on my bunk and stared straight ahead for a long time. I thought the fresh sense of isolation would crush me. I'd been reading my Bible, writing in my journal, doing my best to keep my mind occupied. But then a human being had come into my cell and conversed with me, and when she left, her absence magnified my solitude exponentially. I knew there were other blocks nearby with women in them. The agony of being *alone* in this situation was the hardest part.

But, of course, I wasn't alone. Not for a moment. Even though I couldn't see the Lord – couldn't, at that moment, feel His presence – He was with me. I recovered a bit and, wrapping my blanket tightly around my shoulders once more, I sat down on the bunk, leaned back against the wall, picked up my tote lid and resumed writing.

As time ticked slowly by, I started wondering if I'd be allowed a visitor. I'd already been here several hours and I thought probably someone would have asked to see me. Had anyone asked and been turned away? Did the judge's order say, "No visitors?" How did it work? As I recalled, when Larry was arrested he'd seen our pastor very quickly. It would have been my pastor who brought my Bible and my prescription. Why hadn't they let him see me?

I was stewing, writing and reading, getting really hungry, when my cell door opened. This time it was a female guard who told me to come with her. It was time to get me booked in. I snuck a peek at her watch. Five o'clock. Almost evening. No wonder I was hungry.

The guard led me across an open area and directed me to stand between a camera and a white backdrop, within touching distance of a large fingerprinting contraption I instantly dubbed *Igor*, because Igor sounds scary, and that machine looked scary to me. Another female deputy arrived and asked me if I had any tattoos or other distinctive markings. I explained that I did have a couple of tattoos; since I was still in my long-sleeved turtleneck, they couldn't see them, so they permitted me to just describe them.

The two women then discussed at some length whether they should take my mugshot (Mugshot?!) with my glasses on or off. They decided they would take it both ways. The memory of Congressman Tom DeLay, smiling in Texas for his own mugshot, floated to the surface of my mind, and I wondered, *Smile? Don't smile?* Representative DeLay said he smiled because he knew the mugshot would become public, and he didn't want it to *look* like a mugshot. I was seriously tempted to do the same, and sent the necessary instructions to my facial muscles, but they failed me. There was nothing to smile about here and my face knew it.

I never did get a proper look at my mugshot, but at one point I craned my neck and caught just enough of a glimpse to confirm the worst. My hair mussed, and with no nose powder or lip gloss, having sat in my cell cold and scared for six hours, not to mention having the weight of the world on my shoulders, I looked a wreck. No wonder mugshots are so awful! The person being photographed is having the worst day of his or her life.

Photo shoot completed, we turned our attention to Igor for fingerprinting, 21st Century style: no ink. Maybe we can blame years of tapping away on my steno machine, but my fingerprints did not want to reveal themselves to Igor's digital eye. A twenty-minute battle ensued. Adding injury to insult, this process was further impeded by the fact that I'd broken my right wrist years before, undergone three surgeries, and to this day do not have full mobility in that wrist. I can flop it up and down quite well, thank you, but roll it side to side? No can do.

The print diva got the fingers on my left hand done without much difficulty, then took hold of my right. To perform the process requires that you place the side of your finger on the scanner, then roll it over to where it's lying on its other side. This action requires a rolling wrist motion.

I pointed out the scars on my wrist and explained it wouldn't roll in the direction they needed for an accurate finger scan, but I don't think she heard me. She had a job to do, and so we plodded on, trying again and again and again, until I broke out in a sweat from the pain. I dipped my shoulder downward, trying to force my wrist around so the scanner could scan my entire finger pad. Persistence and dumb luck prevailed, with both of us vastly relieved each time Igor chirped that he was pleased with an image.

And so: Mugshot, Done; Fingerprints, Done.

But there was more to come.

Having finished with Igor – no love lost there – the deputy led me to the booking desk, a large counter, and instructed me to sit down on a small, round stool before it. She told me to extend my left arm onto the counter, and then she clamped a handcuff onto my wrist, the cuff permanently affixed to the countertop. I'd hoped that once I was safely transported and locked in, I'd be done with shackles. It was a horrible feeling to learn otherwise.

I wondered if the cuff would close far enough to feel uncomfortable. Like many women, I have little wrists, but mine have always been kind of a family joke. When she wanted my compliance on any given matter, my big sister used to take both of my wrists between the thumb and forefinger of one of her hands and squash them together, so everybody teased her that she'd stunted my wrists from developing. I shop for bracelets in the children's section, and when my broken wrist came out of its cast, the doctor was obliged to fit me with a child's splint, after first spending thirty minutes mutilating an adult one in an attempt to make it fit me. I'd have to let Dana know that standard-issue handcuffs do indeed shrink down plenty small. *Ouch*! again.

As the deputy was gathering forms, my mind drifted to all of the women I'd met here, and I envisioned them sitting exactly here, on this stool, left arm stuck to the counter. Some of them were sent here from overcrowded jails in other counties. Some hadn't been sentenced yet, and were awaiting the hearings that would decide their fates. Each and every person who came into this jail as an inmate had sat here during processing, alone with their fear, anger, or despair.

I'd witnessed people, men and women, crying and struggling in the back bay as I was on my way to the library for church. I remembered one woman, in particular, who was so frightened, she was tearfully begging the guards to listen to her, to understand that this was a mistake. She was trying to make them let go of her, pleading with them to not bring her inside and put her into a cell. I don't know what she'd done, or had been accused of doing, but I'd been moved with great compassion for her then, and I understood far more now, as I sat in her place.

Most people who arrived here didn't know how long their stay would be, and now I was right here with them. This was March. Would I be out by summer or would the best months of the year, the opportunity of seeing my grandsons, be lost to me? My attorney had warned me that if I was ordered here, my time could be lengthy, unless of course the commotion he planned to make in the news media worked as we hoped.

My ruminations were interrupted by the deputy handing me forms to sign. First there was an inventory of belongings they'd taken from me when I arrived. I looked it over and signed that, yes, this was correct. My few things: my sweater, earrings, and watch, my wedding ring...all were listed. I felt incredibly sad, but no, nothing was written there that shouldn't be, and nothing was absent that ought to be present. I'd given my handbag to Larry before they took me into custody at the courthouse. I hadn't arrived here with much. How I wished, now, that I had given him my ring, as well.

The deputy proceeded with other things to sign, other questions to be answered. She gave me a rulebook and a pamphlet on what to do if I felt sexually threatened or harassed by anyone in the facility. I shuddered. Did that kind of thing happen here? If so, could you really *tell* someone about it?

Other than that, I really don't remember a single question or piece of paper. They had their procedures, information they needed to compile, and I muttered my way mechanically through all of it.

A movement behind the counter caught my attention. *Oh, no!* Captain Harris, the person in charge of this entire establishment, had entered the room. I wanted to slink away. Maybe he hadn't seen me yet. I didn't want him to know I was here. I was one of his church volunteers! He had personally interviewed me and introduced me to the portion of the jail's interior to which I had been allowed access. It had not occurred to me that he might see me and learn that I was here as an inmate.

As it turned out, he not only knew, but that's why he had come to booking. He was waiting for the process to be complete so he could speak with me.

The deputy finished up and stepped aside. Captain Harris stood behind the counter, facing me. I squirmed on my low seat as he towered over me, leaning on the counter and looking straight into my eyes.

At last he spoke, not unkindly. "I need to know why one of my volunteers is in my custody."

I drew a breath to steady my voice and looked up into his eyes.

"Captain Harris, the prosecutor wants me to testify against my husband. Months ago, I was ready to do just that. But everything has changed."

I stared unhappily at my manacled wrist and continued, "Judge Jordan said he would keep me here, held in contempt of court, until I agree to speak. He warned me that I could be here for a very long time."

"I know," came the Captain's somber reply. He didn't question contempt of court for a spouse in my position.

Maybe he knew his next words would be a blow, so he waited a moment and delivered them gently. "Diana, I have to inform you that, because you've now been incarcerated here, you will no longer be allowed to bring church services into the jail. It's policy. Your privileges have been revoked, and you won't be able to volunteer."

A strangled cry very nearly escaped me. My world was imploding.

"I can't change that, Diana," he continued, "but I would like to hear the story from you personally. What happened?"

Jail Journal Entry:

For I am persuaded beyond doubt (am sure) that neither death nor life, nor angels, nor principalities, nor things impending and threatening, nor things to come, nor powers, nor height, nor depth, nor anything else in all creation, will be able to separate us from the love of God, which is in Christ Jesus our Lord.

(Romans 8:38-39, AMP*)*

CHAPTER **TEN**

COUNTY JAIL, DAY ONE: ABOUT 5:45 P.M.

I winced as the cell door closed me in once again. Unbearable as it was to be remanded back into my lonely quarters, my heart warmed slightly at the sight of my Bible and writing tools. I knew that, at least until lights-out, I would be able to keep myself occupied.

Very unexpectedly, before I had returned to this hated place, I had been allowed to make a phone call from a corner of the booking area. There was a single utilitarian phone mounted on the wall, with one of those permanently affixed, institutional stools sitting beneath it. When the deputy asked me if I would like to make a call, I had stood frozen, nonplussed. I didn't know how to make a phone call from here. I didn't know *who* to call.

Larry had told me that his attorney had forbidden him to visit me, to avoid even the appearance of witness tampering. But no one had told *me* I couldn't at least speak to *him*. I processed this, being a slow decision maker by nature. Ultimately, I decided that *of course* my call would be to my husband.

It is not an easy matter to make your first phone call from jail. It requires you to jump through lots of hoops in order to establish your identity within the facility. It also requires that you have money deposited to your *jail* account, so you can appropriate funds into your *phone* account. If you don't have such accounts, the person you call had better have a credit card close at hand. That way he or she can immediately credit your phone account with dollars that can be used to call that phone number only. In these days of cell phones, a collect call from jail would be a last resort, as it could be very expensive for the recipient. A direct call is best.

I received some instructions from the guards, after which I began the lengthy process of establishing my phone account, even though I couldn't yet fund it. I entered a bunch of numbers into the phone and repeated my name into the handset so many times I lost count. These maneuverings were necessary so that an unseen computer in some unseen place could verify, in untold layers, that I was indeed the inmate I was claiming to be. After all that, I wasn't sure my attempt would succeed, because it would require that: 1) Larry hear his phone; 2) he'd be able to act quickly enough to press the right buttons; and 3) he would grab a credit card and input money into my account, so my call would be put through. It seemed like a lot to ask, since he didn't know I'd be reaching out to him.

As I waited, I stretched my back, noticing that my body objected in earnest to all the cold, unforgiving surfaces in this place. Despite my discomfort, I enjoyed my chain-free state.

I'd been here only about six-and-a-half hours, yet already I'd become acclimated to my confinement. It had seemed odd to be pointed in the direction of the phone, with no one leading me and no fetters anywhere in sight.

Finally, finished with my identification efforts, I placed my call. After a moment, I was able to hear ringing on the other end. *Please answer, Larry…*

CHAPTER **ELEVEN**

I met Larry in 1993. He had hired me to handle the administrative side of his high-end dental lab, where he manufactured porcelain and gold crowns and bridges. He wasn't a dentist. His clients were dentists, and he worked long hours to keep his clients happy and his business booming.

It was Larry's voice that first caught my attention. It was a deep, resonant voice, with a quality that exceeded mere volume. Perhaps it was his *confidence* that I noticed, although that's a poor descriptor. Larry has always had *presence,* and his voice is a part of that. It was impossible to overlook him in a crowd. In addition, the words he spoke were always decisive, often brazen, usually colorful.

I began my job one year after his prior business burned to the ground. One of the first things I learned about Larry was that he had rebuilt his dental lab, albeit in a temporary location, within a week of a fire that left the old building, and his lab with it, a total loss.

Larry had received a phone call from his security company shortly after 2:00 a.m. in early July of 1992, only to inform him that their alarms indicated a fire. He dressed quickly and hurried to the freeway, where he saw a distant red glow so massive that it appeared as if a bomb had gone off. His stomach sank as he raced toward the inferno.

Upon his arrival at the scene, he could only stare in mute helplessness as fire crews worked against the odds. They were able to conquer the fire, but the building was reduced to rubble. An employee named Carlos, always an early starter, showed up for work at 3:30 a.m., unprepared for what he would find. Standing at Larry's side, he gazed at the scene in silent horror. Larry's eyes never left the building as he quietly asked Carlos, "Did you remember to turn off the ovens?" Carlos thought he had, but in the face of such devastation, who could be sure of anything?

Larry and his employees set to work as soon as the embers cooled, combing through the ashes to salvage what they could. Amid the pile of soaking ash, they found one set of teeth, unharmed by the fire, gleaming white and mounted on a large articulator. The hard plastic case housing the articulator had melted all around the finished crowns, but Larry was able to cut the plastic away and deliver the crowns to a relieved dentist.

I'd heard that if you must choose between losing your business and losing your home to a catastrophe, you should always choose to lose your home. Lodging can always be found, as long as you're earning money. If, however, you lose your business, it follows that you may lose your home as well.

Larry wasn't going to let that happen. I wasn't there to see it in 1992, but I've since come to know the single-minded purpose with which Larry can accomplish anything to which he sets his mind. He eventually learned that the fire had been caused by a neglected water heater elsewhere in the building. He consulted an attorney regarding the loss, and turned his mind to more immediate concerns.

He rented a space and filed an insurance claim. Larry's business prowess and iron will held his operation together, and he lost no customers. He convinced his clients that, in spite of his loss, their work could be handled without interruption. He worked nearly around the clock for months, but he was as good as his word.

When I met Larry in 1993, he had already procured a small business loan and built a beautiful, state-of-the-art lab in Lake Forest, California. He had filed suit regarding the destruction of his original lab, but the judge ruled that the building owners were not liable for the fire. Larry didn't recover a dime.

* * *

Sometime after we met, I learned that Larry and I had both been born in the same California city, although he got there eight years before I did.

Larry was the second of four brothers, all born about one year apart. In fact, he shares the same birthday with his younger brother Ed.

When the boys were older, the family moved to Huntington Beach. Larry played some high school sports, but his independent streak revealed itself early when he decided to move out of his parents' home at the age of 17. Still in high school, he got a job and moved into his first apartment. Initially, he worked for Gemco, unloading trucks and stocking shelves. From there he got a job at Stater Brothers, where he unloaded fresh inventory, organized produce and other goods, while his friends slept. He worked nights, went to school during the day, and partied when he could.

After high school, Larry looked to the future and weighed his options. He wanted to be a dentist, but he couldn't afford dental school. His goal was to finish college and set himself up in business shortly thereafter. Since the dental field had captured his interest, he decided to study dental technology.

Orange Coast College in Orange County, California, offered a three-year dental tech training program. Larry jumped at it, and it was during these college years that Larry developed one of his most unusual habits.

Years after we were married, Larry told me of a time he had taken his current flame and another young couple to his parents' cabin at Big Bear Lake. The foursome had planned a relaxing afternoon on the lake in the family boat. Everything was smooth sailing until Larry noticed a lone water ski lying in the boat's stern. He hadn't brought a swimsuit, but Larry wasn't about to pass up the chance to ski. He decided to wear his boxers backwards (for obvious reasons), pressing them into service as swimming trunks. Larry then taught his friend Dan to drive the boat while pulling a skier. They practiced for a while, and soon Larry got in the water and readied himself for action. Dan, however, being a novice boater, got spooked easily and repeatedly stalled the boat. Each time the boat's engine died, the craft drifted farther away from Larry.

This happened until the towline was stretched to its breaking point, and Larry was literally "at the end of his rope." A more experienced driver would have circled around to bring in the line and let Larry regroup. But Dan was new at this boat thing, so when he managed to restart the engine, he took off. Larry heard the motor and felt the lines tighten for the umpteenth time, so he quickly gripped the handhold and prepped for success.

By this time, however, Larry's cotton boxers had been in and out of the water several times. The swift ascents and crashing descents had strained his improvised swim trunks to their limit. In a final attempt to get Larry upright, the boat stalled once again. As the line flew out of Larry's hands, he fell down hard on his ski, his backwards boxers tearing right up the middle.

By now, the boat had drifted out of reach. Another boater saw Larry floating in the water and zoomed over to offer him a lift. Aware of the state of his shorts, Larry said no thanks, he'd rather stay in the water. That seemed odd to the Good Samaritan. Larry was alone, his own vessel stalled and quite distant. The kindly boater just said, "Let's have no nonsense, son. Get yourself up in this boat."

Further refusal seemed foolish, so Larry attempted to hold his boxers together as he climbed the ladder. Squatting down, he miserably took a seat on the boat's small ski deck. Making matters worse, there were two cute young girls seated in the boat's prow, trying to get a look at him. Mortified, Larry fixed his gaze astern, gripped his shredded boxers tightly, and placed his ski across his lap for added security. He'd never been so embarrassed.

When Larry told me that story, his funny little habit finally made sense to me. Whenever Larry packed for a trip, the first thing to land in his open suitcase was a pair of swimming trunks. He never left home without them. And, if the trip he was taking was an important one, the trunks were certain to be brand new.

* * *

Larry completed his college courses, and by the time he was 21 he owned his own flourishing dental lab in Huntington Beach.

Larry was young and his business was thriving. He got married, became the proud father of twin daughters, and life seemed unstoppable for him. He purchased a nice home in Southern Orange County, decided he didn't like the commute to Huntington Beach, and built a new lab in Mission Viejo. Larry focused his business on high-end, beautiful dental restorations that attracted top-notch dentists as clients.

Larry's motto never changed. It has always been, "If I don't want it in my mouth, it's not going out my door."

It was in 1992 that the business in Mission Viejo burned down.

One year later, I applied to work as his office manager and got the job. Larry threw me off balance the moment I first arrived at work by saying, "Hey, you don't mind if I call you Di, do you?" No one had ever called me that. Larry didn't wait for a response. Maybe he wasn't used to people saying no to him.

If that put me off balance, I nearly keeled over when he walked right up to me, took hold of my face in one hand, and said, "Let me see your teeth."

WHAT??? I froze. I had only just returned home after 13 years in the mission field. I wasn't used to having a strange man put his hands on my face. He was standing too close!

Then he insisted, "Open your mouth, I want to see your crowns." I was embarrassed! The crowns on my front teeth were rather a sore spot in my psyche. I remembered, just in time, that this was a dental lab, and teeth were Larry's business, so I managed to stifle my near squawk of protest. I hadn't arrived this morning with my crowns on my mind, but he'd noticed them first thing, and he didn't like them.

I stood there like a sheep waiting for slaughter and let him look in my mouth, wishing the floor would open up and swallow me. But he just said, "We're gonna have to do something about those. You'll love the crowns I can make for you."

I finally piped up, "I need new crowns?"

"Well, of course," he chuckled, "if you're gonna be working in my front office."

As he walked away, I stood there with my mouth agape. I hated going to the dentist! Was my job on the line if I wouldn't go? When I was a teenager, my mom practically had to sedate me before any dental appointment, a situation that eased only when she found a dentist who would dose me liberally with nitrous oxide. That backfired big time, though, when his dose was so liberal that I got high as a kite, believed myself to be flying around the operatory, and then puked all over the place.

No, I didn't want to go to the dentist. But that first encounter set the tone of our early working relationship. Larry would say something that would shock the tar out of me, and then he'd walk off and leave me scrambling to assimilate what I'd just heard. I'd never met anyone like him. Big, bold, confident, with a booming voice and a certainty of his own rightness. About everything.

He was a delegator. He had to be, as a business owner with five employees. Here I was, a person who wouldn't say "boo" to a goose, working with a man who would breezily tell someone on the phone, "Oh, I'll just have you swing that case by on your way home today. My driver's off." I was right. People rarely told him no.

He called me Di, almost without exception, from that first moment in the lab. I'd spent my life telling people my name was

Diana, not Diane. He bypassed all of that confusion and just created a new name for me.

To really know Larry, however, you'd have to look past all the hard work, the drive, the bravado. You'd need to ignore some foul language, unartful speech, and the occasional inability to listen well. You would turn a blind eye to his frequent bad moods and irritability. Dig past the often gruff exterior and you would find a man who would *never* leave a motorist stranded on a highway; you'd see a guy who, upon learning that you had a problem, would move mountains to solve it for you; you would find a person who could accomplish anything he set his mind to, whether that be re-inventing his laboratory from the ground up in record time, or fixing a leaky faucet.

And, as I was to learn later, you would find a man with a bruised but romantic heart.

CHAPTER **TWELVE**

I'd been working at the lab and attending night school for three years when, in March of 1996, my mom died. Within weeks of her death, I filed for divorce from my first husband. My mother's death was so unexpected, so painful, that I felt empty on the inside. I had no reserves of strength left to help me cope with my unhappy marriage.

I had been going to night school to become a court reporter because I knew that, should my marriage fail, I would need a career substantial enough to support myself and my girls.

When Mom died, I met with an attorney. We crunched some numbers, and I learned that I would be able to get an apartment and leave an increasingly difficult situation.

As for Larry? He had gone through his own divorce, and we began dating far, far too soon. I mentioned Larry's bruised heart. That's an understatement. He still appeared to be a tower of strength, but on the inside he was bleeding.

We were both hurting. For me, it was my unhappy marriage, my mother's death, and my own divorce that caused my pain. I never went back to my church after my first husband and I separated. Bill still felt at home there, and my presence would have been awkward. I had never told anyone there my side of the story. I was therefore churchless, and when Larry and I began dating, I slipped far too easily into the world's enticements.

I wanted to feel good, and with Larry, I did. He arrived for dinner dates well-groomed and nicely dressed. He always held doors open for me. At restaurants he asked me what I planned to order, and when the server arrived, Larry would hand him the menus and say, "The lady will have the chicken piccata, no rice, just veggies. And a glass of your best Chardonnay." Then to me, "Would you like a salad to start?"

When I needed a jacket, he held it out for me to slip into. When I needed new tires, he arranged it. He also took care of everything when one of the new tires was faulty. He came to my apartment and fixed the showerhead. He knew he'd have it done far sooner than the apartment manager would.

Confidence, confidence, confidence. I ate it up.

But while he was happy with our new romance, other aspects of his life were very stressful. His divorce had forced him into bankruptcy. He was losing touch with his children. His life was a turmoil of highs and lows. Even *he* couldn't grapple with that for long.

That was when Larry met Jesus Christ.

Larry had a friend and client named Andrew, and Andrew could see that Larry was in trouble. He went to Larry's house and explained the Gospel. Andrew told Larry that he'd tried things his own way long enough, that he needed to give his life to God.

I would have loved to be a fly on the wall during that conversation, but I wasn't there when Larry, in tears, surrendered his life to the Lord. I was, however, thrilled! I felt a little ashamed that I hadn't mentioned anything similar to Larry myself, but you can't preach the Gospel if you aren't living the Gospel, and I wasn't living it just then.

* * *

Larry proposed to me on Christmas Eve in 1997. By early summer, we were making plans to move to Idaho and leave fast-paced Southern California behind. Larry knew I wouldn't move in with him until we were married. Since I had to give up my apartment or sign a new lease, something had to happen soon.

He arranged for a weekend trip to Loews Coronado Bay Resort near San Diego for the four of us: Larry, me, and my daughters, Amy and Bethany. We jet-skied around the bay all day, then enjoyed a sumptuous dinner. When our meal was nearly finished, Larry took my hand in both of his, smiling broadly.

"How would you like to walk across the border tomorrow and get married?"

And that's exactly what we did. The next day the four of us (after a short bus ride), walked right into Tijuana. We spent the day nosing around the shops, purchasing keepsakes, and hunting for a place where we could tie the knot.

At last, we found ourselves in a small, hot law office, where the lawyer, after a brief exchange of vows, pronounced us husband and wife. Weeks later, we received our Mexican marriage certificate in the mail. It looked very official, having been typed on thin pink paper and covered with purple stamps.

We had another ceremony in Las Vegas a few years later, just so we could have a certificate that "spoke English," as I put it. But the little wedding in Tijuana, with just the four of us, and one Mexican lawyer, will always be the one near to my heart.

* * *

That's what I was fighting for, here in this Idaho jail. That man. My marriage. We'd been to hell and back recently, and the outcome was still swathed in mystery. But we'd found something real to hang on to, in both our faith in God and our fresh love for each other. I knew I would do whatever it took to reclaim the life we had nearly lost.

CHAPTER **THIRTEEN**

COUNTY JAIL, DAY ONE: 5:25 P.M.

I sat on my plastic stool, staring at the concrete wall. My hands were clammy as I held the phone to my ear. *Please pick up...*

"Hello?" Larry's voice.

I exhaled. I'd felt so isolated, so alone, and here was his voice! I knew him to be a couple miles away, but hearing him made him seem much nearer. He said nothing about not being allowed to talk to me. He was so happy I'd finally called. His joy at my phone call could not, however, hide the depth of his sorrow at my predicament. Throughout our conversation, his voice cracked and caught as though he were fighting back tears. I knew he was trying to hold it together for my sake, but I wasn't fooled. He was devastated.

I'd had no particular plan when I'd initiated the call. I knew we would steer clear of whether or not I would testify tomorrow. As our conversation progressed, however, I realized that all I wanted to do was to reassure *him*, and, through him, the rest of my family. He'd reached out to everyone, friends and family, to let them know what had happened. I told him that, although at first it was very rough, I'd soon found my writing supplies and received my Bible. I'd made up my bed and managed to create a lap desk. I had asked for and received both a sweatshirt and my glasses. I was much more comfortable now.

Definitely the right thing to say! He was so relieved. He said he would call my daughter Amy right away and let her know that I was okay, or at least doing better. He sounded more hopeful at the thought of having some good news to pass on.

Until that moment, I had been unaware of the anger and grief my incarceration had brought to my family and friends. I was so caught up in my own experience and shock that I never considered that others felt pain on my behalf.

I learned from Larry that Pastor Mark had indeed brought my Bible. As I'd feared, he'd asked to see me, and had been turned away. He was told they needed to process me, and that he could come back later. I wondered if it was policy not to allow visitors right away. After all, I'd sat alone in my cell for nearly six hours before I was brought to booking. Maybe that was part of the "process."

At any rate, I was *relieved*. I would be allowed a visitor after all! I told Larry it would be best if Pastor Mark came around 6:30 or 7:00, so dinner would be over and visiting hours re-opened.

Our twenty-minute phone call flew by far too quickly. Larry informed me he and his attorney were trying to work out a deal with the prosecutor, but they weren't even close yet. They would resume their efforts in the morning. Larry was desperate to plead guilty to something and get me out of here. I still didn't want him to plead guilty to a felony, though. The stakes were, oh, so high.

As our call came to a close, we did our best to encourage each other. I was the one in jail, but he sounded so *sad*! I felt terrible for him. It felt nice to take my eyes off my own fears for a moment and try to strengthen my husband.

"God knows exactly where I'm sitting right now, baby," I murmured into the phone. "I trust Him absolutely."

"Yeah, I do too," he managed shakily, brightening a little. He sounded lighter when we said our good-byes and hung up – not quite as miserable as when he'd first answered the phone. That, along with the promise of a visit from my pastor, lifted my own spirits greatly.

It helped me endure being shut back into my cell after my phone call.

Firmly set now in my routine, I pulled my blanket around my shoulders, eased myself onto my lower bunk, and sat with my back against the wall. I pulled my tote lid onto my lap and proceeded to describe recent events to my journal. By now I was famished, which seemed odd, since I often lose my appetite in a crisis. But it was nearly 6:00 in the evening, and I'd eaten nothing since the egg whites Larry had scrambled for me early in the morning. I'd been here well before lunch was delivered, and I'd heard the trolley rolling along. I could smell a hot lunch being handed in to other inmates, but there had been nothing for me. The cooks hadn't known I was coming.

Any thought of a hunger strike vanished as my food slot opened and an inmate worker handed a dinner tray through the door. A guard asked if I wanted juice. Juice? Okay. I handed out my little cup. They poured something red and sugary into the vessel and handed it back. I took my dinner tray and my juice and set them down on the concrete bench, My Personal Arctic Circle. I didn't want to risk spilling anything on my bed, such as it was, so I opted for the bench and sat down to survey the fare.

They certainly weren't out to starve us. There was salad and cornbread and coffee cake and a beige-colored bean dish – pinto beans, maybe, with a brown, bologna-shaped mystery meat floating through it. I decided the salad would be safe to eat. When I'd finished that, I nibbled on some of the cornbread, throwing dubious glances at the bean dish. That was clearly meant to be the protein portion of the meal, but I didn't want a stomachache later from bean consumption. I gave it a try, but after a bite or two, decided I wasn't hungry anymore.

I did want to hold on to the coffee cake, in case the munchies hit before lights out. My rulebook, however, said that keeping food was not allowed, and I knew I was on camera every minute. So, whether I'm a big chicken or just a stickler for the rules, I regretfully watched my cake go away when my tray was retrieved. It was really just as well. As I've said, I am gluten intolerant, and I'd probably already done enough damage with the cornbread. Now what? Dinner hadn't been very exciting, but at least it was something to do. Long hours stretched ahead of me before lights out at ten, and my spirits plummeted. I didn't want to sit back on that bunk. I didn't want to write anymore. I was cold. Every joint in my body ached. I couldn't stand it here in this brightly lit, chilled and isolated concrete box with nothing to do and no one around. Fear and loneliness threatened to crush me.

Time for a deep breath. Contemplating my circumstances was making me miserable. Reading and writing at least kept me busy, so I snugged my blanket back around my shoulders and sat down with my journal, Bible, and wobbly pen. I'd left off with:

> *Here's what I know: I won't be here forever. This is temporary and You, Lord, are with me.*

I carried on writing:

> *Later (but not much). I read my Bible for a bit and then dinner came. There was a salad, which I was grateful for. I ate that and the cornbread. I had a little of the bean dish, apparently the main course. I left the cake alone. Pastor Mark is supposed to visit me tonight. That will be nice, though it will be too short. Maybe not for him. And there is a small chance that I will get to go to the library sometime this evening. No promises, but maybe. I hope one of the copies of "John, Son of Thunder" is in there. If it is, Lord, help me find it.*

In the early '80s, while living on the ship, I had read a book by Ellen Gunderson Traylor that powerfully impacted my life. She'd taken the Bible and other historical documentation and had masterfully woven together a gripping novel based on the life of John, beloved disciple of Jesus Christ. John was first a follower of John the Baptist, but when Jesus arrived on the scene, John the disciple and Andrew, brother of Simon Peter, took their emotional leave of the Baptist and found their way to Jesus.

I so identified with young John. He was a younger brother, and as such was perhaps discounted by society just a bit. John possessed a seeking, yearning heart, and he was drawn to Jesus like a moth to a flame. John grew to love the Man he called Master and Teacher in the way that I, too, was growing to love Him.

Throughout the story, John, in spite of his great love for his Teacher, struggles to understand Jesus. At times, he even wants to flee from Him, as unfathomable events and teachings follow one upon another. Why did Jesus speak to a Samaritan woman? Why did He say people must eat His flesh and drink His blood? Didn't Jesus know these things were making Him unpopular? At one point, many other followers really did desert Jesus. Where was His army, and when would He establish His kingdom and rid the Promised Land of Romans and other oppressors?

John struggled with pride and insecurity, and he probably squabbled some with the other disciples. But, in him, we see a man who grew closer to Jesus than anyone I have ever heard about. He stood at the foot of the cross and heard Jesus tell him to care for His own mother, Mary. He ran to the empty grave in wonder, and later beheld our risen Savior on more than one occasion. In John, we feel the Lord's heartbeat, His great love for people. At least I do. And John grew in love and devotion until, as an elderly man on Patmos, the last things were revealed to him and he wrote them down. He finished the book with his own words, saying, in Revelation 22:20, "Amen, come, Lord Jesus." My favorite Bible verse.

As a young woman in my early twenties, I'd known that I wanted that kind of relationship with Jesus. I decided that if John could be that close to the Lord, so could anyone. Throughout the journey of my life, that desire has remained in my heart, though on the outside you may have had cause to doubt it.

I have certainly had some dark moments in my life. After my divorce, I plugged my ears to the Lord's voice and lived for myself and for the moment. I strayed terribly from the best that God had for me. But God never gave up on me. He knew that I belonged to him, and it was always His plan to bring me back into His arms for good.

As I sat in this dreary jail, I wanted to re-read the story that had meant so much to me. I had purchased two copies of the book and donated them to the jail's library some time back. Unless other inmates were reading them, I should be able to find one. I hoped I would be allowed to visit the library. The two female deputies who had booked me in were going to try to arrange it.

CHAPTER **FOURTEEN**

COUNTY JAIL, DAY ONE:
PROBABLY ABOUT 7:00 P.M.

As I sat pondering these things, my cell door clanged open and one of the guards announced, "*You've* got a visitor!"

Guards in jails and prisons try to maintain a professional aloofness when interacting with inmates. They aren't there to coddle you. But I caught the whisper of a smile crossing the deputy's face as she emphasized the word, "*You've.*" She knew this was good news.

I hurried into my shoes and, taking my pen and paper, I followed her back through the booking area and around several corners. At last, she directed me to have a seat in front of a small computer screen. Our visit was to be conducted via closed circuit TV, with me seated upon yet another hard and backless stool. I picked up the telephone receiver and waited. Soon I saw my pastor on the monitor. He looked relaxed and easy in his casual shirt and baseball cap. I was unspeakably comforted that he would take the time to come and see me.

How often I myself had come and sat where he now sat, paying visits to inmates I met in our church services. I had done my best to encourage them and feed all the love I could through the camera and handset. I could picture exactly where he was sitting. As glad as I was to see him, some of the shock returned as my mind battled with the reality of my own situation. I sat there in my County Jail sweatshirt, which was pale gray and had its size written, in black marker, right across the front of it.

His first words were his typical, warm greeting, "Hey, Diana." My first taste of "normal" all day. Then he looked to the side and I heard a puzzled chuckle. He'd never thought this would actually happen.

"Larry told me that you're back in court tomorrow," he began, "and this time I will *be* there." The emphasis was due to the fact that he hadn't come to court today. He'd been concerned that someone might throw a curve ball and try to get him on the stand himself. The prosecutor, however, wanted nothing to do with attempting to question clergy. I was still surprised to hear that Pastor Mark planned to be there tomorrow. The thought that he or anyone else might come to court at all was both encouraging and disconcerting.

My mind's eye fast-forwarded to tomorrow, and if that didn't go well, to all the subsequent days. I would have to make my daily obligatory appearance in court and reiterate that, no, I still wasn't going to testify. I envisioned dirty hair, no makeup, and chapped lips. Maybe I didn't want people coming to court after all. I'd be a mess!

I tried feebly to express my concerns, and I will never forget Pastor Mark's response.

"You know, Diana, sometimes families see each other that way." My church was my *family*. My throat closed up as emotion flooded through me.

"You also should know that people are lining up to come and see you, starting with DJ." The thought of my friend made me smile. Such a sweetheart! But who had told her? How was word getting around, so that people were "lining up" to come and visit me? Alone in my trauma, I hadn't thought about phone calls, reactions, more phone calls, and people wishing they could come and visit.

But then a concern hit me. "Well," I said, "will you let them know that I am only allowed one visitor per day? And will you coordinate? Most people won't know it's just one a day." He assured me that he would, and my mind raced. I wanted to see *everyone*! I wanted to go *home*!

But, for now, I needed Scriptural strength pumped into me.

I mentioned that to Pastor Mark, and asked him if he wanted to share any scriptures with me. That's why I'd brought my pen and paper along. He smiled. "You know, I was thinking about that on the way over here, and I do have one for you, if you have an Amplified Bible. You really need the Amplified for this one."

I was surprised. It was he, after all, who had delivered my Bible to the jail earlier in the afternoon. He either hadn't looked closely at it, or didn't remember, so I assured him that, yes, the Bible I had in my cell was an Amplified. He told me to look up 1 Corinthians 15:58. He also pointed me in the direction of Psalm 37:1-11. To say I was eager to read them would be an understatement.

I don't remember everything about our conversation. The trauma of the day and my circumstances had left me pretty shell-shocked, and my mental digestion was subpar. I don't remember stating anything obvious, like, "I'm scared." I do know I said, "I haven't cried yet," to which he replied, "No, don't cry."

I also remember mentioning that it was cold inside the jail, and that I was freezing. He asked if I'd be able to get an extra blanket. I told him I didn't know, but that I'd ask.

Snippets. I remember the beginning of our conversation, and I definitely remember the end, but otherwise I just remember snippets.

The big takeaways from that visit were: 1) the scriptures Pastor Mark suggested; 2) the fact that people on the outside knew what was happening to me, cared, and wanted to come and see me; and 3) the pastor's relaying that, "Larry was so proud of you in court today! Man, if he loved you before, he *really* loves you now!" As he told me this, I could see him smiling at some remembered conversation with Larry.

Larry? Proud of me? Larry had expressed a similar sentiment only a few times before in our marriage, and those times usually pertained to some particularly fearless piece of motorcycle riding I'd managed. But, he was proud of me in court?

This morning, while I was cooling my heels in the jury room after my attorney's visit, Judge Jordan had unexpectedly decided to reconvene all the parties in court. When the bailiff had returned me to the courtroom, I had felt very awkward and clumsy. Still in handcuffs, I was forced to negotiate my way back to the witness stand with my hands glued painfully behind me. The witness chair was on a swivel, facing the wrong direction. I had to use my knees to turn it around, and then took careful aim before I lowered myself onto it. Hardly my finest moment. (Perhaps there is an art to sitting down in handcuffs, but for the uninitiated, it's pretty graceless.)

When all the players were reassembled in the courtroom, the judge spoke to me directly. Lowering his gaze to look at his desk, he said in his rough, gravelly voice, "I have been trying to come up with some lesser thing that I can do to you to convince you that you must answer this man's questions. I've brought everyone back in here so I can put a question to you. Is there anything else, anything less than incarceration, that will convince you to testify?"

How odd. If the threat of jail wouldn't open my mouth, why would something less severe have any effect?

At that moment, sitting awkwardly on the witness stand, craning my head to get a glimpse of the judge's face, I felt completely powerless.

I was reminded of a time when I was living in Prague and needed to see a doctor for a mammogram. I was, mildly stated, *unprepared* to disrobe for the exam without a hospital gown to hide behind. The nurse instructed, "Put *off* your clothes." A desperate search through the changing room had yielded *nothing* to put on!

When the attendant came to fetch me, I simply followed her. I feared that any obvious embarrassment would just make things worse. Wearing only my jeans, I walked past the office staff as if this were the most normal thing in the world. Indeed, it seemed to be a typical moment at the office. No one gawked.

The doctor conducted his entire exam and consultation while my upper person was *in puris naturalibus*. Eventually a nurse took pity on me and wrapped a towel around me as the doctor's discussion droned on. I thought of doctors' offices in the States and silently cried, "My kingdom for a paper gown!" At least I didn't have cancer.

I re-lived that vulnerable moment as I found myself trussed up and crooked on my seat, trying to make myself heard. I stammered to the judge, "No, your Honor. I can't think of anything less severe that you can do to me that would change my mind. I'm sorry."

The whole thing was so humiliating, so uncomfortable, that I couldn't imagine what Larry had found to be proud of. Maybe that I'd stood my ground, fear and manacles notwithstanding?

I related the *can-I-do-less-to-you* story to Pastor Mark, and he couldn't make any sense of it, either. He just reiterated to me that he'd be in court tomorrow, and that I should hang in there.

Finally – and this is etched in my memory – just before our time was up and the screen turned to blue, Pastor Mark said, "If you want to read about Joseph, that's in Genesis 37."

Joseph?! You may be very familiar with the Biblical story of Joseph, son of Jacob, also called Israel. Joseph had eleven brothers, and nine of them conspired together to sell him into slavery. His eldest brother had thought to rescue Joseph secretly, for their father's sake, but he failed. Joseph was therefore sold to the Midianites, who then sold him to a top-ranking man in Egypt named Potiphar. Potiphar's wife found Joseph attractive and wanted to sleep with him. When he refused, even ran away from her, she, a woman scorned, lied and told her husband Joseph had assaulted her. Potiphar believed his wife and threw Joseph into prison!

So Joseph, at just 17 years of age, was kidnapped by his own brothers, sold into slavery, and then imprisoned for *years* for a crime he hadn't committed.

Niggling in the back of my mind was the outcome of Joseph's ordeal. God never abandoned Joseph to endure prison alone. Rather, He was with Joseph, and built him up in wisdom, in dream interpretation, and in stature with his guards. He was eventually put in charge of the prison, though he wasn't allowed to leave it.

There came a time when his counsel was needed before Pharaoh himself. Joseph's counsel was so accurate, so wise, so miraculously inspired by God, that in a moment's time, Joseph was raised from prison and placed in command of the entire country, second only to Pharaoh!

Could I go back to my cell and read this story? Though the account of Joseph was filled with promise and a wonderful outcome, given my situation, it was the scariest story on earth. Some might say I shared unfair imprisonment with that mighty patriarch. But he was locked up for years! As my life right now ticked by minute by excruciating minute, I couldn't envision what would become of me if this dragged on for days, weeks, even months. Years…I couldn't think about.

I would look up the other passages Pastor Mark had shared with me, but the story of Joseph would have to wait.

Our visit over, I hung up the phone, stretched my back and rose stiffly from the tiny stool. On the one hand, I dreaded a return to my cell, but, on the other, I was keen to get to my Bible.

Both would wait just a bit longer, however.

The two deputies approached me and queried, "Would you like to go to the library now?"

Would I ever!!

CHAPTER **FIFTEEN**

COUNTY JAIL, DAY ONE: VERY CLOSE TO 7:20 P.M.

I followed the guards through a number of hallways and finally arrived at a place I knew very well. Patty and I had walked through this same corridor every Sunday afternoon, carrying my guitar, a red folder full of song sheets, and two Bibles apiece. We had, however, always come in from the other direction and of our own free will. I knew right where the library was because that's where we held our church services.

The guards and I stood outside the library and waited for Control to acknowledge the deputies' request to unlock the door. *Click.* One of them pulled the door open, and we were inside. No lights. The library was closed for the evening. A shiver went up my spine. It was so eerie here at night!

Patty and I always came when the library was open. We would set our things down and begin setting out chairs for the ladies. Once the chairs were arranged, Patty would pass out song sheets and I would tune my guitar. I tuned away while the ladies arrived, chitchatting and carrying their Bibles. They would wave at us through the glass as they waited to come inside. I was always so happy to see them!

Tonight was different. Even after the lights came on, it was far too quiet. Inmates all over the jail were locked away in their pods. Programming was over for the day. Dinner was over. My visit was over. The silence was unnatural and I paused, looking around the library from an inmate's perspective. I stood, quite literally, in their shoes. Orange ones.

I shook myself to clear my head, and moved toward the bookshelf that would most likely contain *John, Son of Thunder*. I'd helped someone search for this same book once, so I knew where to look. And there it was! It seemed to have a homing beacon attached to it, drawing my attention. I scooped it up and hugged it to myself gratefully.

The guards wondered if there was anything else I was interested in. I told them no, this was all I'd hoped to find.

Now there was nowhere else to go, nothing else to do but walk with the guards back through several hallways, through to booking, and into my solitary cell.

But I was better equipped now. My bed was made up, and while not inviting, at least it was neat and the green foam mat wasn't showing. I had things to look up, things to write down, and my favorite novel to read. It wouldn't do any good to think about the hours remaining until lights out, to worry about whether I'd be able to sleep, or to think about being here until the court appointment the next afternoon.

Those thoughts *tried* to creep in, causing my heart to pound and my head to swim. I pushed them aside, donned my blanket shawl, and eased myself into my writing nest on the lower bunk, back against the wall, tote lid on my lap, rubber pen in hand. My Bible was on my left and my book was on my right. I took stock of my setting and thanked the Lord that I was in a good facility. I wasn't particularly warm, but I was dry, safe, and my cell was clean.

The first thing I did, when I was settled in, was look up the verses Pastor Mark had given me. Wow! I'd always known Pastor Mark's brain was an encyclopedia of the Bible, and here was further proof. In the Amplified Bible, 1 Corinthians 15:58 says this:

Therefore, my beloved brethren, be firm (steadfast),
immovable, always abounding in the work of the Lord
[always being superior, excelling, doing more than
enough in the service of the Lord], knowing and being
continually aware that your labor in the Lord is not futile
[it is never wasted or to no purpose.]

Pastor Mark was telling me to stand firm, be steadfast, immovable in what I believed was right before God and my own conscience because nothing, not even this horrible experience, was futile. It would not be wasted or to no purpose.

I wrote that out, and turned to Psalm 37. The words leapt off the page to comfort me in my forlorn state.

Do not fret because of evildoers...
Trust in the Lord...
Delight yourself also in the Lord.
Rest in the Lord...cease from anger...
for evildoers shall be cut off...
but the meek shall inherit the earth and
shall delight themselves in the abundance of peace.

(Psalm 37:1-11 NKJV)

Abundance of peace. Could I ever have that? After all the turmoil, shame and fear of the last months, nothing sounded better to me than an abundance of peace. Whether or not my pastor thought that evil had been done to me by the ones who threw me in jail, he seemed to know that *I* might look at it that way. I was reminded of how King David was pursued, threatened, and mocked. Enemies conspired against him ceaselessly.

David brought it all to God. When he had a complaint, he poured it out. He never avenged himself. He knew his only hope was to delight himself in the Lord. "Delight yourself also in the

Lord," verse 4 says, "and He shall give you the desires of your heart." This passage was so rich! I drank it in, then wrote it down.

My journal was filling up. I set it aside for a bit and picked up *John, Son of Thunder*. I remembered when I'd first brought two copies of this book into the jail. I'd been happy to find them, as this book had originally been published in 1979, over thirty years before. I'd found these at an online megastore before I stumbled across the author's website. I promptly ordered three from that website to give as gifts. When I received the ones from Ellen Gunderson Traylor's site, I found that she'd signed them, including at times the word, "Courage!" and other times the word, "Peace!" I loved it!

I savored the feel of the glossy paperback for a full minute before I turned to Chapter 1. The familiar words washed over me, and for just a moment, I forgot my surroundings. As I read, I was transported to a distant land, to a time more than 2,000 years ago. I traveled to the most pivotal time in the history of the world, when everything man had ever known was about to change. The book begins with John the Baptist, and then Jesus makes his slow, slightly mysterious, and absolutely delicious de-but within the pages.

I knew that debut was coming. I wanted to take my time and savor it, but before I was even fifteen pages into the book, my eyes began to sting. I shut them regretfully, setting the book down beside me. The day had been too much for me, and I was very tired.

Keeping my eyes closed and leaning my head back against the cold wall, I imagined opening them to find that my own home surrounded me. At this time of evening, I would normally be in my reading nook, with a book propped open before me, my legs curled comfortably beneath and a nice mug of tea close at hand.

I didn't want to open my eyes and dispel such a wonderful vision. I also couldn't risk nodding off for even a moment. I would need to be monumentally sleepy when the lights went out. I didn't suppose that I would sleep *well,* but I hoped that sheer exhaustion would allow me to sleep *some.* As it was several hours before lights out, I knew I mustn't take even the slightest edge off my drowsiness. I was going to have to open my eyes.

As I forced my eyelids up I found that the glare of my cell and the harshness of my surroundings were all the worse for having been shut out temporarily. The air whooshed from my lungs as reality knocked the wind out of me. My bare metal toilet laughed at me from a few feet away, taunting me. *"Miss Priss, eh? So said your family. Always so prim. You hate using public bathrooms, and now look! You're on Candid Camera! Modesty won't help you in here! It'll just tear you apart!"*

I glared back at my toilet. I silently informed it that I was made of sterner stuff than to be afraid of a little, low, seatless commode. I was an inmate now. I would have to adapt like everyone else.

PART **TWO**

THE PAST

Create in me a clean heart, O God.
Renew a loyal spirit within me.
Do not banish me from your presence,
and don't take your Holy Spirit from me.
Restore to me the joy of your salvation,
and make me willing to obey you.
(Psalm 51:10-12 NLT)

CHAPTER **ONE**

"Adapt?" my family might have asked. "Diana? Adapt to zero privacy?" I could almost hear the chortles. When I was growing up, my mom would often look at me, hands on hips, and wonder aloud, "Oh, Diana, how are you ever going to get married? *Everything* embarrasses you!" I'll note that she was always smiling when she said such things. She was so open and free herself, she didn't know where I'd come up with all my ideas of privacy. I probably just wanted to avoid teasing.

My family consisted of Mom, Dad, and six kids. We were a mixed bunch, the product of a blended marriage. When my parents married, Mom had two children: my sister Dana and, of course, me. Dad had three teen-aged kids of his own: Annamay, Kenny, and Kyle. Kenny was the eldest, but without fail, we referred to them as Annamay, Kenny, and Kyle, or, for short, The Kids. After Mom and Dad had been married for three years, they brought home our new baby brother, Kirk.

Prior to Kirk's arrival I had been the youngest, and was thus the target of most of the family teasing. Kirk never did get his share, in my opinion. I probably asked for it, being a finicky little thing who wouldn't get her hands dirty. While Dana made mud pies, I played with Barbies and small tea sets. Somewhere I picked up the nickname Miss Priss, which I *hated*, but there was no dissuading them. Particularly Dana. Worse, whenever I ate or drank anything, my pinkies would spring to attention of their own volition. This involuntary trait earned me the dubious distinction of being the family's prime member of the Pinkies Up Club.

Target. On. My. Back.

Follow me into my teens, and you will find the family pranksters now thought a gathering was only fun if someone pushed me into the pool. I had long blonde hair and sunned myself regularly. I never got into our backyard pool because the chlorine would turn my hair green and fade my tan. My refusal to get in the water was just asking for trouble with this bunch. Nearly everyone had a go at me, at one time or another, except maybe my little brother (though I'm pretty sure he asked permission!).

This tradition even spread to my mother. My mom was a kind and merciful woman, and there was no question that she loved me. Still, one Easter Sunday, when I was 15 and hunting eggs in the backyard with my little brother, she began dropping hints about an egg she'd spied on the pool floor. Had one rolled in there? As I leaned over to investigate, she snuck up behind me and gave me a good poke. In I went, fancy dress and Easter basket notwithstanding. I spluttered to the surface to find my mother holding her sides with laughter and reaching for a camera. The rest of the family stood in shocked silence before they, too, burst out laughing. Hmph!

Well, by the time I was 17 it had gotten a bit out of hand. When The Kids, all in their twenties now, arrived for Thanksgiving that year, Dad told everyone sternly that no one was to push Diana into the pool. Not even Mom. He meant business. It was a Solemn Decree.

Later that evening, well fed, dishes done, we were all relaxing in and around our Jacuzzi. I knew I was completely safe due to the Solemn Decree, so I was dangling my legs in the hot water, enjoying that we were all together. Without warning, Kenny sank low in the water and began imitating the scary music from Jaws, murmuring, *Duh-da-duh-da-duh-da-duh-da* as he sliced through the water in my direction.

No one knew his plan until he made a quick lunge and scooped me up in his arms. He was out of the Jacuzzi in a flash, heading toward the rim of the main pool. Holding me firmly cradled against him, he leapt high in the air and tucked his legs, preparing to make a huge cannonball splash!

Noteworthy in this particular scene is that the culprit involved was Kenny, my eldest brother, whom I loved fiercely. Everybody did. Our family depended on him to bring a breath of fresh air wherever he went, and no party really started at our house until he arrived. He took me for rides in both his tiny Lotus Esprit and his big rig. Whether we were zooming along, hugging the curves in his sports car, or sitting aloft in his tractor-trailer, I was always thrilled just to be with him.

I could never be angry with Kenny. As we went crashing together into the pool, he was forgiven before we hit the water.

As we came up for air, we saw Dad, leaning over the pool with his hands on his hips, an angry frown on his face. "What the *heck* did I say!"

Kenny, grinning ear-to-ear, just tossed his wet hair out of his eyes. Throwing an arm around my shoulders, he said angelically, "Hey, Dad, I didn't push her in! I just jumped in with her!"

* * *

I mentioned earlier that my entire family was shocked when I made the decision to travel to Greece with my sister Dana. To understand their surprise, we must leave poolside incidents and go back in time a bit – well, a lot, to August 17, 1962 – the day I arrived and changed Dana's life forever.

At first, my entrance into the family wasn't *too* cataclysmic for her. Mom even took a cute picture of 18-month-old Dana on her tiptoes, trying to peek into my bassinet. The photo only shows her from behind, but I don't think she was scowling.

The changes in Dana began to manifest when our parents split up and our birth father moved out. And when I say moved out, I mean disappeared. I was one and Dana almost three, and we had no way of knowing why Daddy was there one day and gone the next. We couldn't understand that, in addition to the divorce, our father had been pulled away to the war in Viet Nam. It would be years before we were able to re-establish our relationship with him.

These events impacted Dana far more than they did me, as I was still a baby. Dana was old enough to experience pain and frustration over the loss of her daddy, and that pain would manifest itself in earnest, later on.

In the beginning, however, she was a good big sister. She watched out for me, quite protectively at times.

In 1965, Dana and I were four and three respectively. Mom was going to visit her friend Donna, and had dolled us up in navy sailor dresses with white trim and fluffy skirts. We had on little white ankle socks and small patent leather shoes. Our blonde hair was carefully combed and held with cute barrettes, so we were picture perfect as she paid her call.

Donna lived in a Los Angeles neighborhood where the streets were lined with matching duplexes, two-stories high and side-by-side. They nestled uniformly along the streets, each with two strips of grass out front. Each home had a concrete footpath leading between the strips of lawn and up to its front door. There was no variation between the buildings, the strips of grass, or the footpaths.

While Mom and Donna were drinking coffee and catching up, Dana and I got bored and asked if we could go outside. Mom gave permission, but we were to stay right outside the door. Had we done that, we would have been okay. But Dana took my hand and we walked 15 feet down the footpath to where it met the sidewalk. We then turned around to get our bearings.

That's when it hit us. All of the doors looked just the same! Never mind that our toes were still touching the very footpath we'd just walked on to reach the sidewalk. We were too little to reason that out. No, we were now on the *actual* sidewalk, and we had no idea which door was the right one!

That's when we knew…we were *LOST!!*

We burst into tears simultaneously, frantically wailing into the air, "We're L-O-O-O-O-O-ST! We're L-O-O-O-O-O-ST!!" I didn't want to be Lost! Holding hands again, we set off down the street, making an incredible ruckus, crying at the top of our lungs, and declaring ourselves to be Lost!

Imagine the bemusement of the nearby resident who finally called the police. He or she surely wondered how these two well-groomed and obviously well-cared-for little girls had come to be all alone in the neighborhood, bawling their heads off and crying non-stop into the air, "We're L-O-O-O-O-O-ST!"

When the police arrived, the officers tried to calm us. They told us they would help us, and said that we should come with them in their police car. But Dana wasn't having it. "NOOOOO," she wailed. "You're a *Stranger!*" And she resumed her crying with renewed vigor.

The well-meaning officer then turned to me, offering me ice cream if I would just get in the car. He promised that once I was in the car, he could help me find my parents.

Well, *sniff,* ice cream sounded all right, *sniff.* I decided I would go with him and get some ice cream. But Dana grabbed me and held on tight, saying, "You can't take her! You're a *Stranger!*"

By now a small crowd had gathered, and everyone was trying to figure out what to do. The poor officers were probably about to call for backup by the time Mom came running down the sidewalk. Struggling to make haste in high heels, she waved her arms and cried frantically, "Wait, wait! They're mine! They're mine!"

No further verification was needed as we caught sight of her and ran pell-mell into her arms. As she stroked our hair she asked, "Why didn't you just turn around and come straight back in?" All the while we, between hiccups, tried to tell her that all the doors looked the same. Dana explained importantly that the *Stranger* tried to *take* Diana, but Dana wouldn't let him!

I don't remember if Mom got us any ice cream after that, but I expect she did.

Sadly, that was the last sisterly love story Dana and I were to tell for quite some time. That love remained in our hearts, of course, but there was little evidence of it in our daily lives.

Dana, the nice big sister, caring and protective, would change completely. Only one year after the Lost incident, when inner frustrations and pain found no other outlet, she became my personal, bullying oppressor.

We were very young when Mom remarried, and I thought all the changes were wonderful. I liked our new house. I loved my three new siblings. We thought the world of our new dad. But Dana had known a different life – one she still valued. Our "real" dad, as we described him, was still in Viet Nam. She missed him.

Divorce, remarriage, new house, new family…Dana had a lot to deal with that she had no way of voicing. With no outlet, she became increasingly frustrated, and as we grew up, she took more and more of that frustration out on me.

By the time I entered kindergarten, Dana dominated my every moment. She picked on me, teased me, and bullied me at every opportunity. On the other hand, she always knew how to behave sweetly in front of others. No one ever caught her twisting my arm behind my back. She told me no one liked me, and by the time I was five I was convinced that I was a ridiculous pest who shouldn't be allowed near other people. Where had nice Dana gone?

When I was six and learning to write, she scrawled my name, in my exact newbie printing, in the dust on Dad's car. I got in trouble, and no one believed me when I said I hadn't done it. As punishment, I had to wash the car with a toothbrush. Armed with an old toothbrush and a beleaguered attitude, I imagine I did more harm than good to Dad's paint job.

When we were older, Dana did not allow me to hang out with her friends, even when she wasn't around. She forbade me to have a crush on her favorite TV stars. She never allowed me to speak up for myself or disobey her demands. I wanted to take guitar lessons, but Dana pitched a fit. That was only for Dana.

The only other instrument in the house was Mom's old accordion. Mom agreed that I could have lessons, and even hired a teacher for me, but it didn't last. *No one* wants to hear a kid practicing an accordion, and our parents never asked for an accordion recital at a family party – not when Dana could render everyone misty-eyed as she beautifully played "Dust in the Wind" on her guitar.

When we entered a roomful of people, Dana would reiterate into my ear that no one in here liked me, so I'd better watch myself. At various times she threw me across rooms into walls, dragged me by my ankles so my elbows got horrible rug burns, slugged and pinched me incessantly, and scoffed at everything I did.

In Dana's defense, I must add that, although she felt entitled to pick on me, no one else was. If anyone on the playground messed with me, he was likely to get a punch in the nose from my big sister. This was a serious deterrent, as Dana was the elementary school tetherball champion, and stood a head taller than most of the other kids.

Not long ago Dana put some of our childhood troubles into her own words: "Part of our difficulty was the obvious difference in our personalities. We were polar opposites: I was strong, you were weak; I was very tall, you were normal sized; I liked dirt, you liked dolls; I loved dogs knocking me over, you were afraid of them; I wore jeans, you wore dresses. If we had not been sisters, I doubt we would have chosen each other as friends. Add into the mix our emotional turmoil over the divorce, and I became the perfect tyrant to you – the perfect victim."

Mildly stated, I was *not* developing a positive self-image. Indeed, I was heading into a corrosive view of myself that would last for decades. Then, just when I thought life couldn't be harder, it got worse.

One summer day, shortly after my 10th birthday, Dana and I had gone to a movie together and were waiting for Mom to come and get us. Dana was very athletic, always sure of herself, and very strong. Spying a low brick wall, she began leaping over it, landing three feet down in a sunken patio area. She did it over and over, and finally convinced me to give it a try. I was not athletic, coordinated, or strong. All the same, I finally made my leap, caught my toe on the bricks, and flew face-first into the patio. Dana rushed to my side and helped me up. Her face paled as she discovered that my upper lip was the size of a golf ball and that my shattered upper front teeth were embedded in it.

The dentist put long, fat silver crowns on what was left of my two destroyed teeth. He told my parents to leave those crowns on as long as everything stayed calm – no sense disturbing the roots if they were healing. I wore those silver crowns for three years.

Let me give you a clear picture: I had huge, silver, rabbit-like teeth in my face from age ten to age thirteen. Pre-adolescence is NOT a good time for a young girl to become wildly hideous.

When orthodontia time came around two years later, they put my braces right on top of my silver crowns. Everyone called me Tin Grin. In junior high, no one would speak to me. They were either appalled by my appearance or thought I was too much of a goodie-good. I had one friend, Suzy, who had known me before I broke my teeth, and she stuck with me. Unfortunately, she didn't attend my school.

As a result, I hated junior high. I became more and more insecure, more of a homebody.

The tide started to turn a little during my freshman year of high school. I had finally gotten out of my braces and into some crowns that looked like normal teeth. Dana joined a Baptist youth group that, every lunch hour, fearlessly dominated a large circle of grass on the high school lawn. She was reluctant to let me join (see above rules about not hanging out with her friends), but some of the group members met me and insisted that I be allowed to come along. Bless them.

Soon we were fully involved in this youth group. We met weekly, and attended Christian concerts every Friday evening at Calvary Chapel in Costa Mesa. We got to see Keith Green and Benny Hester and Bob Kilpatrick, to name only a few. No longer looking like a freak, I made some friends and tried not to interfere in Dana's circle. Things improved slightly at home during that time.

In my sophomore year they improved even more, for both of us. Dana was accepted as a Foreign Exchange Student. She flew off to Uruguay for an entire year. I no longer had someone watching and criticizing my every move. During that year I got a job, a car, and a boyfriend. When Dana returned home, she was ill with something akin to dysentery. She was horribly thin, and couldn't remember she should speak English to us.

I, on the other hand, was nearing the end of my junior year, was working and going to school. I was healthy and more in-dependent. I spent all my extra time at the beach, and I had a busy date life. I had come into my own, during her year away. Unfortunately, my self-image hadn't changed much.

Dana eventually recovered from her illness, and after gradu-ating from high school, she quickly became restless. She'd seen something of the world, and wanted more. Never one to take small steps, she signed herself up with the Merchant Marines, deciding she'd ship out and make her own way in the world. Dana was packing her duffle bag when Mom learned our church was sending a group of people to volunteer aboard a missionary ship in Greece.

Filled with excitement, Mom told Dana about it. She was thrilled at the thought that Dana could "ship out," without joining some cargo vessel filled with who-knows-what kind of shipmates.

Together they spoke to our church, and in very short order Dana was accepted as a volunteer with Youth With A Mission. The church and my parents promised to send monthly support, totaling $100 a month.

As it turned out, Dana's adventure was about to change my own life forever.

CHAPTER **TWO**

Dana did her Discipleship Training School (DTS) on the island of Cyprus, delving into the Bible and building lifelong relationships. She and several others from the ship had been sent to Cyprus to get the mandatory YWAM education under their belts.

When I later joined her on the ship and began my own DTS – the first ever held aboard the *Anastasis* – it was a new beginning for me, too. What amazing teaching! What hard work every afternoon. What strong friendships we built during that time!

They say it takes five years to form a strong bond with another person, unless you are together in crisis. Though the ship wasn't a place of crisis, it *was* a place of challenging living conditions. The power was cut every evening at ten o'clock in order to save fuel. It was turned back on every morning at 6:00 a.m., at which time the toilets held surprises for the unwary.

Having had no power during the off hours to maintain water pressure, the toilets settled in for the night and developed air pockets in their pipes. If you weren't careful to bleed the air out slowly in the morning, the first flush would cause the toilet to explode, spraying water, and the bowl's contents, all over the bathroom. Probably all over you, too.

We all ate together, worked together, and prayed together. We froze together when the winter wind sent the ship tugging violently on her anchor. The chill permeated right through her steel hull and into our bones. We learned rules of etiquette, such as not to shine our flashlights into people's faces when lights were out. It blinded them!

That rule didn't apply to me, though. I got used to finding my way around in pitch-black hallways and staircases, as a flashlight was a luxury I did not possess.

We enjoyed feasts, celebrations, guest speakers and lots of hot tea out on Aft Deck. Although there was no crisis, we bonded together with the stickiest of glue. Those relationships remained and gained strength throughout my next 13 years in Youth With A Mission, ten of which were spent living aboard the ship.

These events stemmed from that first, adventurous trip to Greece in January of 1981. Those early days on the *Anastasis* were a time of work, a time of learning, and a time of sacrifice. We learned to do without most of the things we took for granted in our home countries.

It was also during those early days in YWAM that my world was rocked to the core by family tragedy.

I was 18 years old, and I'd been with Youth With A Mission a mere six months. Most of that time was dominated by my five-month Discipleship Training School. Our DTS had just finished its outreach phase, and I'd been living in a hostel in downtown Athens for two months. We had joined forces with schools from across Europe, and we had a large gathering of young people spreading the Gospel in Athens that year.

We had taken over the entire hostel, divvying up the sleeping quarters. Young singles were divided by gender and assigned to huge dorm rooms. We covered most of the floor space with our mats and sleeping bags. There were probably twenty girls in the room I shared, sleeping on thin mats on the floor, shoulder to shoulder. Our belongings were stowed near our feet. Smaller rooms were allocated to married couples and families.

Every day we met on the roof for announcements, teaching, and, best of all, worship. One day, some of the neighbors approached us and said it sounded like angels were filling the streets with music every time we sang. They'd never heard worship songs like ours, and would open their windows just to listen. We dubbed our hostel the Lighthouse. Our goal was to shine the light of Jesus in an otherwise dark downtown area.

Our outreach finally concluded in late May, and while other students returned to their home countries, I moved back aboard the ship. While I'd been on my outreach in Athens, Dana had become engaged to a shipmate. She was planning her on-board wedding, and we set our minds on things to be done. We were preparing, not only for the wedding, but for our mom's arrival. She was traveling all the way to Greece, and would stay on the ship for the big event.

On the morning Dana was scheduled to go into Athens with her fiancé to pick out a wedding ring, a call came in to the ship's shore office. Unfortunately, the news got jumbled as it was passed among too many people. By the time the ship's chaplain came to give the news to Dana and me, he had only one piece of information.

"I am so very sorry, but your brother has died."

"*Which one?*" I cried. "We have three brothers!"

The chaplain didn't know. He only knew our brother had died. He hadn't known to ask which one of the three.

I sat in my cabin, a ball of confused terror. Dana decided to go ahead into town, and said she would call home from the shore office, then radio back to me. I couldn't do a thing but wait.

My brothers were Kenny, Kyle, and Kirk. Kenny was the eldest, who had picked me up and jumped with me into the pool. The family charmer, he got away with everything. Kyle was our artistic one. He was an aspiring musician and was the family's deep thinker. And Kirk. My baby brother! Seven years my junior, he was only eleven years old!

As my mind jumped to each one, I thought my heart would stop. It couldn't be any of them! I rejected the thought of losing each one in turn. I couldn't bear it.

An hour later I was summoned to A Deck Reception. It was from this area that the ship's business was conducted. Staffed full time, this was our communications hub. There was a radiophone there, and when I arrived I was handed the receiver. Dana was calling me from shore.

"Diana, it's Kenny. It was a motorcycle accident." My knees buckled, my eyes instantly streaming rivers. Kenny was gone? *Noooooooo!!!* I couldn't grasp the scope of it. A world without Kenny in it? I was only 18. I'd never before had to experience the impact of such a crushing blow.

Dana sounded odd to me, too. She seemed to be in some kind of shock that wouldn't allow her to process this news at all. She just said, "Well, I'm going to go on into town. I'll see you when I get back." Where I was a puddle of raw grief, nearly consumed with the weight of it, Dana had pulled away, unable to take it in. She couldn't face it. She stuffed it down inside somewhere for the time being. I knew her, knew how she loved him, and feared for her when the truth really sank in.

Later, when another launch approached the ship, I made the decision to go ashore. I needed to call home for myself. Upon my arrival at the ship's office, however, I found myself unable to place the call. I had to dial lots of numbers on an old rotary phone, but my trembling fingers stumbled over the sequence again and again. Mercifully, the woman who worked in the office finally did the dialing. I reached my mom, and she was able to tell me a little bit more, but it was months before I got the whole story.

Kenny had been on a motorcycle ride with his roommate. Near the end of the day they made a wager about who could get home first. Racing down a winding mountain road, Kenny missed a turn.

Dad got the call that Kenny had been in an accident, and was told the name of the hospital he should go to. It was over an hour away. Before Dad had raced out the door, he'd asked for details on Kenny's condition. The hospital staff told him they were not allowed to give him any information over the phone. Dad, therefore, had no idea of the severity of the accident. Kenny had still been alive when they'd called, but by the time Dad rushed into the emergency room where Kenny lay, my big brother had slipped away, out of our lives forever.

Our family's heart would never beat the same again. Our rhythm changed forever. Our breath of fresh air, our wonderful Kenny's spirit had flown away to heaven.

* * *

We had to carry on after we lost Kenny, as families do, but we never recovered. Dad's hair turned from brown to solid white within a month. Just two weeks after the funeral, Mom came to Greece for Dana's wedding.

It was such a time of highs and lows. I was excited for Dana. I was happy to see my mom for the first time in six months. All the while, my eyes leaked non-stop as thoughts of my wonderful brother flooded my heart.

We spoke about Kenny often at family gatherings in the years that followed. When I would weep, my brother Kyle would say, "It's okay to cry, Diana. Kenny was worth crying for."

CHAPTER **THREE**

While on the ship, I met and married my first husband. Our two daughters, though born in California, each knew only the ship as their first home.

We left the *Anastasis* in 1990 in order to bring YWAM into what is now the Czech Republic, but was then still known as Czechoslovakia. We planned to move to Prague with eight other people, and then to work with local churches. We would formulate more of a plan once we learned the areas of greatest need.

Hearts and hands to help. We'd heard this phrase often from Don Stephens, founder of Mercy Ships. We were bringing hearts, hands, and four children into a country only recently freed from the grip of Communism. Our two daughters were not alone in our mission, because another couple on our team had two young children as well.

Before we could start the work in Prague, however, we needed to spend a year building a team and working on logistics in Amsterdam. We then lived for two years in a beautiful Prague suburb called Hlubočepy, where we tried to learn Czech. By the time we left, I could manage a stilted conversation with Czech friends…if they were very patient.

In 1993, we decided it was time to go home for good. By then my girls both spoke Dutch and Czech, and I had 29 different countries stamped in my passport.

And my relationship with Dana? We've had our ups and downs since that season, but mostly our ups. I've mentioned that during her YWAM training she wrote and apologized to me for making my childhood difficult. During my own schooling, I likewise had things for which I needed to apologize. Now, she and my daughters are my best friends.

I used to joke with Dana that somehow I'd managed to "marry" her twice, meaning I found men who were able to control me with anger and criticism. In some ways, with my first marriage, that was true. My first husband, whom I met on the *Anastasis*, was the eldest of four children. He had been rough on his siblings as they all grew up, just like my sister had been on me. He had told me, before we married, that he had a temper, but I'd never seen any display of it at all, so I didn't really believe him. Sadly, he wasn't kidding, and I, with all of my own insecurities, wasn't equipped to handle it.

When we left YWAM, I was fairly certain that our marriage wasn't going to work. Three years after our return from the mission field, we divorced.

Two and a half years later I remarried, and though Larry was otherwise unlike my first husband, he, too, had anger issues. I buckled under them, just like I always had with Dana.

I was 50 years old by the time I realized that, not only had I "married" my sister twice, I had brought the *kid sister in me* into both of my marriages. I had never learned to speak up. Shoot, I hadn't even learned to *think up*. Awesome teaching and Bible education notwithstanding, I had not yet rid myself of my stunted self-confidence. And on my own, I never would have.

It would take the strong, all-knowing, loving hand of God to turn me around.

CHAPTER **FOUR**
BACK TO THE PRESENT

COUNTY JAIL, DAY ONE: ROUGHLY 8:30 P.M.

I jumped when my cell door clanged open. Staring into space, thinking of my family, I'd thought I was locked in for the evening. The sudden *whoosh* of air took me by surprise.

It was Sergeant Green, a kind man who had helped walk me through the process of becoming a jail volunteer. He was working nights, and apparently someone had filled him in on the inmate in Hold 4, both who she was and why she was there. Seeing him was a wonderful surprise!

Sticking his head and shoulders into the cell, he said, "I came to see how you were doing."

"I'm not a happy camper," was my seriously lame response.

"No, not a happy camper. But you're okay?"

What could I say? I'd never been less okay, but that wasn't what he meant. I wasn't ill. I wasn't hysterical. I wasn't hurt. I was…incarcerated.

I didn't know how to respond, so I just said, "I'm nervous about tomorrow. The judge said he's going to make me stay here for as long as it takes. I could be here a long time."

He was nodding. "I know," he said, even as his eyes were drawn to the naked upper bunk. He didn't say anything about my doubling up of the mattresses, and I was still blissfully unaware that my use of that upper pad was taboo. His eyes took in the little nest I'd made on my lower bunk. He noted my Bible, book, writing things, and blanket wrap. He spoke again, ever so gently, saying, "You won't have to stay in this cell for very long." I felt a highly dangerous lump form in my throat. "In a day or two you'll be moved to one of the blocks."

My eyes grew prickly as the first tears of the day threatened to shred my fragile composure.

He knew. He knew this cell was awful, and he was offering what comfort he could. His next words surprised me even more.

"I want you to know that I really respect you for what you're doing."

It's a good thing I was sitting down. Though I'd been pleased to see him, I couldn't have guessed I'd hear such an encouraging sentiment on this black evening. Just like when Pastor Mark mentioned that DJ wanted to visit, I realized that what was happening with me wasn't happening in a vacuum. I hadn't considered there would be scuttlebutt in the jail about an imprisoned church volunteer.

Then again, maybe Captain Harris had told Sergeant Green to keep an eye on me. Either way, I was astonished to learn that, as I sat in here and tried to cope, one moment at a time, people were talking about me. People had opinions, and not all of them were bad!

"Wow, Sergeant Green," I spluttered. "I didn't see that coming. I don't know what to say except, thank you."

"Sure," he replied. "Hang in there. Good night." And he was gone, closing that dreadful steel door behind him. But he'd lifted my spirits, given me new things to think about. I was waking up to the fact that this thing was bigger than I. People were watching. People were aware.

I closed my eyes and whispered, "Let people see courage from You, Lord. Let them see faith. Help me to hold it together, so that, through all of this, people will see You."

Remembering my earlier conversation with Captain Harris, I knew that, while my faith in God wasn't on the line, my faith for my circumstances certainly was. Captain Harris had informed me that I would no longer be allowed to volunteer in the jail, due to my incarceration. My freedom, my job, and the jail ministry all hung in the balance, and the question was, *Do you believe?*

My freedom? Well, at present I didn't have that. My job? That wouldn't survive any kind of jail term. To maintain a professional court reporter's license requires an annual renewal, during which they ask, "Have you been convicted of anything in the past year?" Well, I hadn't been convicted of anything, fortunately. I was just being *held* until I agreed to speak. However, I didn't need any more trouble if I wanted to work as a court reporter. And the jail ministry was, according to Captain Harris, already gone.

Still, though the captain was a firm man, running a tight ship at this county lock-up, he was also kind. He had asked me for my version of events. Even as he had to deliver the difficult news to me, that my clearance would be revoked, he wanted to know my side of the story. What had happened? Why was I here?

CHAPTER **FIVE**

It was a valid question. Why was I in Captain Harris's custody? Any life is full of twists and turns, of course. For a time, mine had spiraled out of control, though not criminally. I had never seen a jail cell coming my way. But, I wasn't a completely innocent victim, either.

Remember the motorcycle course? Well, after that, Larry and I took up Harley riding in earnest. Every year we took time off in late April and headed to Laughlin, Nevada for the annual Laughlin River Run. There was usually still snow on the ground at home, so we loaded the bikes into our trailer and set off to warm up, ride around, and shake off our yearly dose of cabin fever.

Our route varied some from year to year, but eventually we found that it was ideal to park our rig on the Harley dealer's back lot in St. George, Utah. From there we would ride over to Mesquite, Nevada to spend the night before riding on to Laughlin the next day.

The River Run really gets going on the last Thursday of April every year. By Saturday evening, things that were getting crazy could go downhill fast. We liked to arrive on Wednesday, when vendors were already setting up and a few early birds were beginning to trickle in. We almost always bugged out of there on Saturday morning, leaving well ahead of the wild Saturday-only crowds who rode in from Vegas and Los Angeles.

When I say things got crazy, I mean that 70,000-plus bikers would completely take over that town, rendering it unrecognizable from one day to the next. On the Tuesday before the Run began, it was business as usual in Laughlin. The average day saw busloads of people arriving to eat, gamble, swim, and stay in rooms that cost around $29 per night.

By Thursday morning those nice people had piled onto their busses and fled as the bikers swarmed in. Then the rooms went for $200 per night, with a three-night minimum. Most rooms sold out a year in advance. Though we arrived on Wednesday, that didn't count toward our three nights. We, too, had to pay to keep our room through Sunday morning. We never had any trouble, though, selling that final night to a biker who needed it. In one case, we handed it over outright to my daughter. Fully grown by this time, she had come with a friend to visit us and check out the party.

And a party it was. *So many* people, all geared up in their favorite riding wear. We all hung out, went on rides, and checked out the goodies.

Vendors set up huge tents that housed complete motorcycle shops. They would happily install your new seat, pipes, handlebars, or anything else that struck your fancy. There was clothing, jewelry, and leathers galore. You could buy anything from a tricked-out chopper to motorcycle insurance.

During the day we would ride, relishing the hot weather and the freedom of being on the bikes after a long season in snowy mountains. We rode to Needles, Lake Havasu, Bullhead City, and, my favorite, Oatman.

Oatman was always ready for the bikers. They all loved to ride there, park their bikes and walk around. People could get their pocket knives sharpened or buy beautiful Native American jewelry. The folks who ran my favorite leather shop in Oatman once caught me asking a stupid question and fined me, ordering me to put a quarter into the dumb-blonde basket. Looking around, I saw that, indeed, there *was* a basket labeled, "Dumb Blonde Fines," front and center on their countertop. Gotta love it!

Another memorable Oatman moment happened when I was trying to park my motorcycle, which by now was a nine hundred pound Road King. I had left the pavement and was backing the bike very carefully on the slippery, rocky dirt. I felt a tug, and my bike began moving backward without my say-so. A glance in my mirror revealed the problem. A guy I didn't know, holding a beer in one hand, had grabbed my rear luggage rack and was tugging the bike backwards as I tried to park. He probably thought he was helping!

My huge Road King wobbled as I lost my footing and couldn't regain it in the loose gravel. I yelled at him to STOP IT, and he quit pulling. Fortunately, he didn't let go completely until the bike was steady. *Gee-ma-nee!!!*

The trip to Laughlin was a big event for us for many years. We accumulated lots of stories, both good and bad.

One time we, along with the entire town, were locked down in our hotel rooms while the police investigated and cleared away bodies after a shooting between the Hells Angels and the Mongols. The feud began out in the desert, raged all the way into town, and exploded into Harrah's casino in the early hours of the morning. When all was said and done, four people were dead, with several more injured.

We enjoyed friends, concerts, nice dinners, and good times, but that wouldn't be the whole story. There was also drinking. Lots of drinking. On the worst night, Larry had so much to drink that he hallucinated most of the night away, even while sleeping. He was sick, remaining in bed for thirty hours. He had alcohol poisoning, and missed out on a Foreigner and George Thorogood concert the following night.

On another occasion, after a large meal with, again, lots of booze, Larry paid the bill and left the restaurant ahead of me. He never noticed that I'd gotten separated from him, and a group of bikers closed ranks around me. It's not a good situation when a bunch of inebriated men start saying, "Hey, honey, where ya goin'?" I felt one hand on me, and then another, as they grabbed at me lewdly. I had just decided I was going to have to make a lot of noise when I heard a big voice growling, "What's going on here?"

It was George, our big, burly riding companion. A stonemason by trade, he stood head and shoulders above all of my tormentors. Nobody was going to mess with him as he reached in and pulled me away, his expression grim. His eyes scanned the crowd as he asked me, "Why are you alone, and *where* is Larry?"

I had no answer. Larry wouldn't have forgotten about me if he'd been sober, but for all I knew, he was already back in our room. He'd be asleep in no time. Or angry.

Frustration and pain from past events (childhood trauma, divorce, and the resultant loss of his business and close relationships) had created in Larry a fermenting, permanent anger that lay just beneath the surface. When he drank, it burst out of him. The years of our marriage had seen increasingly frequent incidents of intoxicated anger towards me. Nearly every night, if he didn't fall asleep early, he would yell at me and rage around the house. On countless nights I cried myself to sleep in our guest room.

In many ways, traveling made it worse, because he was enjoying some precious time away from his demanding business. He wanted to relax and have a "good time." Trouble was, the drinking brought out his temper, and he never remembered, next morning, that he had spent the evening shouting at me. Travel was difficult for me because we shared a small hotel room, and there was no guest room to which I could escape.

* * *

Over time, Laughlin and our ventures there became less and less appealing to me. Evenings were no fun – and then, there was that close call we had on the freeway.

As we traveled back to St. George, this particular time, to

load the bikes and go home, I thought for sure I was a goner. A large piece of rusty, corrugated roofing had fallen off the back of a truck. It had sharp, upturned edges, and it filled the lane ahead of me. Zooming along at sixty-five miles an hour, I knew I couldn't ride over it. I swerved to my right to avoid it, which put me squarely behind a white pickup. The driver of that truck panicked at the sight of that chunk of metal and slammed on his brakes!

To avoid rear-ending him, I swerved right again, this time onto the right-hand shoulder. *So did he!* He swerved unnecessarily onto the shoulder, still right in front of me, and inexplicably *stopped!*

I jerked my bike upright, out of its swerve, and locked up my brakes. I knew if I hit him with my bike upright and slowing, I'd have a chance. If I locked up the brakes with the bike leaning, it would squirrel around and wreck.

Never lock up your brakes while your bike is leaning. That was the Second Important Lesson we'd learned in our motorcycle course years before, closely following Important Lesson Number One about Turning Our Heads. Even in that very quick moment, I could hear my instructor's voice saying, "This is when the big boys go down, and it's because they weren't taught this: *Always* get your bike upright before you lock up your brakes."

Now, even braking hard wouldn't be enough. I had no room, and thought I was in for it. At the last moment, the pickup driver saw me in his rearview mirror and gunned it, racing away from me as quickly as he could. I slowed some more, gulping in air and trying to gain better control of my bike.

That's when *I* saw, in *my* rearview mirror, a car that was about to plow into the back of my motorcycle. He was trying to avoid cars in what had become a free-for-all swerve zone around that corrugated roofing. His car was on the shoulder, zooming towards me. His tires were literally smoking as he slammed on his brakes. I had to *move!*

I believe what happened next is a miracle. With all my braking and swerving and breath catching, the bike had slowed from sixty-five mph to maybe ten mph. It was nearly slow enough to put my feet down. But everything had happened so fast that I hadn't had a chance to downshift, which would usually have been my first order of business. I'd been busy trying to stay alive, so I was still in fifth gear. You can't get a motorcycle going from a near stop when it's in fifth gear. It'll stall, jerk, and probably fall over.

When I saw that car bearing down behind me, ready to launch me into kingdom come, I released my clutch and opened the throttle. Though the bike stuttered a little, it didn't stall, and I boogied out of harm's way just in time!

Larry was way ahead of me and hadn't seen a thing.

CHAPTER **SIX**

Coming as it did at the end of April, the River Run at Laughlin rolled out our annual motorcycle season. It was not, however, the season's main event. For years our summer vacations revolved around ten-day Harley trips. We usually stuck to the Pacific Northwest, though occasionally we could be found in the Four Corners region. We stayed in Durango, Colorado, rode around some very scenic country, and even played a little golf.

Actually, Larry played a little golf. I took a lesson. Just one. My instructor was obsessed with the geometry of the game, and that was probably not the best approach for this student. I hate math. I am calculator-dependent. Geometry? No. If golf was math, it was not for me.

The majority of our trips were more northward, though. We rode as far as the Canadian border, traveling with the same friends every year. I think the guys had fun on those long, ten-day rides, but I never should have gone. I was the only female, and my main function, besides making hotel reservations, was just *keeping up*.

In my experience of being the lone woman in the group, keeping up was *everything*. And it was a losing battle. I'll let you in on a secret: people lie. Just as a fisherman might exaggerate the size of his catch, bikers veer off plumb when talking about their speed.

And it can go both ways. It can be, "I was doin' ninety over that pass, slidin' on road worms and nearly losin' control! It was wild!" (Road worms are the streaks of tar that road crews lay down to fill in cracks. In the heat, they get slippery.)

My trouble stemmed from the opposite side of the speed lie. They would ask me, "Why can't you keep up? We're only going sixty!" The truth was that they were doing seventy-five or eighty, easy. Did they think my almost new motorcycle didn't have a working speedometer?

I know one guy who missed his curve and slipped over the center yellow line, right into an oncoming car. When I saw him a week later, banged up but alive, he was baffled. "I have no idea what happened!" he exclaimed. "I mean, I was only going twenty-five!"

I didn't want to be mean about it, since he was hurt, but I could have told him he had just revealed the trouble. I knew from riding with him that his "twenty-five" around a twisty really meant forty-five or fifty. Every. Time.

One of those long trips nearly took Larry out as we were riding along the Beartooth Highway in Montana. I'd told the guys to ride ahead, that I would take the hairpins at my speed and catch them on the straightaways. The scenery was breathtaking, but I wasn't looking around much. I had all I could do to handle my bike.

It was just as well I wasn't trying to ride flat out, because as I came around one particular curve, I saw a motorcycle down. It was just ahead, lying on its side, in front of a car stopped in the oncoming lane. The accident had happened only a few feet from an abrupt cliff edge. I squinted hard at the scene, and saw to my horror that it was Larry's Harley that was down! Then my eyes fell on Larry. He was sitting on a huge boulder, signaling me with one hand.

We've seen two examples where I didn't drop my bike in a pinch: on my practice ride where I missed my turn, and on my near miss with the corrugated roof. Fortunately, my nerves didn't fail me here, either.

I pulled over carefully and shut off my bike, dismounting fluidly, if I do say so myself. The other guys later marveled (in a rare offering of kudos) that I managed to retain my composure and remembered to put the kickstand down.

Larry's bike was on the asphalt, and almost beneath a car's front bumper. He tried to tell me he was okay, but he wasn't. His coat was torn, his helmet scratched up, and a quick survey of his bike showed considerable damage. Surprisingly, his fancy paint job hadn't suffered a scratch. Engine and luggage guards had done their job; in addition to protecting the paint, they had prevented Larry's leg from being crushed when he'd "laid the bike" down.

And indeed, he *had* "laid 'er down." A deliberate crash. He'd been cruising around the winding highway, enjoying the beautiful vistas and the fresh, crisp air. He'd been doing a (biker's) twenty-five mph (see above), when a large rock had come tumbling down the mountain and slammed into his rear tire.

He'd lost all control of the bike, and he was headed for another sharp turn to his right. He knew he'd never make the turn. To miss it would have meant soaring straight off the highway and over the cliff to his death. His only option was to lay the bike down and hope for the best.

As it happened, there was a car coming around the blind curve in the opposite lane, its speed appropriately reduced for the twisty conditions. It stopped just short of Larry, as he slid to a stop. He staggered up as quickly as he could, because, he told me later, he didn't want me to come around the bend and see him sprawled out on the ground. (Very considerate of him.)

In the end, he had torn something in his shoulder. His motorcycle needed new handlebars, a new clutch assembly and left-hand mirror. When we got home, we had to replace his engine guards, saddlebags, and tour pack. He had to tolerate considerable ribbing in the future from friends who liked to remind him, when we would set out, "Rubber side down, Larry."

Rubber won't help you much, though, if you're on only two wheels and find yourself in a downpour. Roads can get slick in a hurry when rain starts, and if it's heavy enough, the water will puddle treacherously on the surface. For this reason, the town of Ennis, Montana would be indelibly etched upon my memory.

We'd been on the road for nine days. Every day was right around four hundred miles, and that was too much for me. In a car, I can drive over a thousand miles to see my kids and think nothing of it, but on a motorcycle it's a different story.

Exhausted, I was eager to reach our Ennis motel. We were still a hundred miles out when the sky started clouding up. We'd encountered only occasional showers on this trip, and so far we hadn't needed to don our rain gear. This particular day, in fact, had been quite sunny. Late in the afternoon, however, we noticed white, puffy clouds dotting the sky. They quickly increased in number and drew closer together. I glanced at them often to see if they were gray underneath, but so far they were harmless puffballs.

It wasn't long, however, before the sky started to darken ahead. I checked my odometer. Still fifty miles to go. I willed the miles to go more quickly. I didn't like the idea of being caught on the highway in a serious rainstorm, fearing the slick roads, spray from other vehicles, and the terrible visibility that would follow.

The sky grew darker. Forty miles. Now the clouds started shaping up and coming nearer to earth. A deep, inky mass moved closer and closer to where we were rolling along the highway. Somewhere deep within the approaching darkness were bursts of jagged light. We were facing not just rain, but a huge thunderstorm!

Thirty miles. Now I couldn't decide if the clouds were black or a very dark purple. It seemed there was no way we could avoid being caught in the impending storm. There was no cover anywhere. If the tempest hit us, we'd have to ride on the best we could and hope to make it to town in one piece.

Twenty miles. My heart was racing. Could it be that we'd get so close and still get walloped? I'd never seen such ominous clouds before. Did they get tornadoes in Montana?

Ten miles. Was that a raindrop on my visor? No, you big, mean storm! Wait to unleash your fury! We're almost there!

I turned my attention heavenward. I felt I had no right to pray. I wasn't living right. I hadn't read my Bible in ages. I had blatantly sinned on occasion, living just to please myself. I had sunk right out of any relationship with the Lord. But I knew He was there. I knew I'd wandered, but He hadn't gone anywhere.

I allowed just the thought of a prayer to form in my mind. *We need Your help, Lord.*

The storm, pregnant with fury, held back, and we rode into town.

We located our motel, got the kickstands down, and the lady at the front desk ran outside to hand us our keys. "Hurry, just get inside! Come do the paperwork later!" Then she scurried for cover.

The first huge, fat raindrops landed on our heads as we quickly grabbed our bags off the bikes, opened the doors to our rooms, and ducked inside. Immediately, as we got past the doorjambs, the skies opened. I had never before witnessed such rain. We were on the narrow main street of town, but we could barely see the buildings across the road through the torrential downpour.

From the protection of our room, Larry and I stared outside, mesmerized. We'd come within a minute of being out in *that…* on bikes!

The street flooded instantly. Water came down so fast and heavy that it couldn't flow away. Lightning bolts and earsplitting thunder struck simultaneously. Such conditions could have been lethal on our Harleys. Indeed, the hand of God had held back the deluge until we were safely inside.

The storm lasted for about half an hour, and we eventually stopped staring at it and got cleaned up from the day's ride. Ready to go relax and have some dinner, we were to meet our group across the street at a bar/restaurant. As it was still raining, we held our jackets over our heads and made a run for it. Once inside, we found that one of our gang knew the owner of the establishment. They were surprised to see each other, and after introductions were made all around, the party was on.

I left fairly early, because it was clear that this bunch was headed well into their cups. When I went back to the motel they were smoking cigars, drinking, and entertaining each other with motorcycle war stories.

But the night was young!

I was sound asleep when, around eleven o'clock, our door flew open and Larry blasted into our motel room, turned on the light and, weaving on his feet, said, "Hey, you got a Band-Aid?"

That's when I noticed he had a towel wrapped around his hand, and it was soaked in blood. What on earth? I couldn't be angry with a bleeding man, so I got up and found him some Band-Aids. He removed the towel and ran his hand under the water.

Good grief!! Even my sleepy eyes could see that his finger looked half severed. Had he been in a fight?

"What *happened?*"

"Oh," he said breezily, "'snothin', 'sfine. Was jus' cutting the end off a cigar."

I watched in disbelief as he dabbed some antibiotic ointment into the cut, and then wrapped the bandages this way and that. He applied pressure and pressed the flesh together until he had a very neatly dressed wound. Amazing. He was reeling on his feet and could barely speak, but his hands were completely steady.

Then, to my complete shock, he reached for the light switch and turned it off, saying simply, "K, I'm going back. 'Night!"

The man was out of his mind!

I crawled back into bed and eventually fell asleep again, only to be awakened once more. This time it was nearly one o'clock in the morning when the door banged open. Again, on came the light, but with a new twist. This time he headed for the television and turned that on, too. He waved airily in my direction. "You don't mind if I turn this on, do you?"

This was a nightmare. It was one in the morning! "Turn that thing off and go to bed!" I was definitely cross this time. What had he been up to? I marveled that he'd even been able to find the right room!

At least he wasn't belligerent. On the plus side, he did manage to shut off both the TV and the light before passing out on his bed.

He really should have been completely hungover in the morning, but the truth is, he rarely ever was. Except for the alcohol poisoning in Laughlin, he usually skated through heavy drinking with no morning-after effects.

* * *

Which doesn't mean there were no consequences to the night's mischief.

Larry hadn't made it back to the motel with his jacket. To restate, I didn't know how he'd found our room at all. Small wonder he'd forgotten his jacket. Its loss was huge, though. First, it was the only one he had with him. Second, his motorcycle key was in one of the pockets.

It was still early in the morning, and the restaurant wasn't open yet. At least we were able to call the owner, and he sent someone to let us in. No jacket. It had clearly been stolen.

Now, as it turned out, the owner of that restaurant and bar, the one who was the long-lost buddy of one of our riding companions, was also a bit of a Godfather in town. He knew everyone, had dealings with lots of people and businesses throughout the area. Every night he could be found holding court in the rear portion of his restaurant.

Folks on the up and up respected him, and the local ne'er-do-wells feared him. When we told him Larry's nice leather Harley jacket had been stolen, he assured us that, without question, it would be recovered.

We loaded up our bikes and got ready to ride out. Meanwhile, word went out that the immediate return of Larry's jacket was required by the "Don" (my word), and that there wouldn't be any trouble if it was returned forthwith.

Fortunately, in our haste to get out of the storm the night before, Larry hadn't locked his bike. He was able to start it right up and ride out with us. And we really had no choice but to leave. Our next stop was a full day's ride away, and the next day we were heading home. We'd been assured that when the jacket was recovered it would be sent to us straightaway.

And that's just what happened. By the time we made our first stop for gas we had a message from our new friend that the thief had been identified. Confronted with the prospect of displeasing the Don, he had morosely slouched over to the bar and handed the jacket in. He'd been stopped the night before by an eagle-eyed employee who'd asked him if that jacket was his. The guy promised, "Oh, yes!" But the employee remembered, and she reported the man's name when word of the theft was put out.

I'd like to say that accidents, thunderstorms, and thievery were the worst things that ever happened on our long road trips. But that wouldn't be true. I'm afraid I got my own self into far more trouble than if all I'd done was wreck my bike.

CHAPTER **SEVEN**

We've now reached a pivotal moment in my story. In the early 2000s, riding around the country in the summertime, I was not a happy woman. My kids, having discovered far too much trouble in Idaho, were back in California. I had thought that moving them away from California would be beneficial for them, but I was mistaken. Teens can find trouble anywhere, and mine easily found it in our new locale.

They went to live with their dad, and to say I missed them would be a grotesque understatement. I'd been ripped in two. Larry worked hard but, as we've seen, he drank a lot, which often led to verbal abuse towards me. He never drank at work, but even sober he was always simmering.

We weren't going to church, but we were going to bars. Almost every night our evening meal consisted of drinks and chicken wings at one of the local pubs. We argued when we got home, and the house grew a little worse for wear. Broken picture frames and fist-sized wall holes were grim reminders of evening troubles.

Larry became my personal Jekyll and Hyde. He kept a grip on himself during the daytime, but slipped into whatever mood the alcohol held for him each evening.

Even his daytime control didn't equate to cheerfulness. Life had creased vertical scowl lines into his forehead. He shook his head like a negating Bobblehead all day long. Nothing was done right, no one behaved right, everything was bad and getting worse. He became domineering over every aspect of my life.

I felt that I wore an Electronic Leash as Larry demanded that he be able to reach me at all times. If I didn't respond quickly to a text or an email, he would get angry. While at home, if I walked upstairs, he would ask, "Where are you going?" He got mad if I stayed up too late. Yet he never asked, "How was your day?" Or, "What's new with the girls?" It seemed that, on the one hand, my every action was under scrutiny, and yet I, myself, remained invisible.

Our relationship was spiraling downward. (That'll happen when you leave God out of your life.) Larry became more controlling, and I returned to my childhood default positions of "roll over" and "take it." Totally unhealthy.

At times I wondered if I should have followed through with a move-out plan I had all but completed one summer. I'd rented a small, furnished studio apartment, signed on the dotted line, handed over my deposit, and shopped for my new life. I bought dishes, a telephone, some wastebaskets and laundry detergent.

But I didn't go through with it. I had once resolved to never divorce again. Getting an apartment and moving out was a big step in that off-limits direction. But in the end, my staying was not because I was strong and resolute. Neither did I stay because I was weak and spineless. I didn't really "decide" to stay at all.

The final nix on the Leave-Larry plan was provided by my sister, Dana. Dana had traveled from California to help me move, but on moving day she decided that I was a *crazy woman who had a nice house and a hard-working husband*. She told me, in no uncertain terms, that, whatever the drawbacks, I needed to rethink my position. She wouldn't lift a finger to help me move into my small apartment. (Fortunately, I was able to get my deposit back).

And so I stayed, and if we weren't *happy*, at least we were *busy*.

I've already described the Harleys, but we also had a boat, ATVs and snowmobiles. We had lots of surface friendships. Everything was superficial. We had no family nearby, no meaningful connections as a couple, either outside or inside of our home.

And so, in the midst of this unhappy state of affairs, I dove headlong into disaster.

We were on one of our summer motorcycle trips in the early 2000s. Larry was in a bad mood and wouldn't ride with the rest of us. He hung back and was unfriendly all day.

He had a way of crawling inside himself where no one could reach him. There wasn't always an event that triggered a sour disposition. It could land on him with no warning, and I never could get him to shake it off or cheer up. I always felt helpless when a mood overtook him, especially when we were on our bikes, far from home.

That was the situation on this day. He grew more sullen as the miles dragged on. I wished I hadn't come at all.

But here I was, on another long trip, riding alone. Our gang was used to enjoying their ride at their speed and letting me catch up when I could. That was at my request. So they were all way ahead of me, and Larry was slipping further and further behind. My side mirrors told me that he was riding almost on the shoulder, inching along like his mighty Road King had become a diseased Moped.

Maybe he was mad because he felt like he had to babysit me? All I knew was that it was a miserable day.

When we parked the bikes, he insisted he was fine, and so off we went to dinner with everyone. It was a night for drinking. Larry ordered drink after drink, as I nursed my favorite cocktail, a Sea Breeze, which tasted far too harmless for my own good. When dinner was over, we started walking around town, stopping at one bar and another, drinking away. And they were nice bars. It's not like we were skulking in the underbelly of society.

But drinking is drinking, and as my inhibitions lowered, I engaged in some mild flirtations with one of our group. He paid attention to me. He was nice to me, made jokes, and seemed to enjoy talking to me. It had been a long time since I'd felt "seen" by anyone. I liked it.

Suddenly something went off inside my head. *No one owns me.* A lifetime of pent-up frustration bubbled to the surface. I foolishly reached for what I saw, at that moment, as independence and self-assertion. I didn't want to be invisible or irrelevant anymore.

I make no excuses for myself here. It is to my deepest shame that I admit that, what began as an intoxicated flirtation, exploded into outright rebellion. Later that evening, when everyone else had gone to sleep, I took myself off to the other man's hotel room.

I couldn't know then that, in throwing off the *imagined* shackles chaining me to an unhappy marriage, I was locking myself into a spiritual prison where the bars of guilt would prevent forward progress in my life for years to come. And later, the revelation of that fateful night would lead to my being placed in *real* shackles, in order to save that very same marriage.

If we are unfaithful,

He remains faithful,

for He cannot deny who He is.

(II Timothy 2:13 NLT)

Still with me? Things are going to get better, I promise. Unfortunately, they go downhill big time. The me that is sitting in a jail cell isn't going anywhere, so for now we'll travel the road that got me here. I can promise you a ride with some wild twists and turns, and I won't sugarcoat any of them.

CHAPTER **EIGHT**

Larry and I had visited a few local churches back in 1999, shortly after we moved to Idaho. We attended one regularly for a while, but it floundered when its lead pastor moved away, and we hadn't looked further.

Then came my own sin on the road trip.

After that I was too ashamed to take myself off to church. Since Larry didn't mention that we should go, I left it alone. I avoided my Bible, my journal, Christian music, and talking about my past life as a Christian missionary. I'm sure you get the picture.

We met a lot of people and had many friends, but those relationships usually centered around some shared activity. We kept ourselves *busy.* We shared Bratwursts and cinnamon schnapps with chilled but happy comrades during day-long snow machine rides; we went to Halloween parties and New Year's Eve parties and surprise birthday parties; we took the boat out in the summer, having launched the season with a Memorial Day Boat Parade Extraordinaire at Magic Reservoir; we tied bandanas around our faces to keep the dust away as we rode over hill and dale on ATVs with the usual suspects from the Magic Dam Fools Club.

We worked, we played. We took out a second mortgage on our home and built a cabin on our property at Magic.

Our life was full of toys. None of our hobbies were satisfying to me, though, because I was so terrible at them. This revelation was brought home to me rather forcefully on one particular snowmobile outing when my attempts to hang on and keep up landed me in deep snow – face down, spread-eagled, *sans* snow machine. I had no idea where it was. I had asked the impossible of it and my sled had fled.

We were with a group of fifteen or so, all hardened snow-mobilers. They were fearless, capable riders who good-naturedly allowed wimps like me to come along on their all-day trips. We'd met outside Magic's Restaurant/Bar/Dam Fools Club, where we'd geared up, counted heads, and set off. After some time, I noticed that we were traveling along a ledge that held, just to our right, a six-foot drop down to a dry creek bed.

We ran out of open ground as we reached what seemed to be a bend in the waterless creek. The lead machines slowed and came to a stop on a small promontory overlooking the gully, which was now filled with snow, deep, and soft. As soon as we whoa-ed up and turned the engines off, our machines sank nearly a foot into the heavy stuff, which likewise covered our viewpoint.

I took off my helmet and looked around in alarm. Having ridden out onto the promontory, we had nowhere to go. As riders gathered in and hopped off their snowmobiles, I wondered how we were going to get turned around. Ahead of us was only the drop down into the gully, where countless stones were likely hidden beneath the snow's surface.

Directly across the gully was a small, flat area, which, when the creek was in full swing, would have formed a shallow pool or a nice cozy beach. Cliffs hugged the small beach in a horse-shoe-like fashion, the rounded end of the horseshoe being fur-thest from the creek. Not terribly tall, but quite sheer, these cliffs were considerably higher than where we sat on our promontory.

High desert plateaus sat atop the cliffs. They would make for nice riding if we could reach them, but we were on the wrong side of the tiny gorge. I'd had confidence that our leader knew where he was going, but he seemed to have brought us to an impasse which would force us to turn back. Such a maneuver seemed impossible, however, because our machines were sunk into the soft snow. I thought *maybe* we could coax them into forward motion, but I didn't think we'd ever get them turned around in the cramped space. Most snowmobiles are not equipped with Reverse, so backing them out was not an option.

But what was this? Mick, our trailblazer, was speaking: "Now, you'll have to watch me and pay close attention, because the only way this is going to work is if you do exactly what I do, and I'll only be able to show you this once. I'll have Randy come after me, and he'll be waiting at the top to help you if you need it."

Help us? With *what??* Mick was strapping on his helmet and throwing his leg over his machine. Then he was gone! He had literally disappeared!

Oh, no way. There he was! He had dropped straight down our side of the gully, zoomed across the creek bed and the small flat beach area, and was side-climbing the cliff face on the beach's right side. He then zoomed around the inside of the horseshoe, gaining momentum and height through the switchback. His sled careened sideways on the cliff walls like a toboggan on the Matterhorn ride at Disneyland. In his final stretch he straightened his machine *up*, nose to the sky, and cranked his throttle wide open.

He was now headed for the open plateau above, but before he got there he had to surmount the top edge's overhang of snow that threatened to cast him, not up and over the top, but backwards through the air. He would surely be flattened beneath his machine on the concealed rocks!

I watched, horror-struck. But he didn't catch the top curl of snow and fly backward. Against (what seemed to me) *all* probability, he crashed *through* the snowy overhang. Hunkering down low across his handlebars, he pushed his machine forward, over the top and onto the flat land above.

After this wild display, I looked around, hoping the others in our group had more sense. I hoped to see them nosing their machines around, back the way we had come. But they were pulling on gloves and goggles and starting up their sleds, as if… to *follow* him? Were they crazy?!?! Now I knew where the Dam Fools Club got its name!

Larry was speaking to me: "Were you paying attention? Make sure you don't let up on the throttle. Don't hesitate!" (Why were people always saying that to me?) "I'll wait here and make sure you're up before I take my turn."

I stared at him, wide-eyed. All the years the man had known me, and yet he thought me capable of *that???*

Before I could actually verbalize that thought, he was heading back to his own machine. I heard the roaring of another snowmobile and looked up quickly to see Randy dropping off of our small ledge. He quickly crossed the bottom and began his sideways climb. Up, up, up he went, round through the U-bend, sling-shotting his sled through the final turn, then taking aim at the top with the nose of his snowmobile. Gun it! Vroooom! And he was up and over. He made it look almost easy!

I was in no position to turn around. When we stopped, I had been near the front of the pack. Due to my super-wimp status, the leader had told me to follow him and stay in his tracks. Great. I had twelve riders behind me that needed me out of the way so they could go. Peril to the fore, traffic to the rear.

I had no choice. Everyone was waiting. I was going to have to just do it.

Things didn't start well.

My machine had settled into the snow, and I was fairly near the drop off where Mick and Randy had already gone down. I checked and rechecked my helmet, gloves, goggles. I was aware that all eyes were on me, so I took a couple of steadying breaths, opened up my throttle........and plummeted sideways down the gully's wall…

…Where I promptly landed at the bottom with my machine upside down on top of me.

I was unhurt, cushioned and buried in snow as I was.

I hit the kill switch and waited while Larry and a couple of guys dragged my snowmobile off of me. They set it, ski-side down, a few feet away. Larry pulled me up and asked if I was hurt. When I assured him and everyone else that I was fine, I could hear the collective sigh of relief...just before the chuckles started.

My friend Marcia, my faithful companion, asked several times if I was really okay. Then, in the giddiness that comes after a fright that ends well, she recounted for me the scene as it had played out from her point of view.

By the time she was done, and considering the good outcome, she soon had tears streaming down her face. She held her sides in laughter-induced pain, barely able to speak. "We couldn't figure out where you'd gone!" she cried, wiping at her face with her ski hat. "We knew you'd have to ride forward to get to where Mick and Randy dropped in, but we never saw you do that. You just vanished! You were there, and then you weren't!"

Yes, well. Very funny. I even joined in the laughter, but the voice in the back of my mind was saying, *You still have to get OUT of here!*

Gathering myself together, I heard Larry cautioning me that I'd lost a lot of my momentum-building room, since I'd have to start out in the bottom of the gully. *No kidding.* I wouldn't be able to ride downhill and gain speed, since I'd chosen to do that part in an upside-down slide instead.

How could I gain enough speed to grip the first side of the horseshoe and then zoom around to a vertical climb?

Inaction was not an option. Escape was not possible. If I wanted to get myself and my machine home tonight, I'd have to get on the thing and make it happen.

Larry again: "Wide open. Don't hesitate!"

I climbed aboard my snowy sled, pulled on my goggles, checked my helmet strap one more time. I locked my feet in place, opened her up, and went for it.

And I nearly made it. Truth be told, my machine *did* make it. I had taken aim and accelerated full throttle up the first wall, knowing I was sideways but going fast enough to climb. I gained speed as I headed around the inside curve and toward the final leg, that vertical beast of a hill that I had to conquer or....*or???* No! No OR! I'd make it!

I tried to lean over my handlebars (as I'd seen Mick do) when I neared the top, so that I could literally *will* my snowmobile up and over the edge. I blasted through the overhanging snow, my machine nearly vertical. *Push on the handlebars, tell the machine to go forward horizontally.* And it did! All alone! It sailed right out from under me, leaving me way up in the air, no machine beneath me, as I spun around, hoping I'd see a soft place to land.

So there I was…face down in the snow, my machine somewhere in eternity.

As Mick ran after it, I sat up, spitting out snow, digging chunks of ice out of my goggles. Randy didn't know whether to laugh or call for Life Flight. As I brushed myself off, I kept saying, "I'm okay, I'm fine, I'm okay."

Randy then walked over to the cliff edge and shouted to those below, "She's okaaaaay!!! Nexxxtt!"

* * *

Later that night, as I sat with everyone in Magic's bar, Randy strolled over to me and said, "You know, I never thought I'd see anything graceful about a snowmobile crash, but I gotta tell you, when your machine went out from under you, it looked for all the world like you were attempting a pirouette before you fell to earth. "

He roared with laughter as he walked away.

CHAPTER **NINE**

Fun and games aside, around this time I began fearing death. It wasn't just the close calls on Harleys and snow machines that brought this on. I knew in my heart that, as things stood with my soul, I wasn't ready for a face-to-face with God.

Shame. It's not only depressing, it's debilitating. My rock-bottom self-confidence descended to the nether regions, and my old standby insecurities regained influence in my spirit.

I'd lost my way and I needed a rescue. God, being merciful, loving, faithful and *good,* drew me back into His arms as only He could.

Sometime in 2005, I awoke one morning with a song playing inside my head. It was a once-popular song that hadn't crossed my mind or my path in more than ten years. And it wasn't the whole song, which is really just a lost-love song. It was only the chorus, with large helpings of harmony from the backup singers. Those words stayed with me for days, popping into my mind as I woke, as I fell asleep, as I ran the vacuum. They were with me as I drove to work, washed my hair, did the shopping. I'd forget about them, then notice them playing merrily away in my brain for no reason that I could fathom.

Realization finally struck one day as I was folding laundry. Here it was again, loud as could be in my head: "I want you back, it's time that you came home to me."

That refrain from the 1994 pop single, *Home to Me,* was a clarion call seeking to make itself heard. Incredulous, I dropped the T-shirt I'd been folding and spoke aloud to my bedroom, "Is that *You*, Lord?" Suddenly, such peace flooded through me that I knew I wasn't crazy. God was getting my attention and telling me to come home.

Tears poured down my cheeks as I realized the perfection of His choice of lyrics. He knew my shame. He knew my every fault. He knew I'd been avoiding Him, but He didn't yell at me. He didn't rebuke me. He simply said, "I want you back. It's time that you came home to Me."

A fresh journey with my Savior began on that day. I marveled that, whatever else I might be, I was wanted by my Father, the Creator of the universe. He had let me know it in no uncertain terms.

I dug my favorite Bible out, bought a new spiral notebook and pen, and began setting my alarm for a couple hours earlier. I wanted to spend the early morning hours with Him, as had been my habit for many years.

It seemed like no time had passed at all. The Lord didn't sulk or punish me for the years I had shut my ears to Him. He met with me, just as He had so many times before my *lost decade*. I could tell His goal was to *encourage me to draw close*, not to embarrass me and remind me of all my wrongs. This was not the time for Him to be firm with me or to start cleaning me up. He knew that far better than I did. This was a time of tenderness, of a Father welcoming his prodigal daughter home.

His Word came alive to me again, and I marveled at the lessons the Holy Spirit could teach through every piece of Scripture. I basked in the peace of His presence while the day was young and the morning still. I filled journal after journal, morning after morning. He began in me a beautiful process of forgiveness and healing ...

The same process that is available to all who will receive it.

CHAPTER **TEN**

Click.

My computer announced the arrival of a new email. The sound of the email dropping into my inbox distracted me. I was in my home office, seated on the floor next to the window overlooking our backyard and patio. The window was open, and I was studying a curious bee that was hovering just outside the window screen. Perhaps it was drawn by the warmer air flowing *out of* the house. Our upstairs was always quite warm. Hot, really, in the summertime, even with the A/C on.

I had been praying, asking the Lord to show me where to send some money. I knew that being back in relationship with Him meant giving as well as getting, and as yet, I had no home church. I felt bad about that, and I knew that that situation was going to have to be remedied soon. That didn't, however, solve the problem of where to send some money *this* month. My checkbook was lying next to me, with the amount filled out and written in longhand. My name was signed. But where should I send my money? The "Pay To" portion of the check remained blank.

So I found myself, two years after the Lord had drawn me back, speaking to Him about where I could send some tithe money. I wanted to give to a prison ministry, because I couldn't get that off my mind. In Matthew 25, Jesus expresses His heart that we feed the hungry, fill the thirsty, invite the stranger home, and visit those who are sick or in prison.

The *in prison* part leapt out at me every time I read that verse, and there were times I wondered why. We had no prison in our area, and for years our local jail was very small and housed only men. As they wouldn't allow women to enter the jail and hold Bible studies for men, it seemed like a dead-end dream until 2008. That was the year our large, brand new jail opened its doors. Hmmm. And closed them, of course.

But even with the new facility, I didn't know anything about helping inmates. Our jail could have been on Mars, it was so unknown and out of reach to me. I didn't know how to go myself. Perhaps a starting place would be to send money to an already established and reputable prison ministry. But which one?

Rewind with me to the *click* I heard as my new email arrived. As I watched the bee buzzing just a few inches away, I wondered if I should get up from my prayer time and see what it was. For some reason the timing of its delivery had roused my curiosity. I'd heard the *click* just as I uttered the words, "Lord, please show me the *right* prison ministry. I don't know who is trustworthy. I don't know who is doing things *Your* way."

My curiosity won the day, and I lifted myself to my desk chair. Grabbing the mouse, I enlarged the screen for my email program. There it was, sitting at the top of my inbox, an email from Prison Fellowship Ministries, written by its founder, Chuck Colson, inviting me to be a partner in their ministry, and telling me how I could contribute!

That's just a fun story all day long. I had never heard of Prison Fellowship Ministries. They had *never* reached out to me before. I sat there grinning at the computer screen as I read and re-read the email. At last I simmered down enough to write *Prison Fellowship Ministries* in the "Pay To" portion of my check. I addressed an envelope, found a stamp, and headed out to the mailbox.

CHAPTER **ELEVEN**

I sent my first check to Prison Fellowship in 2008, just before the economic world fell apart. The *Great Recession.* Overnight real estate values plummeted, the stock market crashed, people lost businesses, families lost homes. Lives were disrupted and sometimes destroyed all over our nation, and the damage was far-reaching, affecting millions around the world.

Our own Valley was hard hit, though for us it simmered at first, affecting mainly real estate sales and the construction industry. Big tycoon developers went belly up before the rest of us really felt the water heating, and it didn't boil over in our area until 2010. That's when we learned that our county is often two years behind the financial trend, whether that trend is good or bad. I don't know the reason for that, but we saw it play out very personally.

Larry's business lost 75 percent of its workflow within a month, in late 2010, and everyone else experienced the same decline. Shops closed, luxury outlets shut down, For Rent signs popped up everywhere, as restaurants and businesses of all types breathed their last.

Before all of this, back in 2008 and 2009, when foreclosures skyrocketed and the nation struggled, Larry and I were still doing okay. We still had work coming in. We paid our bills. We took small vacations. Life remained somewhat normal.

That meant that I still had money every month to send to Prison Fellowship Ministries (PFM). We did not yet have a home church.

In fact, it was the recession that brought my name to the attention of the Director of Advancement for the Pacific Region of Prison Fellowship Ministries. That's quite a handle, so I'll shorten it to Steve. Anyway, he noticed my small offerings each month, because so many others had dwindled away. Many donors had lost jobs and could no longer contribute.

In early summer of 2010, before the recession hit us personally, I received the first phone call from Steve. I wasn't home, so he left a message on my answering machine. Steve's message left me speechless. He wanted to come up to Idaho and visit me!

I didn't know what to do. Giving is supposed to be in secret! You don't talk about it! I didn't want to be thanked! I didn't want to be noticed at all! But this very nice man wanted to meet me, and he was persistent. I didn't respond to the first message. I felt so bashful. Eventually Steve left a second message, and then resorted to email.

Poor guy. I had to answer him. I replied to his email, and he began proposing dates that he could come to meet me. I told him it was too far. It wasn't necessary. But I couldn't dissuade him. He cheerfully told me when he'd be in town, and that the choice of a restaurant was up to me. He hoped Larry would be joining us.

I had been out of church and out of touch with fellow believers for *years*. Larry and I had smartened up enough to quit going to bars every day after work. Trouble was, now I never left the house in the evenings at all. I had a job, but was otherwise becoming increasingly reclusive. I was seeking God, but my circumstances were difficult a lot of the time. You can read your Bible and support a ministry and still be depressed.

At that time, Larry still found relaxation after work each day in a bottomless cocktail, albeit at home. Although he knew I'd been sending money to Prison Fellowship, he didn't share my enthusiasm for prison ministry. He didn't want to come to dinner with us. I would have to go alone, eat Thai food with Steve, and let him thank me for sending the money that I didn't want to talk about.

I am so glad, now, that Steve was indefatigable in his efforts to see me. He didn't know it, but his visit forced me to come out of my shell, wear something nice, leave the house and talk to a new person. I battled my insecurities as I shared a table with this delightful, effervescent, upbeat man of God. He was so easy to be with that I gradually relaxed. We had a wonderful conversation. We were speaking about something near to both of our hearts, after all, and that was prison ministry.

He told me some of what Prison Fellowship was involved with. Chuck Colson had founded it, and they had volunteers and programs all over the world.

As our evening together drew to a close, he said the words that would impact me most deeply. He'd been explaining various ways people can be involved. Money, prayer, support staff. Then, eyes dancing, he added, "But there's nothing like actually going behind the wall!"

My heart clenched with yearning. I wanted that. I'd been sending money, but what I really wanted was to shelve my own problems and reach out to people who needed a friend. I wasn't an ordained minister or a professional counselor, but I could be a listening ear.

I set my mind to study more, to pray more. I began asking God to make a way for me to go "behind the wall."

CHAPTER **TWELVE**

On Christmas Day, 2010, my daughter Amy flew up from California for a visit. She was expecting her first child, my precious grandson, Caden. My daughters always spent Christmas Eve with family in California, then got up early on Christmas Day, when *no one* wanted to travel, so they could enjoy empty airports and easy flights up to Idaho. Amy came alone this year, as Bethany was unable to take off from work.

Christmas Day fell on a Saturday. As I drove Amy home from the airport, she asked casually, "Soooo, are we going to church tomorrow?"

Amy knew how reclusive I'd become. She also knew there was a church I wanted to attend. Sunday after Sunday, when we didn't go, I felt terrible. I *knew* the Lord was leading me there, but I was afraid: Afraid they might make us stand up and introduce ourselves; afraid people might be falsely polite and promptly forget us; afraid, alternatively, that they might be too observant and notice the scarlet letter on my forehead.

When Amy asked her question, we both knew that what she meant was, "Mom, you've wanted to go to this church for years. It's Christmas. It's a perfect time to go. I am here and will go with you."

How could I refuse? My answer, "Absolutely!"

* * *

True to her word, Amy was up and ready to go to church with me the day after Christmas. We found places near the back. I was quite busy trying to be invisible when a tall man with piercing blue eyes stopped and shook my hand.

He seemed to look right *through* me. But all he said was, "Hi, I'm Mark." Amy said later that, to her, it was immediately obvious that he was the pastor. I think her words were, "I could have seen him from a distance, filling his car up at some random gas station, and I would have known he was a pastor."

I was too distracted to give it much thought. I wasn't used to being among so many new people. And that man didn't even speak that day. It wasn't until the next week, when I returned with Larry, that I learned that he was, indeed, the pastor.

The people in that church welcomed us with open arms. No one ever said, "Stand up and introduce yourselves." Rather, Pastor Mark told the woman in charge of the new church directory to take our picture and include us. He told her, "I have a feeling that Larry and Diana are going to be joining us regularly, now."

Never a public spectacle, instantly included. Lovely.

* * *

Twelve years after our arrival in Idaho, we found our church home. This was a close-knit group of people, but we never once felt like outsiders. People were easy to talk to. We received invitations to people's homes for dinner. For the first time in my memory, I looked forward to going to church every Sunday.

As summer approached, our Sunday announcements included a new item: the School of Ministry would be starting up again in September. I wondered what the School of Ministry was. Not that it mattered. Larry and I still stayed home every night, and so I knew we were unlikely candidates for evening classes.

I was surprised, therefore, when the church's summer barbecue rolled around, and I learned that Larry was interested in attending the school. Pastor Mark approached me during the

August barbecue all enthused. "Hey, Larry told me you guys are interested in joining the School of Ministry. I think that's great! You two will be perfect for it!"

Wow! I wasn't upset, but Larry hadn't said a word to me. And now Pastor Mark thought it was a done deal! He continued, "Do you know Patty?" He pointed to a lady I didn't know. "She's signed up. We should have a good group this year."

He was all smiles, and apparently wasn't looking for a commitment from me. He was just making conversation, happy that we wanted to join in. And I *did* want to join in. But *Larry*? Throughout the weeks of Sunday morning announcements, he hadn't breathed a word of interest!

As Pastor Mark walked off to converse with other barbecue guests, I realized that, in my surprise, I hadn't asked him for any details about the school. What might a Bible course at a small church look like? A six-week program? Probably something like that.

More surprises, therefore, when we actually did commit. When we showed up for Week One of the International School of Ministry, we learned that it was a two-year course!

* * *

Although surprised to learn that the Bible school was a two-year commitment, we decided to jump in anyway. We didn't have any other evening activities, so the two hours on Monday nights seemed, after some consideration, doable. Of course, it turned out to be far more than that. We had assignments, too, but they were wonderful assignments!

First we each had to write a song. That intimidated most of us, especially those not musically inclined. But Pastor Mark said we wouldn't have to sing them for the class unless we wanted to. Really, no one would ever know if you actually put music to your words. The bottom line was that some kind of a poem would do.

Those songs turned out to be a highlight of the school year

for all of us. We had six weeks to come up with something, and we all surprised ourselves. When Pastor Mark first explained the assignment, Larry's shoulders literally slumped. His chin hit his chest in despair. He'd signed up for Bible school, but this was a "bridge" too far.

Even so, it wasn't long before Larry heard a story that resonated with him. Armed with the danger and good outcome of that story, he happily jotted down some very inspired lyrics. He asked my daughter Amy to put them to music. Amy is a talented musician and songwriter, and she was able to create music that captured Larry's personality to a tee. Rock 'n Roll!

I hadn't played my guitar in years, but I pulled it out and tuned it up. I was able to play Larry's song and sing along with him. He experienced a fulfilling sense of achievement at creating a new song, especially since that was the last thing on earth he ever would have thought possible.

He finished his song long before I did. I was completely blank. Couldn't come up with a thing. Finally, with only a week to go before the assignment was due, I decided to speak to the Lord about it. Yes, that should have been my first thought, not my last resort. I told Him that nothing was coming to me, and I needed help.

The very next morning I woke to a lovely melody rolling through my mind. I hummed it absently as I made breakfast and cleaned the kitchen. It gradually dawned on me that it was an *unknown* melody, something I'd never heard before. I grabbed my guitar and figured out the chords, and soon I was humming and strumming like I'd known it all my life.

Now I just needed words. A thought came to me, and I grabbed pen and paper. Thought after thought. A pause to think of a word that rhymed, and then more jotting. The inspiration was surely from the Holy Spirit. Never could I, in one twenty-minute session, have written an entire song that I actually enjoyed singing.

Perhaps I shouldn't have been so surprised. I'd asked for His help, after all.

* * *

Preparing to sing our songs for the class, and we couldn't wait for the assigned evening to arrive. Try to imagine our disappointment when Pastor Mark, who led the school, wasn't even there. There was a church finance meeting scheduled for that night. We and our fellow students had been left in the hands of the two assistant leaders. They, in turn, were shocked when I showed up with a guitar. In years past, most people just handed in their lyrics. No one actually *sang*. No wonder Pastor Mark hadn't minded missing that school night.

To their credit, almost every student had arrived with a fully written song. Once things got going, everyone participated. Larry volunteered to go first. I accompanied him, and since I had the guitar already in my hands, I went next. Motivated now, other students asked to borrow my guitar so they could sing their songs, too.

Patty, whom I'd seen at the church barbecue, was the only other woman in our class. We were prayer partners, and were soon to be much more. Patty didn't consider herself musically talented, but she'd done her homework and was ready to go. She couldn't do it in front of us, though. She was afraid she'd get too nervous standing there, watching us watching her. She went to the back of the room and made us promise we'd face forward. Ha! She was so cute! And her song was beautiful.

It was a wonderful, memorable evening. We were finished performing when Pastor Mark, his meeting over, stuck his head into the room to say hello and goodnight. One of the co-leaders, Bernie, said, "Man, you missed some great songs. These guys all did a really good job!" Pastor Mark looked around at all of us.

"I had no idea," he said. "Usually people just turn them in. I didn't know you guys would actually be singing them!"

"Well," Larry said dryly, "when you give an assignment, maybe you should make a point of being here the night it's due." Everyone laughed. Larry's candor never failed to surprise me. I wouldn't have had the nerve to say anything, though I would have silently *thought* it, really hard.

Pastor Mark was laughing too. "Believe me," he said, "next time I'll be *sure* to be here!"

Then he added, "Can I hear some of them now?" That was unexpected, and gracious of him. It was late, but he stayed and listened. Larry and I sang ours, then a few more people agreed to sing theirs again. Patty returned to the back of the room and gave Pastor Mark the face-forward instructions.

Our school was small, just eight students. But we bonded that night, no longer strangers coming to Bible class. Now we were family.

CHAPTER **THIRTEEN**

In October 2011, just weeks after we'd begun the School of Ministry, a woman stood up in church and informed us of the need for ministry in our local jail. She named no contact person. Nor did she specify what the ministry might look like. But there was a need, and she wanted all of us to know it in case anyone was interested.

I sat rooted to my chair, electrified. I couldn't feel my lips. This was *it*. I knew with certainty that that announcement was meant for my ears. I'd prayed for years for the Lord to show me a way into our jail. When the new jail was built in 2008, I even considered prayer vigils right in the parking lot.

How could I get in there? What would I do once I, in fact, got in?

I knew nothing of prison ministry. What I knew was that the need had come calling at the very church I attended. I was definitely going to have to pursue it.

It seemed a rather daunting task, though, to tackle on my own. *Lord,* I prayed silently as the service continued, *I can't do something like that alone.*

Before I finished my silent prayer, Patty's face rose up in my mind, clear as day. Of course! She'd be perfect! My fellow student in the School of Ministry, Patty was a mature woman of God. She had a heart for the hurting and a longing to serve the Lord. I resolved to speak to her after church. Actually, I practically ambushed her in the church's small kitchen when the service was over.

She heard me out and even expressed interest. She also said she needed time to pray about it.

A few days later she called me up. Yes, she would do it. She'd really known the moment I approached her that she would say yes. She told me the Lord had spoken to her heart when the announcement was made, too. She'd thought, *That's what I'm to do!*

She prayed, and she conferred with a trusted friend, who said, "Patty, you're ready. Go for it!"

Well, cool. We were a team. Now what? I called Pastor Mark and asked him for the phone number of the lady who'd made the announcement in the first place. I placed the call, told her I was interested in jail ministry, so whom should I talk to? She was pleased that someone wanted to jump in, and she gave me the name and number of the police chaplain.

His name was Niko. I stared at my phone for a few minutes before making the call. Did I really have the nerve to telephone someone I'd never met and tell him I was interested in jail ministry, maybe a Bible study, when he didn't know me from Eve? I was not normally possessed of such spunk.

I took a deep breath. I was sure this was the Lord's leading, and I had to start somewhere. I dialed the number.

I reached Niko and explained that Patty and I were interested in starting a Bible study at the jail. He was thrilled! He wanted to know what church we attended. When I told him, he enthused, "Oh, Pastor Mark! You'll be perfect!"

What a nice man! He was so encouraging! He said he had a meeting scheduled with jail leadership early the next morning, and he was going to speak to them about us. He promised to call me when the meeting was over.

I waited on pins and needles all the next morning. How long would their meeting take? What if they said no? More important, what if they said *yes*?

Patty, on the other hand, was waiting for a phone call from *me*, so she could learn the verdict, as well.

My attention span that whole morning was pretty much zilch. I was distracted, dragging my phone around with me everywhere so I wouldn't miss Niko's call. This is what I'd prayed for...for *years*. I knew from Scripture that God has *such* a tender heart for prisoners. Jesus Himself said that when we visit someone in prison, we visit Him. He put Himself in the prisoner's shoes. I didn't know what jail ministry would look like, but my heart burned to begin the work He'd laid upon it.

* * *

My phone finally rang at eleven o'clock that morning. It was Niko. He was very happy and also very serious as he told me that their meeting had been extended. They'd been discussing the prospect of our bringing church (*church!!*) to the ladies in the jail. And they had decided, especially considering their high regard for Pastor Mark, that they would allow Patty and me to hold church services, even though we weren't ordained.

Ordained? Church services? "Niko," I stammered, "we were thinking of bringing in a Bible study, maybe on a Wednesday evening. We never heard anything about a desire for church services!"

"Listen, my friend," Niko was soothing now, "it has to be church. That's what the need is, and it has to be on Sundays. If you can't do that then it isn't going to work right now, because that's what they need. We're gonna work it out so you and Patty come in on Sunday afternoon, and then, after you are finished with the ladies, we're hoping some men will also join and bring services to the men."

Well, this was simply huge. Sunday mornings I attended my own church, and Sunday afternoons were "me" time. They were also "us" time, the only time Larry and I actually had plans to be together.

Now, don't laugh. We loved NASCAR. I haunted NASCAR's website and learned the schedule, the start times and on what channels races would air. I then set the DVR to record each race, carefully adding three hours to the recording time in case of rain delays.

There were races on Saturdays, and occasionally on Friday nights, in the slightly less prestigious series, but the big boys came out to play on Sunday afternoons. Larry and I had our favorites. I'd spent a considerable amount of time combing through eBay to find Bobbleheads of our favorite drivers. On Sunday afternoons we were like kids, lining up the Bobbleheads so they could watch the race with us. It was like decorating a tree for Christmas. We decorated our coffee table with NASCAR driver Bobbleheads. Watching those races was one of the few things we enjoyed in common.

And then there was the nap. As the race zoomed along in the background, we would cozy up on our sectional sofa, a purple affair that joined at a right angle in the corner. Each of us reclining on our own half, we would snooze through a hundred laps or so, I with my favorite couch pillow and sofa throw, and my Jack Russell cuddled beside me.

It was my favorite part of the week, and I had just run headlong into the question of, "*Will you give it up?*"

* * *

Eternity. The word rang through my mind as I pondered a commitment that would change my much-loved Sunday afternoon routine. In the greater scheme of things, in the light of *eternity*, was a couple hours of weekend time so important? I considered facing the Lord when it was my time to go home to Him. Would He ask me, "Why did you hold on to those hours so tightly? Why couldn't you let go? Didn't you realize I was leading you?"

I didn't want to stand before Him and have to answer those questions.

And of course there was the question of *eternity* for the inmates sojourning in our jail. Did a couple hours' ease for me trump their need to hear the Gospel? Were my habits more important than their salvation, their encouragement, their need for love?

When I considered the question in the light of *eternity*, I knew I had to say yes, of course I would do it. Not because I was Sister Selfless Super Saint, either. I was putting one untried foot in front of the other as the Lord opened up the doors. I didn't want to disobey, didn't want to disappoint God. I didn't want to face Him and say, "I'm sorry I ignored You."

* * *

"Is that a deal breaker?" I asked over the phone, once I told Patty our visits would be on Sunday afternoons.

"It might be," Patty replied. "I'm going to have to think about it, and pray about it, and get back to you. I sure hadn't planned on Sundays. Sunday is my family day."

I understood. Patty worked full-time at a bank, which left only weekends to take care of the rest of her life. I knew that her husband was disabled, so most of the household responsibilities, as well as the care of her husband, fell to Patty. Sunday afternoons, after most of the weekly tasks were finished, were precious. How could she make a commitment to give that time away?

Patty, however, had reached a moment in her life where she wanted to be in ministry. She wanted to be, as she put it, "about my Father's business." She'd enrolled in the School of Ministry, and she believed the Lord had quickened her spirit when she heard the announcement about need in the jail. It didn't take her very long to decide that if Sunday afternoons were what was required, then Sunday afternoons would be just fine.

Niko gave me copies of the paperwork we would need. We had to begin our background and clearance checks. We filled those out, handed them in, and got that ball rolling. Within a few days, we each received a phone call that we'd been cleared to go into the jail. Wow! *Was this happening?*

Now we just needed to learn the answer to the ever-present question, What does jail ministry look like? Remember Steve, from Prison Fellowship Ministries? He had taken another job and was no longer with Prison Fellowship, but I was still in touch with him via online social media. I knew that Patty and I would be wise to team up with people who were already involved with prison ministry, people who knew the ropes. I decided to reach out to Steve and ask him what our first step should be.

He was thrilled, and provided me an email address for Mark Hubbell, Director of Prison Fellowship Northwest. We could join up with them, and head into the jail under the joint umbrella of our church and Prison Fellowship.

Thus began our journey.

* * *

Mark Hubbell was enthusiastic when I reached out to him about becoming Prison Fellowship volunteers. He put me in touch with his assistant, Bonnie, who helped Patty and me to get some training under our belts. Prison Fellowship has online training for many different areas of ministry. I almost had to pinch myself when I checked "In-Prison" as my chosen course of study.

The training sessions took only a few afternoons to complete. Mark Hubbell took the time to come all the way from Salem, Oregon to Twin Falls, Idaho, to meet us. He brought us each a book written by Charles Colson, Prison Fellowship's founder, as well as some Bible study guides we could use in the jail, if we chose to.

What a marvelous man! He spent hours with us over lunch, getting to know us, learning about how we'd been invited, not just to visit, but to hold church services in our jail. We quickly perceived that Mark was not only wise in his own field of prison ministry, but he was kind, thoughtful, discerning, and full to overflowing with joy.

He told stories about wonderful things happening in prisons, and also with prisoners who, when released, took the Gospel back to their neighborhoods. He firmed up our understanding of Prison Fellowship's goal, which was to see lives transformed. We weren't going to be just visiting inmates, if you will. We wanted to see people restored by the hope, power and love of Jesus Christ.

Prison Fellowship has a three-pronged approach. First, while an inmate is incarcerated, volunteers bring worship, Bible studies, and friendship behind the wall. Some prisons have fully accredited seminaries within their walls.

Second, when inmates are released, Prison Fellowship has trained mentors to walk beside them. These mentors help former inmates adjust to life on the outside – life without a return to harmful ways and relationships.

The third prong is the Angel Tree outreach. People working and volunteering with Angel Tree deliver Christmas gifts and greetings to children whose parents are incarcerated. Inmates can sign their children up and make requests for appropriate gifts. They write their greetings to their kids when they fill out the applications. Volunteers purchase the gifts, copy down the greetings from Moms or Dads, and take everything – in the name of the parents – to the children in time for Christmas. Angel Tree volunteers also try to keep in touch with the kids throughout the year, providing camps and meaningful experiences for children who might otherwise be forgotten.

Unless the prison world is on our radar, most of us don't realize that the children of incarcerated people suffer as much or more than their parents do.

Caring for people while in prison and watching them become new creations in Christ; mentoring them upon their release and helping them re-integrate into church and their community; and touching the lives of their children...this was Chuck Colson's vision, and it is bearing fruit worldwide.

Patty and I had been cleared to go "inside." We'd finished our training. But, we had one final step, and that was to meet with the jail's commanding officer, Captain Harris. We excitedly told Mark Hubbell that we had an appointment to meet with Captain Harris the following week and that we'd set December 4, 2011, as our start date. Mark, in turn, promised to send a box of paperback Bibles to us so we could donate them to the jail's library.

Things were coming together, and only three weeks had passed since our initial decision to dive in!

* * *

It would be a huge understatement to say that I was nervous as I turned off my ignition and stared at the jail building. In truth, my stomach was doing backflips. I was in the jail's parking lot, preparing to meet with Patty, Niko and Captain Harris. Just a meeting, but where correctional institutions are involved, nothing is a simple affair. I'd never been inside a jail. I didn't know what to bring with me, if anything. Patty's car was already here, so I knew she must be waiting for me inside. Had she worn a coat? Could we have outerwear when we went "inside?" I hated to part with my coat. It was mid-November and cold outside. On the other hand, I didn't want to return my coat to the car if its admittance was denied.

In the end. I left my coat and handbag in the car and made a dash for the door with nothing but my keys. We were to meet Niko in the jail's lobby, and he would escort us "behind the wall" to the meeting. My stomach flopped again at the thought. What would Captain Harris be like? What would the interior of the jail be like? What if we didn't measure up, somehow?

Tugging the front door open, I stepped into the Sheriff's office lobby. Patty had taken a seat at the far end. Niko stood nearby, chatting amiably with her. Patty was ensconced in a massive, ankle-length down parka. Drat! I was going to freeze on my return to the car later; Patty would be warm as toast.

Smiling in welcome, Niko got down to business and told us what to expect. I felt a twinge of vindication when the first thing he told us was that, when we came in for church services, we *couldn't* wear our coats. We were allowed to wear a watch and could bring our Bibles.

"Otherwise," he said, "just you. Don't bring or wear extras."

We wouldn't be in contact with inmates on this visit, however, so Patty was allowed to keep her coat as Niko led us to a door and pressed a button. We heard a distinct click as the lock released, and Niko pulled the door open. When it shut behind us, we found ourselves in a concrete corridor. It was just a small space with a door at each end, and no way in or out unless Control unlocked one of the doors for us. Security. This place meant business. My stomach lurched again.

Control, however, did let us out, and we entered a wider hallway in the jail's interior. Everything was new to me, foreign. I shivered slightly as I took in the guards at their station, the locked doors, the bright lights, the chilly air.

We turned left down the hallway and walked through yet more steel doors before coming to what was obviously a library. Its wide, toughened windows exposed its interior to anyone standing in or walking through this corridor. This was where we were to meet Captain Harris. Niko informed us that this room would also serve as the venue for our church services. Books lined two of the walls, but there was a large central area where we would be able to gather together.

We entered the library and found some chairs. In short order the captain arrived and took a seat on one of the tables that was, for the moment, pushed up against a wall.

This meeting was to be a meet-and-greet, because, of course, Captain Harris needed to be acquainted with all his volunteers.

I was relieved when we were finally introduced and I discovered that he was not a frightening boot-camp-sergeant type of guy. He was certainly very serious, but I could tell there was a kind man in there. It had long been his desire that the inmates be offered church services, so he was happy to have us.

He asked what we would be doing with the ladies. This is where I piped up. "Well, I was thinking I could bring in my iPod with a player, and then we could sing along with songs for worship – "

I stopped. I could see that wasn't going to fly. He shook his head and said, "No, I don't want tech gadgets coming in here. Do you have a Plan B?"

I did, but I was so rusty! I'd played my guitar to accompany Larry's song for school, and to play my own, but I hadn't led worship in 19 years!

"Well," I managed, "I do play guitar. I can bring that and some song sheets and lead worship that way."

Vigorous nodding. "Yep, that's what I want."

Oh, this was going to be more challenging than I'd realized. On the other hand, surely the Lord had already been preparing me. Wasn't Amy, at this moment, creating a notebook full of worship songs, complete with guitar chords, as a Christmas gift for me? I knew about it because she'd needed my input on songs I liked. She'd been working on it for weeks, inspired by the fact that I was back in church and back in Bible school. She wanted to encourage me to get my guitar back out and keep it out, to get back to doing something that had been a large part of my life in Youth With A Mission.

I would tell her that her inspiration had been prophetic. Before she'd known of the need, she'd been preparing to meet it!

* * *

On Sunday, December 4, 2011, Patty and I first stepped into the jail as a ministry team. I'd been playing my guitar like crazy for weeks, trying to get myself warmed up as a worship leader. My main problem was that all of the songs I knew were outdated. Amy rescued me by suggesting three songs that were easy to play, beautiful, and timeless. Patty came to my house and listened to each song. Her excitement grew as she realized we really would be able to have music. We prayed together and agreed on a plan for our first day.

That morning at church, our pastor had called us forward, and the entire congregation had stretched out hands in agreement as he also prayed, "commissioning" us to head into the jail in the name of Jesus.

Patty and I have never looked back. We tried never to miss a Sunday, though that did happen once or twice. We had another partner for awhile, but when she moved away, it was back to just the two of us. We told people that we left there each week more blessed than when we went in. We sincerely loved those ladies, and we made some lasting friendships. Strong friendships form in crisis, remember. And some of these women were in *such* crisis!

We laughed, we learned, we prayed and cried together. And yes, we sang worship songs, lifting God's name high from behind the walls that couldn't keep Him out. I bought a smaller, lightweight guitar that simplified the entry and setup process every week.

When our friends moved on to prison or were released, new faces arrived. When they left, many of them would write to us. We loved them, encouraged them when we could, and looked with them to our one Hope, our one Source of salvation and abundant life – Jesus Christ.

PART **THREE**

THE BOOM

For my thoughts are not your thoughts,

neither are your ways my ways,

declares the LORD.

As the heavens are higher than the earth,

so are my ways higher than your ways

and my thoughts than your thoughts.

(Isaiah 55:8-9 NIV)

CHAPTER **ONE**

Gird yourself. This one's gonna hurt.

* * *

Have you ever dreamed that you killed someone, forgot it for years, and then suddenly remembered? That the secret was going to come out, and life as you knew it was *over*? But then you woke up and realized it was only a dream?

I had such a dream in late September, 2012. My relief was profound as I awoke and realized I wasn't a murderer. I wasn't going to prison for the rest of my life!

In the midst of my relief that I hadn't actually *killed* someone, a man's face rose to the surface of my mind. I sat in stunned silence. I hadn't murdered, but I had been unfaithful to my husband. The "A" word. *Adultery*.

I tried to push it from my mind. That had happened ten years before, and I had sought the Lord's forgiveness many times. I had prayed and asked God if I should confess to Larry, but I'd always sensed a *Halt!* from the Lord when that question arose. I was sure that telling Larry would be the wrong thing to do.

Now, however, I felt the Lord was telling me the time had come. I must confess my sin to Larry. Could that really be true?

I had believed that episode on the motorcycle trip to be over, in the distant past. I hadn't thought about it in years. I'd put it behind me as a huge mistake in the midst of a marriage filled with huge mistakes. So I pushed the man's face right back out of my mind and told myself to quit inventing trouble.

But when God wants to get your attention, He knows how to get it. I know people disagree on whether God speaks to us, but I believe that God is the greatest Communicator of all. Of course He speaks to us. I believe He has many ways to make His will known – ways that usually have nothing to do with audible voices.

He uses His Word, of course, and through it He confirms His desire to communicate with us. Isaiah 30:21 says:

> *Your ears shall hear a word behind you, saying,*
> *"This is the way, walk in it," whenever you turn to the*
> *right hand or whenever you turn to the left.*
> (NKJV)

And Psalm 32:8:

> *I will instruct you and teach you in the way*
> *you should go; I will guide you with My eye.*
> (NKJV)

When the prophet Elijah was exhausted and forlorn, the Lord had him stand on a mountain, and caused first a wind, then an earthquake, and then a fire to pass by Elijah. But the Lord was not in any of them. His was the still, small *voice* that followed. (I Kings 19:11-12.)

In John 10:27, Jesus said:

> *My sheep hear My voice,*
> *and I know them,*
> *and they follow Me.*
> (NKJV)

He can use peace to urge us in the right direction. He uses songs, people, dreams, books, nature, seahorses.

Seahorses?

I remember the first time I really noticed seahorses. They are such unusual little things. They speak to me of God's creativity in action. The males carry the young! They be-bop beneath the ocean's surface, largely unobserved, intricately designed and de-lightful. Evidence of a Creator with – dare I say it? – a sense of humor!

But more to the point, in this case, His voice came to me in the form of *conviction*, a profound pricking of my conscience. My ears didn't need to hear a thing.

Later that morning, as I was trying to pray, I felt a physical sensation as if someone had cracked an egg on my head and let the cold contents run down my shoulders and back. Then again, maybe it wasn't anything landing *on* me so much as a peeling away of something *from* me, and that was the shield that had hidden my sin from the light of day for all these years.

I argued internally as I prayed. I even apologized to God for what must be my wrong thinking here. I hoped I was *imagining* that He was applying this pressure to me. I'll repeat that I'd prayed about this before, and had had *no* peace about confessing. Couldn't I, therefore, be mistaken now? Telling Larry would only hurt him and wreck my marriage. Then what use would I be to God?

But again, there was that immediate knowing within me, as the words came into my mind, *What use will you be to God with this giant skeleton in your closet? Can your marriage grow? Will you ever step out in further ministry? Will you ever reach for more in any Christian pursuit, knowing that this could come out at any time and reveal you for a fraud? Satan can hammer you whenever you least expect it, and you're carrying the weapon he'll use to do it.*

Yes. Very good points. I wouldn't reach for more, wouldn't step into any larger arena of ministry. I'd been in jail ministry nearly a year. I knew I would do that, but no more, afraid that people would learn the truth; afraid, above all, that God wouldn't bless my efforts.

And how could I presume to teach? Jesus said, in Matthew 7:3-5:

> *And why do you look at the speck in your brother's eye, but do not consider the plank in your own eye?*
>
> *Or how can you say to your brother, 'Let me remove the speck from your eye'; and look, a plank is in your own eye?*
>
> *Hypocrite! First remove the plank from your own eye, and then you will see clearly to remove the speck from your brother's eye.*
>
> (NKJV)

Indeed, if God was saying it was time to confess, and I disobeyed, then I was drawing a line in the sand and telling Him I would obey only to *here*, but no further; that I wouldn't obey Him if there was risk, if it hurt.

I couldn't say that to Him. I wanted a close relationship with Him, like John the Apostle had. I wanted no wedge between us, ever.

But this seemed too hard. The consequences seemed too unimaginable.

I wrestled with it all day. I felt like I was walking through thick syrup. Every step was an effort, every activity spent trying to shut out the direction that had come to me this morning. I knew I had a choice, but it seemed unbearable. Obey God and face the consequences? Or disobey Him and risk losing His presence, His delight?

Psalm 32:4 phrases it better than I can:

When I refused to confess my sin,
my body wasted away
and I groaned all day long.
Day and night your hand
of discipline was heavy on me.
My strength evaporated
Like water in the summer heat.

(NLT)

That's exactly how I felt! God, my loving and compassionate Father, was being firm with me, and I found it painful!

I then did what every person does who has a question and a laptop. I Googled it. Assuming both partners are believers, should a Christian spouse confess unfaithfulness?

Opinions were widespread, but in the Christian realm, most of the teaching I found leaned towards confession (unless physical safety was a concern). Pastors and counseling professionals were gentle but firm as they pointed out the damage that prolonged silence could do to both people in a marriage. They emphasized that healing and restoration were only possible when *both* parties had all the information and could choose – or not choose – to continue the relationship.

I was not doing a very good job of talking myself out of it.

Even my evening reading gave me no rest. I'd been reading C.S. Lewis's *Mere Christianity*, and had settled down to enjoy some sound, peaceful wisdom. The first thing I read, however, was, "If you had committed a murder, the right Christian thing to do would be to give yourself up to the police and be hanged."

Oh, come *ON!!* Even C.S. Lewis was picking on me! Confession was everywhere!

I told myself I understood about the murder thing. A Christian can't leave a thing like that hidden. But my sin was different, wasn't it? *Wasn't it?*

The truth is, I didn't want to argue with God. I wanted to believe, really believe that I'd gotten this wrong. But I didn't think I had. In one direction lay confession, and with that thought came peace. Fear, oh yes, but a peace that I was going the right way. In the other direction lay no confession, and I was right back to walking through syrup with my bones wasting like King David's.

On October 1, 2012, I wrote this in my journal: "Good morning, Lord. You are God, and it is not for me to question You. It is for me to obey You, and if I perish, I perish."

Dramatic? Yeah, it sounded better when Queen Esther said it. But it was how I felt. I was going to go out on the biggest limb of my life, and I had *no* way to know the outcome. I wanted to get the next verse in Psalm 32 over with. Psalm 32:5:

> *Finally, I confessed all my sins to you,*
> *and stopped trying to hide my guilt.*
> *I said to myself,*
> *"I will confess my rebellion to the Lord,"*
> *And you forgave me!*
> *All my guilt is gone.*
>
> (NLT)

I did point out to God that the verse clearly says, "I will confess my rebellion *to the Lord*." But no relief. His hand was heavy upon me. I knew that the Lord had already forgiven me, but my obedience to Him was on the line. I would obey Him because I trusted Him. I clung to the words in *The Message* paraphrase of Romans 10:12-13:

> *Scripture reassures us, "No one who trusts*
> *God like this – heart and soul – will ever regret it."*

I would confess to Larry when he came home from work.

CHAPTER **TWO**

Imagine standing above a hole that is six feet deep. It's a fairly large hole, easily ten feet square. As you peer over the edge of the hole, you see, just six feet down, that the floor of the hole is covered with knives, each with its handle embedded in the ground. All of their blades are razor sharp, glinting in the sun, and pointing straight up. They are placed evenly throughout the expanse of the hole's floor, with a mere two inches between each lethal tip.

You see what's down there. You know that, should you fall into the hole, you could die, though perhaps not quickly. After all, six feet isn't so very far to fall. Just the thought of such a fall, knowing you'd be impaled by so many terrible edges all at once, is enough to make you shrink back. You long to flee from that dreaded place.

But you can't leave. Though every instinct recoils and every ounce of reason urges you to run away, you know you have to jump into the hole. Whether the wounds you sustain are mortal or not, you know the pain will be unbearable.

That's how I felt, waiting for Larry to come home. I'd wrestled with what I believed the Lord was telling me to do. I'd argued. I'd done research. Above all, I tried to tell myself that God would not ask such a thing of me.

Yet, I believed that, indeed, He *was* asking such a thing of me. I couldn't foresee what my life might be after I confessed to my husband, but this is what I knew: God is God. He is eternal, and there is no one more important to listen to than Him. God is good. If He wanted me to confess, He had a reason, and He would be with me. He is also holy. I could not put my fear of a person above my fear of the Lord.

I heard the garage door open. I heard our dog Sienna bounding up the stairs from the garage below. As Larry made his way up to our main living area, I looked into the hole, at hundreds of gleaming knife blades waiting to tear into me, and I threw myself in.

CHAPTER **THREE**

Larry dropped my hand like he'd been scalded. "With WHO?" he demanded. His face was turning purple.

I wished with all that I had that I could rewind time two minutes back. This had been a terrible idea. Absolutely the dumbest thing I'd ever done in my life, and that was saying something!

He was inches from my face, waiting impatiently for my answer. I told him who. That made things worse. "I thought he was my *friend*!" Larry was yelling now. My heart was pounding so hard I was sure it was going to break ribs, fly out of my body and land, *splat!* on the floor. What had I *done?*

Well, I reminded myself, what I had done had been done ten years ago. I mentally reviewed the evidence I believed the Lord had given me in order to explain this path I must take, and I calmed slightly. I'd known this revelation could end in divorce. Larry would be within his rights to throw me out of his life. And maybe that was what needed to happen. We certainly couldn't go on living the way we had *been* living. (Bible School was bringing about changes, but Larry's drinking and temper were still with us.)

And so, as terrible as those minutes were, I could feel some of the chains falling away from my soul.

I drew a steadying breath as Larry walked over to the kitchen sink and stared out our small kitchen window. His fists were clenched, and he beat them again and again on the countertop surrounding the sink.

"How could you? How could you? How could you?" His eyes were wild. Tears cascaded down his face, quickly soaking his shirt.

I said I was sorry so many times I lost count. I fell to my knees, weeping, and said I hoped he could forgive me, but I understood if he could not. I hated myself, and I told him repeatedly that I knew I was slime, and that I would leave. He'd never have to look at me again.

I was devastated and heartsick. There was a tiny part of me that wished he could realize that, way back then, all the years before I'd strayed, our marriage had been struggling; that I hadn't known him then as I did today; that I'd been insecure and lonely. But Larry was too hurt to see anything beyond my betrayal. I feared for his very health, as grief threatened to consume him.

The last thing I wanted to do was call someone, to let someone else know what I'd done, what I had confessed. It would be humiliating to call another person and explain what was going on, but I knew that my embarrassment mattered far less than Larry's well-being. He clearly couldn't handle this situation. I knew my life was toast anyway, so if I was humbled even further, well, probably somewhere along the line that would be a good thing.

I picked up my phone and called Pastor Mark. I told him I'd done a terrible thing and Larry was beside himself, not doing well, and we could really use his help. Pastor Mark cut right to the chase and asked me, "And the terrible thing you've done would be?"

Unreal! In the space of ten minutes I'd had to say the awful words twice!

Pastor Mark needed to wrap up what he was doing, but said he could be with us in thirty minutes. Larry and I did nothing while we waited. Larry stayed in the kitchen, staring out the window, pounding his fists on the counter. I waited a few feet away, on the couch. Was the hard part over, or just beginning? I had no idea.

Our small church couldn't afford to pay much of a pastor's salary, so Pastor Mark did outside jobs to help pay the bills. He arrived in his work clothes, took off his shoes and came into our home. He brought a lot of peace with him. I was dreadfully embarrassed, and yet so glad to see him!

He took a look at Larry and asked me to go upstairs so they could speak in private.

I went, wondering if I was to face more endings than only my marriage. Perhaps it was odd to think of it under the circumstances, but I wondered if Pastor Mark was about to ask me to step away from my jail ministry, at this point.

Some might even ask, "Why did you enter such a ministry in the first place, with this sin in your past?" Well, I'd asked God's forgiveness many, many times. I'd certainly repented, which means I'd *stopped the behavior.* My repentance was for real. I would *never* do that again. I didn't care how lonely I got; I wouldn't jeopardize my relationship with God.

Another truth is, until my unfaithfulness had come up in prayer the other day, I hadn't even thought of it in years. I'd sought forgiveness for what I'd done, I'd asked the Lord if I should confess, and had felt that "check" in my spirit. So I'd put it behind me.

I'd been reestablishing my walk with the Lord. Prisons and prisoners had been on my heart. I'd been praying regularly for the Lord to open up a way for me to become involved, and He had.

Fortunately, God doesn't wait until you are perfect to put you to work for Him. But His timing is perfect. Had the Lord reminded me of my sin *before* I had pursued working with inmates, I never would have done it. As it was, the jail ministry was approaching its one-year mark, and *now* God had said that He wanted my secrets revealed, all shadows gone. Surely, the sequence of events had been the Lord's doing.

But would Pastor Mark see it that way? Or would he tell me he could no longer be supportive of me in that position? I didn't know, and fresh sorrow gnawed at me. What a hornet's nest I'd kicked!

After twenty minutes or so, Pastor Mark called me to come downstairs. The two of them were seated at our dining table, and I quietly slid into a chair as well. Pastor Mark told me that Larry didn't want me to leave, because he didn't want to be alone. *Oh,* I thought sadly. *That isn't going to be a good enough reason for very long.* For either of us.

Pastor Mark further said he'd seen many situations like this, and really, our chances of making our marriage work were 50/50, in his experience. He said that once trust was broken, it could be difficult to restore.

I came right out and asked him if he thought I should step down from the jail ministry, but he was already shaking his head. "No, you are the *perfect* person to go into the jail."

I pondered this for a moment, mentally pursuing the implications of his statement. Realization grew in my heart, even as I marveled at the depths of God's wisdom. Here, even in this dark circumstance, "light bulbs" of understanding flickered to life in my mind: I had strayed from the Lord for years; I had sunk to terrible depths of depression and sin; God, in His supreme love and faithfulness, had pulled me back into His fold; He had then sent me to befriend women who needed His love and faithfulness, as well.

They, too, needed to know – from a real Prodigal Daughter – that God has the power *and the desire* to forgive them, to love them, and to heal them.

A weight lifted from me as Pastor Mark confirmed that I truly had not pursued the jail ministry in error.

While I was relieved on that front, the more pressing question was, What was to become of Larry and me as a couple? I felt a twinge of jealousy as I thought of the happy home Pastor Mark would return to this evening. I couldn't envision a happy home in my future, whether near or distant.

But Pastor Mark was speaking again. "Listen, guys," he said, "I don't want you to give up hope. It can be hard to rebuild a relationship, but if you're both willing, I believe God can make a way." He smiled and added, "I know *I'll* be pulling for you."

It was comforting to hear him say he wasn't writing us off. At the same time, everything looked black and uncertain to me. Larry's hurt, his anger, indeed, his *shock* at what I'd confessed — all seemed insurmountable.

I reminded myself, deep inside, that God is a Worker of Miracles. I couldn't let go of that. If nine levels of my inner being were in flaming, self-berating agony — squirming under the fear that Larry would *never* recover from my revelation — then the tenth level clung tenaciously to our marvelous, loving Savior. *Savior.* That's what He is, and that's what He does. He *saves* people. I had been so sure He'd told me I must confess. If that was true, then He'd known what would happen, and He would be with us now. Whether He'd be with us singly or as a couple was precisely the question.

"I need to get going pretty soon," Pastor Mark continued, "but I'd like to pray with you before I leave. And I will *be* here for you as you walk through this process."

We all closed our eyes. I tried to find hope as our pastor's prayer filled our small home with faith, strength and peace. But, to be honest, I was focused on the fact that he was leaving soon. Larry and I would be alone again.

I was trying to rein in my distracted thoughts when Pastor Mark finished praying and looked slowly to Larry, then to me.

"You know," he said, "I believe the Lord is saying that you two are better together than you are apart. Even as I was driving over here, that's what came to me, and it's even stronger now, after prayer. You are *better together* than you are apart. I want you to hold on to that, going forward. I believe the Lord has a plan, and His plan is always good. Okay?"

I hope so, I thought dismally. I didn't doubt God's good plan.

But I was a little concerned with our own ability to make room for it.

Pastor Mark stood up and I thanked him for coming. Larry was still very silent. My nerves amped up even more.

Saying that he would arrange regular times to meet with Larry and help him walk this through, Pastor Mark had to take his leave.

Larry and I were alone.

The moment Pastor Mark was out the door, Larry headed for the liquor cabinet.

When I awoke

I sensed His presence next to me

And then He spoke

In stillness He said, Just believe

This hurt is deep

I'll hold you softly as you grieve

I'll watch your sleep

'Til you remember how to breathe

CHAPTER **FOUR**

The room was dark and quiet in the pre-dawn hour. I came awake from an unsettled sleep, still hyperventilating. When was the last normal breath I'd drawn? Three days ago? Four?

My subconscious barely registered the words from a song singing through my mind:

> *I'll watch your sleep*
> *'til you remember how to breathe*

What was that? I rolled over, my head fuzzy, heavy on my pillow. I didn't want to get up. At the same time, my body ached and yearned for movement, telling me I'd been in bed long enough.

I counted slowly as I inhaled, then counted slowly as I exhaled, trying to get enough and yet not too much air. I knew from my troubled dreams that my hyperventilation had carried on in the little sleep I'd found. Even now, counting one...two...three...four *in*, and one...two...three...four *out*, my breathing found no rhythm. It wouldn't self-regulate.

And the nonstop singing on the floor of my mind, virtually unrecognized by conscious thought:

> *I'll watch your sleep*
> *'til you remember how to breathe*

My mind rolled over the events of the past month. I didn't want to think about what had happened, but everything was too new, too fresh for me to ignore or tamp down.

Thirty-four days ago I had confessed my infidelity to Larry. It didn't matter that my crime had happened ten years in the past. It was new to him, and he had been incredibly hurt. I thought back on all that had happened in the last 34 days, and in particular three nights ago, when all hell broke loose...

* * *

Ever Since Pastor Mark had left our house on C-Day (Confession Day), life had been nothing short of a wild roller-coaster ride. A scary one.

Larry had had several drinks and a few brutal words for me that day before going up to bed at five in the afternoon. I was both relieved that it was done and alarmed that I'd done it. When he left the room, I didn't know what to do with myself, so I just sat very still on the couch until I was sure Larry was asleep. He had no doubt taken some sleep medication and was out for the count.

The next morning, he got up and went to work without a word to me. When he came home, he drank and refused to look at me. He spoke nothing to me but the same words, over and over: "How *could* you? How could *YOU*, of all people?"

I began to see that, prior to my confession, Larry had thought of me as some kind of unicorn in his troubled world; a being that had some quirks, absolutely, but a good person on the whole. His personal princess. Not that he ever verbalized that, and not that he felt I was a princess in a necessarily healthy way. He was quite a controlling prince. But though I hadn't known it, I'd been on some imagined pedestal that stoked, dare I say it, his ego. Though I was only eight years his junior, he'd been proud of his *younger* wife. He had never thought to be wronged by her.

His faith was shaken, not only in me, but in God. We'd found our church, I was involved in jail ministry, we were in Bible school. And now this. He saw me as a person who loved the Lord. How could he reconcile that with the person who had confessed to cheating on him? It was a good question, and I asked myself the same thing many times. How was I, a woman capable of great sin, able to throw myself into God's loving arms and actually believe that He wanted me?

What choice did I have? It was God or nothing. I was all in. God had told me He wanted me back after my years of wandering. He'd worked miracles just this year in getting our large, expensive house sold for our asking price, though the market was upside down and most people were short-selling or just walking away.

He'd also reserved for us the one and only home we wanted to move into, once our old one sold. It was a lovely townhome, one of several that were part of a wonderful community, and all priced to sell. And sell they did. Every single one of them except the one we liked the best, the one we wanted. Placed centrally on the park, this unit overlooked spacious lawns in the foreground, with majestic mountain peaks further off. For weeks, we had parked in its small driveway every Sunday after church, asking the Lord to keep it for us until our house sold. And He did!

God had been with us through so many steps lately, and had shown Himself strong and faithful and near. He hadn't changed. I knew that. It seemed it was time for Larry to decide what he *really* believed, and when he saw me as fallible, it rocked his world.

He came home from work that second afternoon, one day post C-Day, and headed for the bourbon.

In the midst of all our turmoil, we both had jobs to do, and so I stayed upstairs in my home office for as long as I dared, accomplishing nothing. I knew there was a dark, angry presence in the house, and I couldn't concentrate. I finally made myself go downstairs and say "hello." Larry was just sitting on the couch, staring into space.

I was at a loss. I hated myself, not for telling him, but for my original transgression. (Okay, and maybe a little bit for telling him. Had I gotten that wrong, after all?)

The atmosphere in our home was suffocating, but nothing terrible happened that night as Larry, once again, skipped dinner and went to bed early.

The next day I almost caught a glimmer of hope. Larry heard a song about forgiveness on the radio during his drive to work. He called me, very choked up. He said it had hit him out of the blue, the awareness that, not only *could* he forgive me, but that he really *wanted* to forgive me. He was deliriously happy and he couldn't wait to get home. He said something had broken off of him, let him go. He felt free and forgiving and in love with me.

That was a good day. Larry zoomed home from work like a teenager racing to be with his first serious crush. He was all smiles, wanting to hold me nonstop. He beamed ear-to-ear as he recounted his decision to forgive, and the burden that had lifted from him.

I was very happy that he was feeling better. He definitely seemed sincere, and I loved seeing him free of the pain of the past two days.

But I was apprehensive. Nothing seemed *finished.*

It wasn't like we'd talked anything through. We didn't discuss anything of substance, like *why* I did what I did. We didn't ask if there were things we should be working on together. Could we take a look at any of our still-current problems?

Nothing like that happened. I think Larry's true desire to forgive me, plus the work the Holy Spirit was beginning in him, provided both of us a taste of freedom and joy that day. We could be free from secrets, free from bitterness, and joyful in renewed relationship. We saw where our hearts *wanted* to be.

But we didn't talk. We didn't address a thing.

CHAPTER **FIVE**

That one good day slipped through our hands like silky sand at the seashore. The new start Larry had envisioned eroded away because nothing had really changed.

Larry's initial forgiveness was based on a feeling. He forgave me because it was what he *wanted* to do. I'm not downplaying that at all. Like I've said, he was sincere. But because it was a *feeling*, it couldn't last. As soon as he *felt* differently, my life blew up again.

It took only twenty-four hours.

Day One, I confessed.

Day Two, we had silence and an early bedtime.

Day Three was Forgiveness Day.

Day Four was start-off-friendly-but-then-drink-and-yell-at-Diana Day.

For Days Five through Thirty-One, see Day Four.

It was too much. We were still married, but our marriage was crashing out of control. My heart was breaking. I was at fault, of course, for my error, and, some would argue, for revealing it. There were, however, two of us in this marriage, and to this point, only one of us was sorry for poor choices. Though I'd been lonely before and afraid of Larry's temper, now things were worse, exponentially worse, because he felt justified in verbally abusing me. He said as much.

But, it was plain that Larry was hurting, and I still cared for him.

Throughout all the years of frustration and sour moods and difficulties, I saw something in Larry that I loved, even though he probably didn't see it in himself. Not everyone saw the wonderful qualities and sweet potential lurking beneath Larry's tough exterior, but I did.

We were such an unlikely couple. My sister said it was like putting Reese Witherspoon with Tony Soprano.

Tony Soprano got things done! He was no angel, but he definitely took care of business. One of my favorite things about Larry was that when he set his mind on something, he, too, got things done. It didn't matter how hard it was. When I first met him, Larry had a massive cocaine habit. When he decided to quit, he did so. Cold turkey, overnight. Who *does* that?

He was dauntless, powerful in his approach to life. He'd let his earthier side run a bit wild, so his language was untamed, but even that was sometimes refreshing to a person like me who tried so hard to live by the book.

They do say "opposites attract." If you look up that phrase, "Opposites Attract," on Wikipedia, you may see us smiling back at you.

Larry was tough, at least on the outside. People could say things to him that would have sent me into hiding for weeks. Not Larry. He'd just blow it off and say, "Forget him." He wouldn't let the unkind words eat at him. Very impressive!

Since my reunion with Jesus Christ years before, I'd been praying diligently for Larry, living in faith that the Lord would bring him to where he needed to be. He'd committed his life to God years before when Andrew, his client and friend, had seen Larry's life spiraling out of control, and had introduced him to Jesus. Until recently, however, we'd neglected church attendance. Larry was still a very young Christian.

I wanted to see all of Larry's self-confidence, strength and ability directed into channels in God's kingdom. I prayed that we'd be in some kind of ministry together. People looked at me oddly when I mentioned that. They knew some of Larry's edges were *very* rough. All the same, that was my hope and what I was praying for.

Now, in the midst of the most terrible month in my life, I was ready to give up. I'd had enough. It seemed I was doomed to spend the rest of my life as either:

A) *The Lucky Forgiven Woman, or*

B) *The Evil Jezebel Who Deserved Verbal Abuse.*

I hated what I'd done, and I could call a sin a sin, but we were nearly a month out from my Big Reveal. I'd known things could go badly if I confessed, but the word "bad" didn't even come close.

Larry still wouldn't have a discussion with me. He drank and he called me horrible things and yelled at me every night. Scary, towering, in-my-face-purple-rage yelling. He needed to either forgive me all the way, or let me go. And if he wouldn't come to that point himself, I knew that soon I would need to try to recover some kind of a life for myself, for my family's sake as much as my own.

I received one phone call from Ricky, "the other man," during that time. Larry had called him first, right at the beginning, confronting Ricky over the phone. Larry never gave me any details of that conversation, but when Ricky called me, he told me that he had apologized to Larry. He also said that, as Larry had refused to accept the apology, Ricky was concerned for my safety. Knowing Larry's volatility, he wanted to make sure I was alive. I was relieved to learn that Ricky wasn't angry at me for spilling "our secret." He said it had bothered him for all those years, too, and he would tell his wife, as well, at an opportune time. But the reason for this brief phone call was to make sure I was okay. That was it. He didn't think Larry was rational.

I didn't either, and I was falling apart. I didn't eat. I rarely slept. I questioned every decision I'd ever made. My kids and grandkids needed me to be healthier than that. I knew I was ready to move *on*, even if that meant moving *out*.

* * *

It was October 31, Halloween night. Our church was hosting a Trunk or Treat in the church parking lot, and I'd spent the evening there. I'd hoped to help with some of the games, but everything seemed well in hand. I spent most of the evening chatting with my pastor and his wife, as they served hot dogs and pulled pork to parents, princesses, and Ninja Turtles. Lots of food and candy for everyone.

I was one of the few people not in costume. I was probably more of an annoyance than anything, as there wasn't much I could help with until clean-up time, but I didn't want to go home. I couldn't stand to be within the walls of my own house. Larry was okay, reasonably friendly each day, until the first cocktail. After that, all bets were off.

I couldn't live this way. I waited until I knew Larry would be asleep, then I went home and made a phone call.

I had a girlfriend named Juliette who rented a three-bedroom condo that she shared only with her two dogs. I asked her if she'd like a roommate. At first she said no, but then she said, "Wait a minute. For who? Who needs a room?" I told her I did.

My tired, bruised heart and shattered self-worth nearly OD'd on the comfort of Juliette's next words. "*YOU??* Of *course*, if it's *YOU!* When can you come? Do you have a bed you can bring? I have a room that's completely empty. We'll get it all set up for you. I think I know where I can get a dresser. This'll be *easy!* Bring your dog for now; let's see how they all do. Do you need to come tonight? Are you safe? The couch is right here for now if you need to come now."

I was almost giddy. I could get out. I could live somewhere where no one was mad at me. It had been so long since I'd felt hopeful! I told her I was okay for tonight, that Larry had long since gone to bed.

I didn't take Juliette up on her offer of the couch that night. By the next night, it was too late.

CHAPTER **SIX**

My court reporting job took me out of the house for depositions, and then kept me in the house, in my home office, where I edited my deposition transcripts. Earlier this day, I'd been sitting in a law office sixty-five miles away from home, catching every word of the proceedings with my steno machine. Having then driven back, I was exhausted, and I dreaded coming into the house. I'd dreaded coming home for the last month.

I lugged my equipment up the stairs from the garage. I was hampered, as always, by my very excited Jack Russell, Jasmine. "Jazzy," we called her. I set my machine case down and picked Jazzy up for a squeeze. I nearly tripped over my cat, Sheila. Also glad to see me, Sheila was rubbing herself against my legs in figure-eight fashion, purring loudly. Our other dog, Sienna, didn't get up from her (naughty) location on the couch, but her tail thumped wildly.

I loved my pets, and it would have been a great homecoming, but for the silent, brooding man sitting next to Sienna, holding a drink. I didn't know how long he'd been home. It was only four o'clock in the afternoon, so he might have been in friendly mode. But he said nothing. The silence was ominous.

I asked how he was doing. "Fine," was his very clipped response.

I tried again, "Is anything wrong?"

"Nope," was his curt reply. "Nothing's wrong." I wasn't really expecting an honest answer. A better question would have been, *Is anything right? Will anything ever be right?*

He continued to sit silently, staring at nothing. The TV wasn't on. There wasn't a sound in the house except for Sheila's loud and happy purring and Sienna's tail thumping. Sheila bonked more insistently on my legs, clearly feeling ignored. I reached down and rubbed her ears, whereupon she promptly sat down and closed her eyes, happy at last.

Clearly, another bad evening was in the offing, made worse by the fact that it was starting so early. I decided to leave Larry be. I took my USB flash drive out of my steno case and went upstairs. I needed to transfer today's job onto the big PC in my office. That done, I decided to back up the job to my external hard drive, as well. I now had four copies of the day's deposition. Laptop, flash drive, big PC, and external hard drive. It had been a tough job, and I wanted it saved in every way possible.

I'd carried a pile of exhibits up with me when I brought the flash drive, so I opened the transcript on the big PC and used my software to create an exhibit index. That took a little while because I had to describe each exhibit (document) within codes. The codes kept the description hidden unless I opened a dialog box. Pretty nifty software. I could later just use the command to Create Index, and all of my exhibits would line up neatly, with their heretofore invisible descriptions falling into place on the Index page.

I finished that task and decided I'd dawdled around upstairs long enough. It was now nearly five-thirty, and my stomach reminded me that I hadn't had any lunch. In fact, I hadn't had breakfast, either. Stress. It kills my appetite every time.

I couldn't stay upstairs, and anyway, Juliette was ready for me to move in with her. This unbearable situation need not continue. That thought fortified me and I took myself downstairs, thinking I might find something to eat.

It wasn't to be.

As soon as my feet hit the floor in our living room, Larry, with a horrible smirk on his face, said, "You want to know what's bugging me?" I didn't. I said nothing.

He went on, "The church posted pictures of last night's Trunk or Treat, and guess what? YOU WEREN'T IN ANY OF THEM!!!"

What? I was baffled. Did he think I'd lied about going to help at the Trunk or Treat? Why on earth would I do that? This whole mess had started with *confession, coming clean, deciding NOT to lie!* Why would I lie now about something so silly?

"Did you see Pastor Mark in any of the pictures?" I stuttered lamely. "I was standing there talking with him most of the evening. No one needed my help with the games." Then another thought occurred to me, and I continued, "Oh, I wasn't wearing a costume. No one would have a reason to take a picture of me." I thought that would calm him down, but he wasn't even listening.

"And do you know what else?" His face was turning red now. "Do you know what I think about every single morning? I look over at the gym, and I see people in there working out, and I figure as soon as I leave for work, you're going to go over there and get some guy and bring him home. It's all I think about!"

Oh, help. Larry had crossed right over into lunacy. We were done. I'd gotten it wrong, I'd made a bad marriage completely intolerable, and there was no way back.

Back to what? I asked myself. *Back to bad?*

He was yelling now. Again, he'd yelled at me almost nightly before my confession, too. He'd been losing control for some time.

Larry stood up and stormed to the other side of the room, sitting down on a different couch. His chest was heaving, his expression one of terrible pain – pain that was morphing minute by minute into vengeful wrath.

"Here's what I want to know," he demanded. "Has Ricky called you? Have you spoken to him at all during this month?"

Yes. He had called.

Since Larry had asked me a direct question, I told the truth. If you thought I was nuts to confess in the first place, you're probably sizing me up for a strait jacket this time. But I was done with lying. Good, bad, or ugly, I wasn't going to lie. A lie right here would have been *easy.* Nothing would have escalated. But, nothing would have improved, either. All of my options were horrible. So I chose to at least stay clean in God's eyes, and I told the truth.

"He called one time," I answered, "just to make sure I was all right."

CHAPTER **SEVEN**

"OH, HO!!!!"

Larry's blast was triumphant. He felt justified, vindicated in all the terrible things he'd been allowing himself to think about me.

Our downstairs living area was really one big room. It had a sitting area on one side that we called the nook, a dining table in the middle, and another, larger area that we referred to as the living room. I was seated, by now, in the living room, and Larry was on the couch in the nook. When his "Oh, ho!" shook the rafters, Jazzy jumped onto my lap and began shaking. Sheila streaked upstairs. Sienna, a very calm larger dog, cast alarmed glances from Larry to me and back to Larry. My own heart pounded unmercifully in my chest, and I became immediately light-headed. Where was this going?

I didn't have to guess long.

"I'm going to shoot him!" Larry was standing now. His volume increased, and I was truly terrified. He stomped over to where I sat with Jazzy trembling on my lap, and hovered over me, a tower of rage. "I'm going to get my gun and shoot him! That's exactly what I'm going to do!"

"Stop!" I was pleading. "You're scaring Jazzy. You have to *stop!"*

But he didn't stop. The shouting and threatening probably lasted ten minutes, and I was afraid that even if *I* didn't pass out from fright, Jazzy would.

At last, with an awful sneer, he turned very deliberately and headed for the stairs. I was shaking so hard my teeth were chattering. What should I do? I knew I could leave, but with no notice, I didn't know where to go, and I was afraid he'd smash my equipment or do something that would really hurt me. I'd backed up my work, but all of my backups were in the house. And what of my animals? And what of Larry's threats against Ricky? What should I *do?*

I heard a loud thump upstairs and decided (*how dumb could I get?*) to go up and see what he was up to. I was too afraid *not* to know, and part of me still thought I could talk some kind of sense into him.

But sure enough, he'd dragged his gun bag from beneath the bed. He was in the adjoining bathroom, shells on the counter, loading his gun.

I knew he was angry, crazy angry, but was he really willing to throw his life away?

"Larry! You're going to go to prison! Stop it!!"

"I don't care, and you'd better leave me alone." His voice was strangely calm, and after all of the yelling and explosive venting of the past month, this eerie calmness chilled my very core.

I stepped into our large bathroom and looked to see him pick up one shell, then another. I had to try. "Do you have any idea what you're doing? You'll go to *prison!*"

I was standing just slightly behind him, and he lifted his right arm, ready to slam his elbow backwards into my face. Larry is a big guy. Powerful. He made a threatening jab to show he meant business, and, again very calmly, said, "Get out of here. You *don't* want to be in here."

No kidding! I ran downstairs, and you'd have thought I was a headless chicken, with all my frantic running around. I should have headed straight out the front door. But I couldn't. Larry was threatening to shoot a person, a person who had no idea he was coming. My addled brain told me to first hide my phone, so Larry couldn't take communication away from me. I would then find Larry's keys so he couldn't actually leave *with a gun.* He was about to destroy his life and maybe even hurt someone!

The moment I found his keys, I planned to skedaddle. But I couldn't find them. Then, at a moment when I was nowhere near the front door, Larry slowly thudded down the stairs.

I was standing near our dining room table, and Larry came to a strategic halt. He knew he'd placed himself between me and any means of egress. I couldn't get to the front door or to the stairway down to the garage without pushing past him. There were no other exits in our townhome. He was holding his gun down at his side, and I froze at the sight of it. I couldn't move.

His face was smug, arrogant with power. He knew he held all the cards. I didn't recognize him. I'd seen him angry before, many times, but never like this. I was afraid that any tiny move I made might set him off.

He paused, taking in my fear. He knew I couldn't get by him. He began waving the gun around and speaking in that foreign, flat, yet powerful voice. His eyes were completely unfamiliar to me. Mine fixed on the weapon, as he waved it around in my direction, and I realized that if it went off, a bullet could well hit me.

"You'd better not call anyone," he ordered. "I'm going over there, and I'm going to shoot him. I know Ricky's always got a gun with him, and he's a better shot than I am, so who knows what's going to happen. But you'd better not call anyone."

I looked from the gun back to his eyes, unable to determine his intent. Did he mean to shoot me, too?

Suddenly, the gun stopped its waving. Very slowly and deliberately, he raised his Glock and pointed it right at me. I couldn't breathe. I imagined the impact of a huge .45 caliber bullet tearing through my chest. I thought of my daughters, of my young grandson, and the grandson yet to be born. He was due in less than two weeks. Would I never meet little Joshua?

Lord, I cried out silently, *I know You are seeing this. I thought You promised me things, things yet to be. Where are You? Is Larry going to steal me away from my children? My babies? What will they do? How will they survive this?*

The sheer *unfairness* of it shook me as much as the fear did. I felt utterly helpless. There was no need for me to die. If Larry shot me, it would be robbery of the worst sort. He would be robbing not only me, but my family, of my life. And there was nothing I could do about it.

He stood there for some time, gun aimed at me as he deliberated. I say *deliberated*. The *crazy* part of him deliberated. The business owner, the hard-working man, even the grieving husband, were nowhere to be seen. The man in front of me had snapped in the most terrible sense of that word. His "deliberations," therefore, were skewed.

Knowing that didn't make me feel any better. If he killed me, he would regret it in the morning. But right now, tonight, anything could happen. I thought my life was over.

I waited, insides squirming, hoping he would lower the gun again. *Please stop pointing that thing at me!*

But now he was speaking again. "I mean it! You'd better not call anyone." And yet again, *"You'd better not call anyone, or more people are going to die!"*

Yeah, like me, of a heart attack, if not a bullet. The room spun, but I was afraid to reach for the back of a chair. I feared any sudden move could spell disaster.

Then, after a gut-wrenching two minutes, Larry lowered the gun and looked away. He turned around and went down the stairs, heading for the garage and his pickup.

CHAPTER **EIGHT**

His keys must have been in the ignition. No wonder I couldn't find them.

I heard the truck pull out and away from our garage, and I drew several shaky breaths. I retrieved my phone from its hiding place and dialed my pastor. I knew if anyone could call Larry and talk sense to him, it would be Pastor Mark. But he wasn't available, and my call went unanswered. *Think, Diana!*

I called my dear friend, my levelheaded buddy who had already walked through so much of this with me. DJ. True to form, she picked up immediately. As soon as I heard her voice, my emotions boiled. Tears pouring down my face, I choked into the phone, "DJ, I'm in trouble!"

Most of us have friends. Not all of us have friends of the caliber of my friend DJ. I don't know why I was so fortunate, but there you are. She was a blessing straight from God.

The moment she heard my voice and I told her I was in trouble, she was putting on her jacket and grabbing her car keys. "I'm on my way," she said. "What happened?"

I was nearly hysterical by now. "Larry has his gun, and I thought he was going to shoot me, and now he's on his way to shoot someone else, and I don't know what to do!"

"Call the cops," was her immediate reply.

"I don't want to call the cops! Everything will just get worse! He doesn't know what he's doing!"

"Diana, call the cops. You have no choice. Someone else is at risk, right this minute, and you have *no* choice. I'll be right there.

I'm in the car. I'll be there in two minutes. Hang up and call the cops."

I knew she was right. Larry had expressed his intent to me. If I didn't call the police, would that make me an accessory? I couldn't risk it. Larry, impaired or not, was making his own decisions right now. I dialed 911.

I don't have complete recall of that conversation. I know that I explained what had already happened. I revealed Larry's expressed intent. After I'd provided a description of Larry's truck and his destination, the 911 operator told me to get out of the house.

I got confused and started packing. Literally. I had a suitcase out and was throwing in jeans, a toothbrush, my blow dryer. Let's see, socks, oh, this warm sweater...

"What are you doing?" It was the 911 operator. "Diana, it sounds like you're *packing*. Stop it! Don't pick up another thing! Can you hear me? I want you to get out of the house immediately!"

"My friend is on her way here."

"Good. Get in her car and drive away. You need to *leave.*"

Leave my house, all my things, my own car? Unthinkable. What if Larry stayed angry and changed the locks? I'd have nothing with me.

"Can you hear me, Diana? Are you leaving? Is your friend there?"

"She just got here, but I want to take my own car."

"That's fine, Diana. You can take your own car. Just get out, go to your friend's house, and keep your phone with you."

A moment later, "Are you in your car?"

"Yes."

"Are you pulling away from the house?"

DJ saw me, and I called out that I'd follow her to her apartment, so I responded, "Yes."

"Okay. Diana, I'm going to disconnect, but you'll be called right away by a sergeant who is going to take over now. Okay? Promise you'll answer his call."

"I promise."

And with that, she signed off. I glanced at my phone a couple times to see if the image had changed. Throughout my conversation with 911, a big red alarm bell thingy had been spinning around on the screen of my smart phone. Caller ID on steroids. I wondered if, when the sergeant called me, the ringtone would be a siren. It wasn't, of course. When the sergeant called, my phone sounded normal, with the word Restricted in place of the red alarm bell.

Sergeant Shybar went over a lot of information I'd already provided the dispatcher. Larry's truck, Ricky's street, what had happened. He wanted to know where I was going. I named DJ's apartment complex. Okay. He told me to stay with DJ and that I'd hear back from him in a little while. My call with him was winding up as I found a parking space near DJ's home and turned off the ignition.

DJ was at my door, pulling it open. "Come upstairs, Diana. You can stay here just as long as you need to."

I wasn't crying anymore. That had stopped when I'd turned my attention to my packing. But I was trembling from head to toe. DJ told me to hold the handrail as I climbed the stone steps to her second-floor apartment. Once inside, I collapsed onto her sofa and said hello to her husband, Dave. Dave looked extremely grim, not saying much at first. He just stood very still, arms folded tensely across his chest, waiting for me to settle down so he could get the story. My problems had just blasted into their evening, and all they wanted to do was make room for me. They told me they would do anything they could to help. I was so grateful!

I had no sooner sat down than my phone rang again. It was Sergeant Shybar, saying they couldn't find a truck fitting the right description anywhere near Ricky's house. He also told me that they'd gone there and knocked on the door. Only one person had been at home there, a woman, and they'd escorted her away.

Oh *no!* This was getting worse and worse! Ricky wasn't home, but his lovely wife was, and she was now being removed from her home by the police! No doubt they had warned her that a threat had been made against her family. I felt sick.

After that, my phone rang nonstop. First Ricky called. His wife had called him, told him what was happening. He was out of the state, hunting with a friend. He hadn't yet told her of that stupid night ten years ago with me, so he'd had to tell her now. He was calling me because he needed more details. Just how much danger was his family in? I told him that Larry had not threatened his wife. Larry had made the statement that if I called anyone, "more people were going to die," but I couldn't conceive of Larry hurting Ricky's wife. I'd told the police about Larry's statement, though, which is why they'd escorted her away.

He asked if Larry had threatened me, and I said yes.

Our call broke up a few times because of his out-of-the-way location, but eventually he got the whole story, and he was actually very calm. He'd been afraid something like this would happen. He had other calls to make, so, saying he was glad I was okay, we disconnected.

Then Pastor Mark called. "Where *are* you?" he asked. "Are you all right?"

How had he found out? I told him where I was. He wanted to know what had happened, so I went through it again. He said Larry had called him, and they'd been on the phone together when the police came. So *that's* how he knew! Apparently Larry had already gone back to our house, found me gone, and called Pastor Mark.

He told me, "I was on the phone with Larry, and I could hear banging on the door. Larry just said, 'Hang on, the cops are here,' and went to answer the door. The next thing I heard was the police ordering Larry to the ground, and I could hear them arresting him and taking him away."

What a mess. We were dragging everyone we knew into our drama.

Our call was cut short by the police calling me again to inform me that Larry had returned home and been arrested. They said he would be spending the night in jail, and I could go home any time I wanted.

When my phone was quiet at last, DJ asked me if I'd had any dinner. It was over two hours since I'd come down the stairs at home, hungry and hoping to eat something. I'd thoroughly lost my appetite by this point, but DJ had some delicious beef and potato stew on the stove. She promised to keep the portion small if I would promise to eat it. Such a good friend!

Not much later we decided to let Dave have his living room back. DJ followed me back to my own home and spent the rest of the evening with me. It was probably nine-thirty when Pastor Mark called again. Larry had called him from the jail, asking for his medications. I felt ill again. I didn't want the crazed Larry to come home. Just then, I didn't ever want to see him again. There was, however, a part of my heart that grieved at the thought of Larry in a cell, with no dinner and no meds.

Larry suffered from high blood pressure, high cholesterol, and gout, and he took medications to control all three. He also took an anti-seizure medication to help with a facial tic that, left unchecked, drove him to distraction. He needed Celexa to help with his mood swings, and of course he usually needed something to help him sleep.

It seemed such a human thing, to need one's medication. I took no pleasure from the fact that my fifty-eight-year-old husband had gone off the deep end and ruined his life. It was surreal to think of Larry in a jail cell, and not headed for his own bed.

At the same time, I couldn't get the image of the gun out of my mind, and I found I couldn't catch my breath.

I remained light-headed and short of breath as I gathered what I could of Larry's prescriptions. DJ helped me bag them up. Pastor Mark came in just for a minute to get them, but while he was there he asked how much Larry had had to drink. I showed him a bottle that had started the afternoon full, and was now half empty. He told me that Larry admitted he'd also taken an anti-anxiety pill. It seemed the two substances had clashed in his system.

Being arrested had sobered him up, though, and Pastor Mark said he sounded terrible on the phone. He was in for a rough night, without a doubt.

I learned later that the jail nurse had gone home for the day, so he never did receive any of his medication.

Where can I go from Your Spirit?

Or where can I flee from Your presence?

If I ascend into heaven, You are there;

If I make my bed in hell, behold, You are there.

If I take the wings of the morning,

And dwell in the uttermost parts of the sea,

Even there Your hand shall lead me,

And Your right hand shall hold me.

(Psalm 139:7-10 NKJV)

CHAPTER **NINE**

This hurt is deep
I'll hold you softly as you grieve
I'll watch your sleep
'Til you remember how to breathe

There it was again! I'd nearly tuned it out as I remained in bed in that pre-dawn hour, re-living the events of the last month. Still, the words of the song's refrain persisted through my grogginess, and they nearly penetrated waking thought as I smushed my pillow into a more comfortable shape.

Somehow I'd survived the worst month of my life. This was the third morning since the night my husband had pulled a Glock .45 on me. I woke up alone, out of breath, out of hope. Today was Sunday. I hadn't seen Larry since Thursday night, Gun Night. The night, as we've seen, that all hell broke loose.

I opened my eyes and could just make out the first hint of dawn peeking through the window shade. My chest hurt from my relentless hyperventilating. I closed my eyes again. I knew I needed to get to church, to be among people, but I didn't feel at all well.

'Til you remember how to breathe.

Oh! My eyes flew open again as a different kind of dawning arose in my mind. I was instantly wide awake. *The Lord was with me!* That was *His* voice singing that lovely, healing song into my spirit. He was telling me that He'd been watching my sleep, that *He knew I was having trouble breathing!* HE KNEW! And He also knew my prime emotion these past days had been *grief.* Not anger, not bitterness, but horrible, oppressive *grief!*

Who but God could come up with such perfect lyrics – lyrics designed to soothe my tired, aching heart? I didn't even know who the actual artist was. I jumped out of bed and ran to my computer to Google it. There! I found it, and immediately bought the song online. That done, I synced my iPod and sat, mesmerized, as the song played.

More tears, but not from sorrow. I knew with certainty that God was with me, that He understood *everything.* He was in control, and my only responsibility was to remember how to breathe. Other things would come later, but at that moment I could almost hear Him coaching me:

"Breathe gently in, Diana. Now gently out. I watched over you all night, and I am with you now."

I sank to my knees, hit the back button so the song would replay, and wept until I was spent. God didn't hate me! He wasn't mad at me! He was *with* me. He was *comforting* me, even *me*, the horrible cheating woman who had ripped her husband's heart out as she tumbled off her pedestal.

I began to understand mercy just a little better as I sat and played that song, over and over and over again. The Lord's presence was all around me. I knew – I *knew!* – that not only was He comforting me – He was assuring me that everything was in His hands. And His hands were infinite. I was His daughter, I was forgiven, I was loved, and He held the reins.

I didn't ponder the nagging question of whether or not I'd been right to confess. That was too heavy a load, so I left it in the vault for now. I'd been sure at the time that the Lord had been guiding me, and now He was helping me, reminding me that He was in control.

I thought back over the past few days. Even in my frantic activity following Gun Night, the Lord hadn't allowed me to do anything to make matters worse. At least that was something!

* * *

Larry had spent Thursday night in jail. On Friday morning I was up and busy early, certain that Larry would be arraigned at one o'clock and home by early afternoon. As I didn't know his frame of mind, I wanted to be safely away. DJ came over and helped me choose what to pack for an extended stay away from my life. Her husband Dave had cleared out space in an extra room in their apartment, and I was moving in there temporarily.

After we decided what I couldn't live without and how many kinds of boots and/or shoes I might need, DJ had to go to work. It was up to me to get the stuff into suitcases and into my car.

Our garage is two floors below our upstairs bedroom area, so I had quite a task ahead of me. I took several suitcase loads down to my car. I then went back upstairs to my office. Time to begin the laborious task of unplugging and moving my computer down to the car as well.

I'd already taken the animals to boarding for now. I couldn't bring them all to DJ's, so I had put the cat in her crate, put the two dogs in the car, and dropped them off. I felt terrible for them, especially Jazzy, who hadn't stopped shaking since Thursday's drama. She'd followed me around all morning, whimpering and creating a tripping hazard on my stairs.

I hadn't yet reached out to Juliette. I hoped she still wanted me to come share her condo. I was sure she would. I didn't feel I deserved such wonderful friends. At any rate, this move, and my pets' stay at boarding, would be temporary.

Once my car was packed to the gills, I drove to DJ's and reversed the process, lugging everything up her stairs, one heavy load at a time. I deposited everything in her spare room and checked my watch. I had an appointment with an attorney at one o'clock, and it was now eleven forty-five. I had just enough time, I hoped, to purchase a new phone, complete with a new number. My old phone was tied to Larry's business, and I wanted a fresh start. My own private phone was a first step.

I was able to get an inexpensive Smartphone because I was signing up for a new account. We had our transaction finished just in time for me to dash to my attorney's office. I was in uncharted territory, and needed to speak with her ASAP.

* * *

"I wish you'd spoken to me earlier, Diana. You didn't need to move out of your house."

I sat back in my chair, depleted. *I didn't? All that work, for nothing?*

Caryn continued, "Larry has probably been arraigned by now, and there will be an automatic no-contact order put in place. He won't be allowed to come within three hundred feet of you or your house. You can stay at home."

My new divorce attorney leaned back in her chair and watched me for a moment before turning to pick up the phone. Somehow, she knew just who to call. "Hey, John, I'm calling about a gentleman who was brought in last night on a gun charge. His name is – oh, you've got him? Larry. Yes, that's him. Has he been arraigned yet? I see. And what was the order? And Sam's there now? Okay. Thanks."

She replaced the handset and turned back to me. "Larry has bonded out," she said, "but he has a no-contact order, so you won't have to see him. He told the judge that he will be living at your cabin at Magic Reservoir." She steepled her fingers and locked my gaze. "I have to ask, are there any weapons there?"

There were. I told her there were two guns at our cabin. I didn't know the makes. A rifle and a shotgun, I believed. No handguns.

"Is there any way you can go get them so he has a place to go? He'll be breaking the law if he goes out there and the guns are on the property."

Was there to be no let up? I was exhausted from my morning move, and now I faced moving it all back again this afternoon. And in the meantime I was being asked to drive forty-five miles out to the cabin to get, of all things, *guns?*

"It's really the best solution, Diana, if you can manage it," Caryn continued. "Is that something you can do?"

I reached for my handbag and reluctantly withdrew my car key. "I guess I'll have to," I said.

She was nodding. "In the meantime, I'm going to put together a list of everything I'll need you to compile if you're going to file for divorce."

"Oh, I am," I said, as I stared out the window. "I have no choice." I'd been planning to move out anyway, I thought dismally. I'd only stayed through the awful month of October because I felt so guilty myself. I'd kept the vain hope alive that Larry would change, maybe really forgive me. Maybe he would even recognize and apologize for some of his own stuff. Never did I think that my husband, whether in a fit of temper or not, would point a gun at me. I saw no way back to relationship after that.

"Well, you'd better get moving, because he can't go out there until you've removed the guns." She stood up, a clear sign that I needed to get going. She promised to email me the list of documents I would need to gather, and I stepped out into the chilly November air.

* * *

At least it wasn't snowing. It was still a bit early in the year for that, and I was thankful that my drive out to Magic was dry, uneventful, and peaceful. Peaceful, that is, until just before I pulled up to our drive. That's when my old cell phone rang – the one

Larry knew the number to. I usually screened calls like everyone else, but under the circumstances I felt I should answer it.

I instantly regretted picking up. It was Sam, an acquaintance, who also happened to be the local bail bondsman. As soon as I picked up, and without my permission, he passed his phone to Larry. My hands shook at the unexpected sound of Larry's voice.

"I don't want to talk to you," were the first words out of my mouth.

"Baby, I'm so sorry! I'm so sorry! Where are you? I'm so sorry!"

My heart wasn't ready for sorries. I wasn't ready to talk to Larry. I told him he wasn't allowed to talk to me because of the no-contact order.

"Yes, baby, I'm allowed to talk to you on the pho – "

"No, you're not, and even if you are, I don't want to talk to you."

Then it occurred to me that I didn't know where he kept his guns at the cabin. I felt so aggravated. I didn't want to have a conversation, but I did need to know where the darned guns were!

" – and I need to tell you how sor – "

"Larry." He wasn't listening. He kept talking. "*Larry.*" No good. He wasn't hearing me. I raised my voice, "LARRY!" That worked.

"I just need to know where your guns are in the cabin. I had to drive out here because you can't stay here if the guns are on the premises. I don't want to have a conversation! Just tell me where the guns are, I'll get them out of here, and you're on your own. You should stop at the vet's and get Sienna if you want her with you. They're all there at the moment."

"Okay," he said, "but can't we at least – "

"No! You aren't listening to me! I don't want to talk to you! Where are the guns?"

He heard me at last, and told me where to look. I asked him to wait on the line until I was sure I could locate them. When I found them, I asked him to put Sam back on the phone. Larry finally realized I wasn't ready to hear from him, so with one help-less, "I love you," he returned the phone to Sam.

Sam was all business. "So you're out at Magic now. How long will it take you to get back to town?"

Feeling pressured, I replied, "Forty-five minutes."

"Cool," he said. "When you get home, we'll need you to pack a bag for Larry, as he can't come within three hundred feet of the house. Just pack up some stuff for him, and put it in his truck. Then you'll need to drive the truck down the street so he can retrieve it without violating the order to stay away from the house. We need to get him mobile."

I was still inside our cabin, and I slumped down onto a chair. I was out of gas. My body was exhausted due to very little sleep, a non-stop racing heart, a near-total move-out from my home, and now a dash to Magic Reservoir for gun retrieval. Now I was being instructed to go pack a bag and take care of a man who had scared the living daylights out of me not twenty hours before!

But what was I going to do? Refuse? I'm not the type to get mad at my husband and throw all his belongings out into the street. And the words angry, mad, whatever, didn't fit with my emotional state, somehow.

Annoyed by this request, certainly…but mainly, I was in shock. I was frightened. I was sad, and I felt unable to cope with my own situation. But I wasn't angry. That's why I didn't tell Larry, "I hate you," or, "leave me alone." All I could come up with was, "I don't want to talk to you."

So of course, I told Sam I would do as he asked. We arranged it so that I would call when I got to within ten minutes of town. He and Larry would head to a designated spot. They would wait while I parked the truck and walked back home.

* * *

Packing my husband's suitcase increased the post-traumatic grief that was settling in. I knew he had a few things out at Magic, so I focused on clothes rather than toiletries and underthings. I chose some T-shirts and work shirts, an extra pair of jeans, several sweatshirts. I included some nicer sweaters in case he wanted to go to church somewhere. Black shoes for the same purpose. I packed his Bible, then tucked in his iPod, along with its charger. I'd long since filled his iPod with contemporary Christian music, and I thought he might value having it.

Finished, I lugged the day's umpteenth suitcase down two flights of stairs and into the garage. I put it in his truck and climbed behind the wheel. Our arrangement involved my driving the truck to the end of our townhome's alley, and leaving it on the street. Once I had returned to our home, Sam would drive Larry to retrieve the truck.

They were parked just down the street, a safe three-hundred-foot distance away. I learned later that Larry watched as I parked the truck, got out and walked away. That was the last sight of me that he had for six weeks, and I didn't see him at all.

I waited in the garage for a few minutes so he could get in his truck and drive away. Then I got back in my own car and headed wearily to DJ's apartment. It was time for me to move back in to my own home.

* * *

And so went Friday, November 2nd. By Saturday morning I could barely move. I'd overdone it. All that moving and running around had left me sore and worn out. I'd retrieved Jazzy and my cat, Sheila, from boarding shortly before six o'clock the evening before. Larry, as I'd suggested, had picked up Sienna on his way out of town.

I spent a considerable amount of time that Saturday on the phone, with Jazzy on my lap and Sheila next to me. A number of people called to check in and see how I was doing. DJ, ever practical, told me to go shopping and get myself a pre-cooked chicken and some easy things to have in the house. Pastor Mark called and advised me to remember to eat, at least protein bars, whether I felt like it or not. People knew that it's easy to forget to eat while in crisis mode.

It was all good advice, and I tried to take it. I did buy a chicken and some protein bars. I just forgot to eat them.

I took Jazzy for a walk, then spent hours trying to gather all the paperwork my attorney had requested. Some stuff I had in the house, some things I was able to print off the internet. The rest was in the office at Larry's lab. I still did all the books there, and I knew I'd have to carry on doing them for a while.

Due to a bankruptcy after Larry's divorce seventeen years before, we'd had to use my name to get the business going when we moved the lab to Idaho. All the bank accounts and credit cards, as well as many of the lab's vendor accounts, were in my name. It behooved me to keep the bills paid. I would need to make the twelve-mile trek to the lab and get some work done, but I didn't want to think about it now.

One part of my conversation with Pastor Mark kept coming back to me throughout the day. I had told him I was filing for divorce. He wanted me to take some time, to avoid rushing into anything. But I told him no, that this was too much. My home life had been terrible for years. I'd dreaded coming home every day for a long time. The past month, since I'd confessed, had been unbearable.

"And," I added, "with what's happened, people won't *blame* me. Maybe I won't have to lose another church family."

It was Pastor Mark's reply that came back to me over and over. "Diana, you sound almost *relieved*."

To which I had replied, "I'm *sad*, Mark, but at least I feel I can make a decision. I've been staying, and he's been drinking, and raging, and it's not just about the last month. It's been far longer than that. I never wanted to get divorced again, *ever*. I've stayed, and I've prayed, and I've been holding on to the hope that Larry would change. He's been coming to the Bible school, coming to church, and I was hoping. I know my part in this is terrible, and I'm not making any excuses for it. But I won't stay where it's unsafe."

I had a hole of loss inside of me that was larger than any bullet could have made. I wasn't innocent in any of it, but enough was enough. I had kids and grandkids to think about.

My marriage was over.

Blessed are those who mourn, for they shall be comforted.

(Matthew 5:4 NKJV)

CHAPTER **TEN**

Larry's preliminary hearing was set for November 14th. I'd met with the prosecutor to tell him what had happened, and I'd cried throughout the telling. The Victim's Representative met with me as well, and sat in on the meeting so she could hear my story. They had a copy of the statement I'd given to the police, stating they had plenty of evidence to charge Larry with a felony. They had, in fact, already charged him.

That surprised me. I was not only the sole victim, but I was the sole witness. No one had asked me if I wanted to press charges. I learned that I didn't have to. The State pressed charges. This was all so incredibly serious.

I found myself thinking over and over, *What have you done, Larry?*

The prosecutor's office emailed me my subpoena for the hearing. I wondered what that day would be like, going to court, seeing Larry, taking the stand. Pastor Mark asked me what I was going to say. Baffled by the question, I just said, "I'll just say what happened. I won't exaggerate or anything. But I have to go, so I guess I'll just answer their questions."

He looked unhappy at this answer, but he didn't press me.

I had other things on my mind, too. My grandson Joshua was due any day, and I was heading to California as soon as he arrived. I would stay with Amy for ten days and be as helpful as I could. That would mostly entail caring for little nineteen-month-old Caden. Not a problem for me! I never got nearly enough time with him. The thought of leaving this place, leaving my problems, and just holding babies, was tremendously soothing.

In the meantime, I had plenty to keep me busy. I asked for as much work as my firm could throw my way, as I was single now. I had to go to the lab, get the mail, do the banking, and pay the bills. I could only go when Larry wasn't there, which meant late afternoons and evenings. No fun.

And then when I thought I couldn't handle any more, more came.

My dog, Jazzy, carried on shaking. She never recovered from her fright on that terrible night. Fourteen years old and nearly blind in one eye, she could still "talk" to me. Jack Russells are an intelligent breed, and Jazzy had always been very communicative. As she got older, she became more nervous, but I loved her. She'd been my baby since she was six weeks old.

And now she was asking me, "Where are Daddy and Sienna? Why are you so sad? Why is my world all wrong?"

She panicked when I would leave the house, literally screaming, it seemed to me, with that horrible high-pitched panicked dog bark. And I had to leave her a lot, because, as I've said, I was working more.

I came home every day to find urine all over the house. Everywhere. She was losing control. Her shaking was so bad that sometimes she would stumble. She was miserable. She was sick and getting worse. I had a very painful conversation with a dear friend who said, "Diana, you need to do the right thing for your dog. She's suffering, and it's not going to get better."

All I could think was, *not another one!*

* * *

I called them my bookends. Salt and pepper dogs. The first bookend was my white Jack Russell, Jazzy. The other bookend, Havana, had a Jack Russell mama, but her daddy was pure Labrador. Havana was all black except for a white spot on her chest. She looked like a thick, very short black Lab, yet she often leapt high in excitement like a Jack Russell. Her litter had been a mistake, with no one intending the Jack Russell mama to be courted by the resident Labrador – the Lab that was penned-up to prevent just such a catastrophe. The two got together, though, even through a chain-link fence. The result was a large litter of unsalable pups.

Shortly before Larry's birthday in 2004, an ad had appeared in the paper: "Lab/Jack Russell mix, free to good homes."

I called and learned there was one female, and that was that. I went and got her. For some time Larry had wanted a mid-sized dog to keep him company at work. When I surprised him with that black puppy, she was so small she fit neatly into just one of his hands.

My cigar aficionado hubby naturally named her Havana, because, of course, Cuban cigars are the best.

Six months later, while staying at our cabin at Magic Reservoir, we acquired Sheila. She-bee, She-she. The kitty had many names. Larry had opened the front door to let the dogs out, and a tiny kitten began meowing loudly at him. She had taken refuge in the wheel well of his truck and was perched upon his huge truck tire. Magpies were after her, and she knew Larry could help her.

He called me, told me there was a kitten out there, and I went to look. Larry shooed off the birds and called the kitten. She zoomed over to him immediately, ran up his clothes and into his hands. He immediately handed her over to me.

I was entirely unfamiliar with cats. My parents were allergic and we had *never* owned a cat. We never even *visited* people who had cats. I didn't know what to do with this little baby. But she did. I held her up at eye-level to get a better look at her. She promptly put one little paw on my face and used it to push herself back, the better to size me up. I must have passed muster, because she then leaned forward and started licking my face!

I took her inside and gave her a bath (she was filthy) and discovered that she was all white but for a gray patch on her head. She had startling blue eyes and no tail. She was a Manx. I had some puppy chow at the cabin and she scarfed that down in no time. I left the doors open to the cabin all day, hoping she'd go home, but she didn't. She followed me around, never more than a foot from my ankles. When Larry sat down at the end of the day to watch TV, she curled up around his neck and went to sleep.

We couldn't just leave her out there on her own when we went home on Sunday. We hadn't seen it coming, but we were apparently, now, cat parents.

We later learned her story. She'd been abandoned by a guy who became unpopular for having done so. At least we knew we hadn't stolen her.

* * *

For some time we were a family of four pets. Our Golden Retriever, Koki; my Jack Russell, Jasmine; our little mix, Havana; and one cat, Sheila. Koki died in 2010 at a ripe old Golden Retriever age of twelve, and so we became a family of five. Mom, dad, and three fur-kids.

Havana went everywhere with Larry. She went to work with him. At home when he stood up, she followed. They adored each other. She had a huge heart and loved everybody. Because of her unusual appearance (super-short Lab) and sweet nature, everyone who met her loved her as well. She used to sit with her head on Larry's feet or in his lap when he would relax on the couch.

In late July of 2012, we were in the middle of a move. Our house had sold, and we were moving to a townhome that had far less space than our 2,300 square-foot house. We needed to downsize. Some things we sold, some we gave away, and of course we discovered an awful lot of plain old trash. Larry filled truckload after truckload with junk to be thrown away in the huge bins in the back parking lot at work.

On one such day, Larry left the trash in the truck bed when he got to the lab. He had a lot to do, and he could dispose of the trash later. At noon he finally took a break and drove the truck around to the trash bins. He got out, unloaded all the garbage, got back in the truck, and re-parked it near the lab's front entrance.

He went back to work, packing up cases for delivery. He was quite busy for two hours. At two o'clock, he noticed that Havana wasn't in her bed or following him around. He looked everywhere for her. He went outside and called her, walking around the building. Where could she have gone?

At last, with a sick apprehension, he decided to look in the truck. There he found her. She'd followed him when he left the lab with his arms full of empty boxes. She had climbed up into the truck and into the back seat without him seeing her. She'd done this before, slipping up into the truck, and then hiding on the floor of the back seat. Havana was black, the truck's interior was black. It was a good hiding place. We tried to keep eagle eyes on her, but she was just too smart, and she didn't want to be left behind.

It was late July and 95 degrees outside. She didn't have a chance. When Larry opened the driver's door, he found her, already stiff, right there on the floor. She'd wanted to get out and had come to the front door.

I'd never seen a more devastating sight than that of Larry when he walked into the kitchen later that afternoon. He was holding her collar, trying to get the words out because I didn't know yet. All I knew was that an employee had called me and said that Larry had taken Havana to the vet, that something was wrong. I was completely unprepared for my grief-stricken husband to tell me, with uncontrolled tears pouring down his face, "She's *dead*. Havana's *gone*."

* * *

Larry was inconsolable, and who could blame him? Havana's loss was huge, and right in the middle of such a very major move. We had all we could do just to cope.

He didn't want another dog, but in September, after we'd settled into our new home, I noticed how lonely Larry was at work every day. He tried taking Jazzy with him because he couldn't bear to be dogless all day, but she was old and she didn't want to go. She started cowering down when he called her to come with him, so he gave up.

I found a mid-sized mixed breed at the Humane Society, and I went to meet her. I took some video footage with my iPad. Larry watched the video, saw a nice, gentle, four-year-old doggie who needed a home. He agreed that we could adopt her. Sienna. Her name is her color, reddish-brown. She learned quickly to leap up into Larry's truck, and she went to work with him every day. Sienna was such a good dog, right off the bat, that Larry's heart began to heal up just a little.

So then we were five again. Mom, dad, and three fur-kids.

Until Gun Night. Until Larry had to leave and Sienna went with him.

Then, in the house, we were three: Mom and two fur-kids.

And now Jazzy was sick, clearly at the end of her life. I couldn't leave her alone, screaming and peeing all over the house. I'd lost Havana just four months earlier. I'd lost Sienna because she was with Larry. Now I was going to lose Jasmine.

I took her to the vet myself, barely able to drive for all my tears. I knew it would be painless for her. I knew she was suffering, physically and in every other way. It was time to say "goodbye" to my doggie of 14 years. Many of you, reading this, have had to do the same. I know you understand.

My house was now a home to two. Mom and one fur-kid, my kitty.

* * *

Perhaps I should have known Sheila could never cope with all of the changes in her world. Within two weeks, we'd gone from a full house to an empty one. She was alone all day while I took jobs. There were days I traveled and didn't get home until late. She began attacking me in the evenings, and I knew she was frustrated by all of her own loss. She usually waited until she saw me head upstairs to go to bed, and then she'd launch herself at my leg and bite and claw me (we'd only had her front claws removed). I'd be gushing blood all over myself, with fresh injuries to patch up every evening, just when I wanted to go to sleep.

The final straw came one night when she was seated on the couch next to me, purring loudly and letting me scratch behind her ears. She'd settled deep into the leather, a picture of feline contentment. Then, just as I turned a page in my book, she sprang at me, grabbing my arm with all the power she could muster, and that was a lot. She was a big cat. She tore into my bare arm with teeth and claws and then leaped away, darting up the stairs before I could rebuke her.

I was a mess, with damage to both legs and now my right arm. This couldn't go on. Sheila was grieving, confused, and was taking it out on me.

I had a preliminary hearing to go to, a divorce to prepare for, my own grief at the loss of my marriage and three dogs, and I fell apart. I was at the end of everything. I took Sheila to our animal shelter the next day and asked them to find her a home with other pets and other people. She couldn't stand to be alone.

And that's what they did. She was successfully adopted in short order.

Now, in my house there was one.

I was *alone*.

CHAPTER **ELEVEN**

I surrendered Sheila on November 13, 2012, and the next day was Larry's preliminary hearing.

All my nervous questions about whether Larry would be there, what I would say, et cetera, were for nothing. Larry's attorney asked for a continuance, asserting that he'd not had time to adequately prepare his defense. He was so sure the continuance would be granted, in fact, that Larry hadn't even come.

Prosecutor Wilson informed the Court that I would soon be flying to California, to help with a new grandchild, and he asked that at least my testimony be put on record. His request was denied.

The judge then conferred with me about the possible timing and length of my trip. The math told us that, even if Joshua's arrived later than expected, I would still be home by the first week of December. He reset the "prelim" for December 12, and sent us all on our way.

Larry's attorney was pleased with the outcome, because he wanted as much time as he could get between the evening of "the event," and my taking the stand. Long experience taught him that testimonies can change as emotions cool. For the same reason, the prosecutor was decidedly *not* pleased, and that was why he had tried to get my testimony on the record *now*.

As for me, I just figured Larry was buying time. Maybe his attorney could put together a good case, but I didn't feel that his outcome had anything to do with me. I'd begged him to put the gun away, had warned him of trouble. I'd never wanted any of this for him. When I learned that they were charging him with a felony that carried a five-year prison sentence, I felt terrible for him, but it was out of my hands.

I was, after all, facing my own sorrows, walking through the "fires" of finding myself suddenly single, with my own life and future cloaked in fearful mystery.

There was nothing I could do for Larry.

...Do not fear, for I have redeemed you;

I have summoned you by name; you are mine.

When you pass through the waters,

I will be with you;

and when you pass through the rivers,

they will not sweep over you.

When you walk through the fire,

you will not be burned;

the flames will not set you ablaze.

(Isaiah 43:1-2, NIV)

CHAPTER **TWELVE**

You might well be asking, "Where was God in all of this?"

I can assure you, He was everywhere, all through it, all the time, every minute. When I woke up each morning, His Spirit was feeding me a new song for the day. I found myself dreaming the song, and as I awoke it was playing through my mind and spirit. It was a different song every day. Songs about hope, freedom, forgiveness, restoration.

I was frazzled by loss and grief and an uncertain future, so not everything sank in properly. All the same, the Lord was nurturing my spirit, holding me near His heart, and I knew it.

One particular song about mercy flooded my mind one morning, but I couldn't remember its name. It was a brand new release and I'd only heard it twice. How was I to find it? I wanted to listen to the whole thing! At last, I prayed about it. I said, "Lord, you brought that song to my mind. It's about being held by mercy. I can't find it, so I'm asking for your help. Please let me hear it in the car today so I'll know how to look it up."

Two hours later, while backing the car out of the garage, my radio found its signal and came to life just as a familiar, older song was ending. Before my car had fully left my small driveway, the song I'd asked the Lord about began to play. It was the immediacy of this answer to prayer that struck me. If this song had played during my long drive to Twin Falls, I would have been happy, but I wouldn't have known whether it was orchestrated by the Lord.

But this! It could not have been timed more perfectly to ensure that I didn't miss a note. I was very aware of and overwhelmed by God's tenderness at that moment. I put the car in park, tears streaming, as Jason Crabb's beautiful song, *Let Mercy Hold You,* filled my heart.

I was also careful to get lots of time with God every morning before the day started. I knew that without Him, I'd be sunk. I loved and relied on my early time, with just my Bible, my journal, and my coffee. Something special would always jump off the page and speak to me, and I filled page after page in my journal with wonderful verses, such as this one on November 9, just eight days post Glock:

> *Yet I still dare to hope when I remember this:*
> *The faithful love of the Lord never ends!*
> *His mercies never cease.*
> *Great is his faithfulness;*
> *his mercies begin afresh each morning.*
> *I say to myself, "The Lord is my inheritance;*
> *Therefore, I will hope in him!"*

(Lamentations 3:21-24 NLT)

That's what I was doing. I was taking one step at a time, waiting expectantly on the Lord, Whose tender compassions fail not. Sometimes depression threatened, and self-recrimination attempted to swallow me whole. As long as I never missed my morning appointment with God, I was able to put one foot in front of the other.

Several people hinted at it, but nobody asked me outright, "Are you sure you did the right thing by confessing?"

I will admit that I now asked *myself* that, a lot. I always came back to the same thing, though. My growth in the Lord would have been stunted if I believed I was directly disobeying Him. I

wouldn't step out in further ministry when I had a black secret –
a secret that was bound to come out sometime, if only by talking
in my sleep.

There was no way to move forward toward a good marriage
with a huge lie hanging between us. And yes, it now looked like
our marriage was over. But maybe there was more honesty in that
than in the way we'd been living before.

Even so, I slowed down a bit. I decided not to file for divorce
just yet. I didn't think I could handle a criminal trial and divorce
proceedings at the same time. I also thought it might factor into
a judge's decision-making if he knew things were so bad the wife
was divorcing. I had no desire to make Larry's case worse than it
already was.

CHAPTER **THIRTEEN**

Joshua arrived on November 17, 2012, a Saturday. I managed to book a flight, and Monday evening found me on Amy's couch with a new baby in one arm and a toddler cuddled up in the other.

I planned to spend ten days with Amy, helping wherever I could. At the same time, I was enjoying my own time of refreshing.

Amy's home was a tiny apartment, and, during my stay, there were three adults and two little ones. Yet there was never a harsh word, not so much as an impatient gesture in our midst. Her home was small but joyful, and as peaceful as it could be, considering that we had a new baby in the mix.

My time with Amy's family spanned Thanksgiving, and I spent a blissful holiday surrounded by my loved ones. Nothing was resolved yet in Idaho, but for this time, the love and support of my family poured soothing oil onto the troubled waters of my soul.

I carried two phones with me, trying to update people with my new number when they called the old one. I didn't tell Larry about the new number because I had cut all communication with him. That didn't mean *he* stopped trying to reach out to *me*.

During my initial meeting with my divorce attorney, Caryn, she had explained that the no-contact order meant *no contact at all*. The piece of paper Larry received from the Court, however, was incomplete. The judge had ordered no contact at all, but he had forgotten to check the boxes that would confirm, Not by Email, Not by Phone, Not by Computer.

Larry took some advantage of the loophole that the judge's mistake afforded him. He knew I wouldn't take a call, so he emailed me. He wasn't obnoxious about it, but he was persistent, and he began well before Joshua's birth and my trip to California.

At first, his communications to me had been grief-filled, shattered. He was broken by his own behavior. That worsened when his attorney read him a portion of the 911 transcript.

On November 5, Larry emailed:

> *Diana,*
>
> *Oh my God. How can you ever forgive me?*
>
> *My attorney just called and read to me what you said that I said. I am on my knees crying and apologizing to you and can't breathe. I am not questioning you at all, these are things I don't remember. I don't know what to say. That wasn't me.*
>
> *What do I do?*
>
> *What do I do?*

He emailed me again two days later, and I could hear the cry in the written words, "Have you taken your wedding ring off?"

I had.

"Are you going to divorce me?"

I was.

He asked me three times what had happened to Jazzy. My daughter Bethany had written a post online that said, "RIP Jazzy," to our little doggie, so Larry knew about her death even though I hadn't told him.

"What happened to Jasmine?" he wrote. "Please talk to me. Please."

I was unmoved, but not, I hope, uncivil. I sent him a short reply that explained what had happened.

His attorney tried twice to call me, but I refused to answer or return the call. I was gasping for air myself, and saw no upside in speaking with his lawyer. I wasn't going to reconcile with Larry, and there was nothing I could do to help him.

Larry had been sorry before. He'd been remorseful after incidents of rage that threatened to shake the house down. But he was never sorry enough to change. It had taken fifteen years and the barrel of a gun to get me here, and I'd had my fill.

* * *

The first half of November 2012 was surely the saddest, the most traumatic, and the most exhausting span of time I'd ever known. From November 19 to November 29, however, when I was with Amy's little family, I experienced healing in my body, soul, and spirit.

First, there was healing in my body, because Amy made me eat. Even when he picked me up from the airport, Dean, my son-in-law, said he was under orders to stop for food. No ifs, ands, or buts. I was eager to see the baby, but I complied when he stopped at one of their favorite restaurants. I ordered a chicken salad to go, and we were back on the road in no time. I was touched that he chose to point me in the direction of *good* food, as opposed to a burger, against which my tummy would have rebelled.

Dean is also a talented chef, and throughout my stay he prepared wonderful, flavor-packed meals. He added thoughtful touches, like saving the most perfect Diana-sized pork chop for me. I caught him red-handed in that act of kindness when someone else tried to pick up that chop. They wanted to cut it up into pieces for nineteen-month-old Caden. "Wait," he said, "I have this smaller piece for Caden, and I saved that one for Diana. It's perfect for her."

It was perfect for anyone. He'd set aside the best one for me.

Second, there was healing in my soul – my mind, will and emotions. My mind luxuriated in the tranquil atmosphere. My will, my inner turmoil and decision-making could take a rest. I had nothing to do but laugh with my daughter and enjoy my grandsons. As for my emotions, those were oh so weary. I needed peace, and I found it in my beloved daughter's little home.

I mentioned 'little home'. To be clear, saying eight hundred square feet might be stretching it. I slept on the couch, and we all shared the only shower. None of us, not even my son-in-law, ever complained once.

Third, my spirit likewise needed refueling. I was able to spend time reading a Bible I borrowed from Amy; praying as I steered Caden down the street in his little stroller that looked like a car; and letting God refill my depleted spiritual tank.

* * *

By the end of November, I began to notice a change in Larry's tone when he emailed me.

His earlier emails all required either responses or decisions from me. He told me how much he missed me, loved me, how he wanted us to be together. Above all, he wanted to talk to me, meet with me, let me see all the changes in his life. He was remorseful, saying over and over again how sorry he was. He made a lot of promises about the future.

With each communication came the pressure of deciding whether I would respond or ignore, care or not care, or maybe even *convince myself* that I didn't care.

Sometimes he needed real decisions, like what he should do for money, since that had been my department. He needed me to pay his employee or talk to the computer guy or let him know what billing address we used for credit cards. Any number of things that didn't stop just because our relationship had bottomed out. Still raw from our in-house super explosion, I found all this unwanted interaction draining.

Near the time my family visit was coming to an end, however, I noticed that Larry no longer pleaded with me to talk to him. He didn't ask me for anything. He asked after my welfare and told me a little bit, not much, about changes he was walking through. He expressed to me how much he was enjoying reading Ephesians. His reading showed him that he hadn't been the husband he should have been, but he was quick to add that he wasn't expecting anything from me. He knew I wasn't ready, and he would be patient while I took whatever time I needed. He was kind, friendly, and undemanding. This was new, and very unexpected.

I had come to fear his emails, because I was taking a break, enjoying some time away from my mess. I didn't want to constantly reassert, to a heartsick husband, my decision to end our marriage. But as his tone changed, so did my response.

Rather than avoiding the email inbox on my phone, I began checking it deliberately, albeit surreptitiously.

My family was extremely angry at Larry at that time. They weren't privy to the subtle changes I was detecting in his communications, and nobody wanted me to reconcile with him. My girls had lived with their dad through their high school years, and then on their own throughout most of my marriage to Larry, but they weren't blind to all of the aforementioned problems with drinking and anger.

This last straw had not only broken the camel's back, in their opinion; it had nuked that camel right into oblivion.

I'd fully agreed with that assessment. But as I've said, I'd stepped off the divorce fast track, and decided I wasn't in a hurry to set anything in motion that would further disrupt my world. I had Larry's preliminary hearing, Prelim No. 2, coming up on December 12. I knew that would be harrowing enough, without any more legal sprinkles added.

And now Larry's emails were kind, even mildly amusing on occasion. He was taking care of the business, and doing a good job of it, especially considering that the office computer crashed while our drama was unfolding. The thing just blew up internally, and there was no saving it.

I had backups of our bookkeeping files and important documents, and I'd ordered a new computer the week before Joshua's birth. It arrived even as I was flying to California. Our go-to computer guy, the ever helpful and awesome Clyde, went to the lab to unbox it and make it functional for Larry.

Throughout that ordeal, I never heard an impatient word from Larry in any communication, though it was surely frustrating for him to deal with a new computer without me. The office was my responsibility. I knew where I kept the software; I knew how to access our cloud-based lab program; I knew where the backup flash drive was and what was on it. He didn't know those things.

Through all that, I heard not a peep of peevishness from him. That definitely got my attention and begged the question, *What was happening in Larry's world?*

PART **FOUR**

THE REDEMPTION

For I am about to do something new.

See, I have already begun!

Do you not see it?

I will make a pathway through the wilderness.

I will create rivers in the dry wasteland.

(Isaiah 43:19 NLT)

CHAPTER **ONE**

On November 29, 2012, I flew home. Back to work, back to responsibility, and back to decisions. I might also add, back to isolation and an empty house. I felt anew the pressure of Larry's upcoming hearing, Prelim No. 2.

Remember, I had not pressed charges against Larry. No one asked me if I wanted to. The State pressed charges, and so the case was filed under the name of State of Idaho vs. Lawrence Weinberger.

Larry was to have a preliminary hearing before the magistrate judge. If that judge decided the case was strong enough to go to trial, he would bind it over to be tried. The trial date would be set in the district court, before the district court judge.

If the magistrate judge decided there was insufficient evidence to warrant a trial in district court, the case would be dismissed and Larry would be free to go.

Everything hinged on the findings in magistrate court. It was before this court that I'd been told to appear on December 12. The date, remember, had been set after the first prelim, when Larry's attorney was granted more time. During that first prelim, you'll recall, I'd shown up, ready to testify as required.

As the new date approached, I realized I wasn't as ready anymore. Larry was charged with aggravated assault, a felony that carried a five-year prison sentence. I knew personally of a young man who, charged with the same thing, had served every day of his five years in prison. And that man had used a toy gun. Didn't matter. It looked real, and the State was serious about this kind of crime.

I began to picture myself taking the witness stand, with Larry sitting at the defense table. My words could deliver the blows that would essentially take his life away. If found guilty, Larry would possibly emerge from prison a 63-year-old man with no wife, no job, and no home.

I had no intention of reconciling with Larry, but I didn't want to send him to prison, either. As December 12 approached, a sense of impending doom tried to penetrate my waking hours.

My pastor called me on the phone, and he again asked the question, "What are you going to say?"

What was he asking me? I knew he wasn't expecting me to lie. I told him I was feeling the strain of the upcoming prelim, and that I didn't want to testify, but the court date was set and I had no choice.

I was edgy and skittish, so my pastor chose his words carefully. "You know, Diana, Larry's attorney believes that, if you want to, you can call the prosecutor and ask him to reduce the charges."

Excuse me?

I certainly hadn't seen *that* coming! His suggestion caught me by surprise.

My time in California had been so peaceful, so restorative in many ways. Back at home, however, I'd found that fear and depression still lurked in the shadows of my mind. It didn't take much for them to wake up and tug at the edges of my attempted stability. My inner resources were focused on just hanging on, being "held by mercy," stepping carefully through one day at a time. My reserves of gumption were drastically depleted. I couldn't see myself making that phone call.

"I can't do that!" I bleated lamely. "They won't listen to me!"

Seemingly oblivious to my discomfiture, Pastor Mark spoke again and stressed his point. "Larry's attorney is sure that your opinion will carry a lot of weight, and you are the only person who can do it. They aren't going to listen to anyone else regarding this."

He seemed so sure. Moreover, he seemed sure that Larry's *attorney* was sure. It was a lot to take in. Apparently, the heavy load of Larry's pending court case was mine to bear!

I felt that, unless I made a daunting phone call, I would disappoint my pastor and Larry's imprisonment would be my fault. I was suddenly very tired. Rubbing my forehead, I sat down on the nearest chair.

Pastor Mark can be powerful in the pulpit, but with me, that afternoon, he was soft-spoken. *Firm*, mind you. But soft-spoken. "Listen, Diana, all you have to do is call and ask that the charges be reduced. If they won't do it, well, you tried. But Larry and his attorney are sure that if you'll try, they'll listen to you."

Normally not a pushy guy, Pastor Mark wasn't going to let me off the hook. I knew he was trying to point the way, and also help me overcome my fear. He knew I didn't want Larry to go to prison. Nobody wanted that. And he was right: I couldn't let my current timidity rule the day.

With that thought, my glacial decision-making process gained speed. I settled down and pictured myself making the phone call. I thought to myself, *What's the prosecutor going to do? Crawl through the phone line and bite you?*

I smiled a little. It was just a phone call.

Shortly after my call with Pastor Mark concluded, I scrolled through my contacts and tapped Prosecutor Wilson's number.

* * *

December 5, 2012. Well, I'd done it. I'd called the prosecutor, but to no avail. Mr. Wilson had told me no, he wouldn't consider reducing Larry's charges. I did argue with him, to the best of my ability. I don't like to argue, and I'm no good at it. I always lose arguments. But then does anyone ever really *win* an argument?

You may prove you are right, you may even get the other person to back down, but then there are all the residual hard feelings.

In this instance, however, when I say I argued, I mean that I tried several different ways to make myself heard, to make a case for a reduction in Larry's charges. I didn't just ask once and hang up. But Mr. Wilson was firm in his position, and he wouldn't budge.

"This is a serious case," he told me. "There's no way I can consider reducing the charges at this time."

Considering the weight of what Larry was facing, my stance toward my husband softened even more. I went further than checking my inbox more frequently. On December 5, when Larry sent me an instant message via the computer, I answered him.

That was a first. Prior to this I'd set the rules at strictly *email*, and said the email must only be about the business. As we've already seen, Larry had no intention of toeing that line, but I didn't mind anymore. Indeed, I now looked forward to his emails. An *instant message*, however, was like a conversation, and, until now, I had not been ready for that.

All the same, I wanted him to know I'd tried with the prosecutor, so that evening, when I saw his little instant message scout lurking in the corner of my computer screen, I responded. I told him I'd spoken to Mr. Wilson, but I'd been turned down. I told him that our Bible school had prayed as a class that the Lord would soften the prosecutor's heart, but so far no change.

Larry didn't seem to care about that, he was so happy to be speaking with me – if you care to call computer messaging *speaking*. However you define it, we wrote back and forth for hours. I realized I *missed* him! Was something wrong with me? What kind of woman would miss a guy who'd done what my husband had done?

I still didn't want to see him, still didn't want to talk about reconciling. I didn't believe that anyone could change as drastically as Larry claimed to be changing. Would this conversation make me sadder than ever? Larry was being nice for now, but I knew our marriage was still over. Was all this talking a mistake?

Then I received an early email from him the next morning.

> *Di,*
>
> *I know you're really busy today. I'll make it quick.*
>
> *Thank you for spending time talking yesterday and starting to communicate. I think it did both our hearts good.*
>
> *It was the first night of sleep I've had in five weeks.*
>
> *Thank you and I love you.*
>
> *Larry.*

Who could find fault with that? I'll confess I began that day with a more genuine smile on my face, too.

* * *

We spoke via computer every day after that. I remained unwilling to speak to Larry on the phone. I liked this slow pace. I was only sticking a toe in the water, after all, to see if it really was fine.

Two things I knew about Larry. One, I'd always been drawn to him, so I didn't trust my own common sense when it came to him and his persistence in regaining my heart. Two, I had fifteen years behind me of drinking, anger, volatility, and far too much negativity. Jekyll and Hyde. Good and bad. I'd always loved my Dr. Jekyll. I was no longer willing to live with my Mr. Hyde.

Larry knew that, so he didn't push me. He quietly did nice things, however, which gave me pause. Small, thoughtful gestures weren't really the old Larry's way. One day, when I'd been at a deposition all day and was exhausted, I received a text message on my (old) phone. It was from Larry, saying to check the porch. When I did, I found an entire salmon dinner, carefully laid out on a plate, everything wrapped up, with cooking instructions written in Sharpie on the foil wrappings.

Salmon, with olive oil and lemon and tomatoes, sealed up in foil with the words, "25 minutes at 425." I sautéed the mushrooms he'd packed with chopped garlic and a dab of butter, and warmed up the veggies. It was wonderful!

He hadn't been to the house. Not allowed. Someone else had delivered it to the door for him. I was very touched.

* * *

December 10, 2012. Two days before Prelim 2. This one was going forward, and I was to appear and testify. Today was Monday, and I had no jobs lined up. I was fretting around the house when I heard Larry's IM (instant message) chime on the computer. He only meant to say good morning, but I had something gnawing at my mind.

"I'm nervous about court on Wednesday," I wrote. "I don't want to testify against you. I don't know what else they're going to use, but I don't want them to use me to send you to prison."

"Baby, baby!" Larry wrote back. "You won't have to go near the witness stand!"

I won't?

"I have it all worked out with my attorney," he continued. "I told him no matter what happens, you are not to be put on the witness stand. I won't put you in that position. I'm just going to plead guilty. I've wanted to talk to you. You haven't been ready, but it's all set. My attorney has a call in to the prosecutor to ask if I can plead guilty and skip the preliminary hearing. If that works, you won't even have to go to court! If they do insist on the hearing, at least you won't be testifying. Please stop worrying. I don't want you to worry. This is my problem, and I'm taking care of it."

I sat very still, quietly listening to a clock tick as my world turned around on itself.

Larry was willing to risk a prison sentence, rather than let me endure the court proceedings? Larry wanted to protect *me*, the woman whose confession had tipped him into full-scale madness in the first place?

He'd been clear, but, as my mind tilted, I wanted to verify. Had I read his message correctly?

"You mean you already have it worked out, you've told your attorney to keep me off the witness stand? You're going to plead guilty instead of having a trial?"

"Yes!" he returned, clearly happy that I was catching on. "So you can enjoy your day! Nothing to be afraid of or nervous about. I know you've been having a hard time, but you can relax! I'm the one who brought this on. I'm the one who has to deal with it."

This was unexpected.

How's *that* for a whopping understatement?

I didn't know I could feel so warm and fuzzy inside. I didn't recognize this guy, but I liked him. Up until the past few days, I'd been ignoring him, rebuking him, even, for trying to push the email limits. I'd insisted, while I was in California, that he go to the house with a police officer to get his clothes. I then told him he needed to find somewhere else to live and start his life over. I'd made it abundantly plain to him that our marriage was finished, that I wouldn't consider meeting with him and our pastor.

And while I was shutting him out and telling him to move on, he was making plans to shield me. I hadn't yet considered the cost to myself personally if I testified and saw him hauled off in chains. *He had!* And he didn't want that for me. Not even if it meant prison for himself.

It was a lot to take in. But even as I relished the chivalry of his plan, I balked.

"Wait," I said. "You'll march into court and plead guilty to a felony!"

"Don't worry about it, sweetie. You don't have to think about it at all. I'm taking care of it."

"But I don't think you should plead guilty. We need to think this through."

"Believe me," he wrote. "I've been through it all, over and over."

We've all seen *Law & Order*. Most first-time offenders don't plead guilty to the maximum that a prosecutor has charged them with. Larry's plan seemed out of balance. There had to be another way. Also, what if they still wanted to go through all the motions, just to seal up their case? I said as much to Larry.

"What if they insist on the hearing? On the other hand, I know your attorney thinks they should accept a plea agreement. Don't you want to try harder for that?"

Our conversation went on for a while. After the initial impact of Larry's selfless decision, I began to fret. I knew I couldn't let him throw his life away. He heard it in my tone, even though our words were written, and not audible.

"Hey, it sounds like you're starting to worry again. I think if you met with me, you'd see that I'm fine with this. I'm totally calm, peaceful, and happy. You really don't need to worry."

"We can't meet. There's a no-contact order."

"We can meet if Pastor Mark is with us. It'll be okay."

"I don't know. I don't know what to do."

"Meet me, baby."

That stirred my heart, pure and simple.

I told him I would see him if Pastor Mark would come, too. He immediately set it up for three o'clock that same afternoon.

CHAPTER **TWO**

I tried to stay busy in the hours before our meeting, but my stomach was filled with butterflies. I was curious to see Larry, to find out if he really was "calm, peaceful and happy". But the last time I'd seen him had been Glock Night. Hence the butterflies.

I cleaned up the house and dressed in a simple black sweater and jeans. As three o'clock approached, I was pacing around the downstairs living area. What were we doing? I didn't want to get Larry's hopes up.

And then they arrived. At least, I *thought* it was they. Pastor Mark I recognized. But who was the other guy? As they came through the door I stood absolutely still, flabbergasted. Was that *Larry*? He'd lost at least thirty pounds. He had on a light yellow sweater, and his face glowed softly as he stood before me. Pastor Mark smiled hugely, but he was also watchful.

We sat at our dining room table, much like we had on the terrible day of my confession. But what a difference! Larry seemed so relaxed, so ready to laugh! I didn't feel an ounce of pressure from him, even when he shyly asked, "Can I touch you?" I nodded slightly, and he reached out and touched my arm where it rested on the table. He stroked my hand with his fingertips, and said, "You are so beautiful."

I didn't know where to look, especially with Pastor Mark sitting right there, but it certainly wasn't a *bad* thing to say. I couldn't help smiling.

Larry told me some of the things he'd been doing, including counseling with a pastor and his wife. They pastored a different church, and were skilled in the counseling arena. He'd been going to AA, reading his Bible. He'd also been reading a book called, *I Really Want to Change, So Help Me God,* by James MacDonald.

He told me he'd confronted, with that pastor's help, issues from his childhood that had fomented the simmering, just-beneath-the-surface rage in him. In confronting those painful things and then bringing them to God, the Lord had broken their hold on Larry. His anger was gone.

I noticed that his brow, always furrowed before, was now smooth. There was new light emanating from his eyes.

When he finished explaining some of the things he'd been learning and studying, Larry grew thoughtful for a moment. He stopped tracing my hand with his finger. Instead, he gently took my one hand in both of his and looked into my eyes.

"Baby, I am so, so sorry for all I put you through. I know how I scared you with the gun that night. And I'm sorry, too, for all the years of verbal abuse and yelling at you. I understand now that verbal abuse is the same as physical abuse. You never should have had to live with any of that.

"The AA meetings are in addition to my other counseling. I haven't had a drink since that night. I haven't even *wanted* to have a drink.

"I'm asking you for another chance. I want you to take all the time you need to get to know me as this new man. I've come to recognize the courage it took for you to confess to me the way you did, and I want to spend the rest of my life treating you the way you deserve to be treated."

That sounded nice, but I was still skittish.

He went on, "I can promise you, as far as what you did, I will *never* bring it up again. All of that is behind us. I've done this with my counselor, but I want to say it to you, too. I believe I share some of the responsibility for what happened with you ten years ago. I never should have insisted on those motorcycle trips, where you were the only woman in the group. Everyone was drinking, things got out of hand sometimes, and I can see how it happened. I hope you'll forgive me for only thinking about what I wanted to do, and not about what you would have liked to do for a vacation. If you'll give me the chance, I'd still like to take you to Hawaii."

My circuits were now thoroughly overloaded. I was torn! I appreciated his recognition that those trips were just too *male*, too raucous for me, and I never should have been there. On the other hand, I thought he was going a bit far, taking responsibility for my sin. I was pretty sure that one was still on me.

The bottom line, though, was that I'd never heard Larry speak like this to me. This was not a man trying to convince me that he was sorry, that he'd be good in the future, and to please let him come home. This was a man transformed. He'd hit the bottom, and had at last humbled himself before God and cried out for help. It had taken years and an absolute catastrophe to get him there, but now the change was evident. God had done a work in him that no human could accomplish on his own.

I was utterly blown away.

* * *

Our meeting led to a number of different things. I agreed to go on a date with Larry at some point when it would be legal to do so. Right now the no-contact order was still in place. (Technically, I suppose, we may have crossed the line by even having our meeting.) I also realized that this man shouldn't go to prison for five years. I didn't know how we were going to avoid that, but I didn't think he should waltz into the courtroom and plead guilty.

The next morning I said to him, once again via computer, that he should go over other options with his attorney, but that skipping a trial and entering a guilty plea should come off the table. A little while later, and with my permission, he called me (still on my old phone.) His attorney was concerned the prosecutor might try to force me to testify at the prelim, now just twenty-four hours away. He explained that, if I really didn't want him simply to plead guilty, I should be represented by my own attorney. He named two attorneys I might contact. I already knew and liked one of them, so I called and made an appointment for later that afternoon.

CHAPTER **THREE**

On the morning of December 12, 2012, hearing day, I swung by DJ's place at seven in the morning and picked her up. We were heading to breakfast. Our breakfast place of choice was sixty-five miles away in Twin Falls. It would have been impossible to make that trip, enjoy a leisurely breakfast, and still get back to court by nine. But then, I had no intention of going to court.

I'd had a brief meeting with my new defense attorney, Greg Coburn, the day before. He didn't tell me to skip court. Ethically, he could advise no such thing. But one unintentional word slipped out as he was pondering my situation and making a plan: *If.*

He was in the middle of explaining to me that, since I was unwilling to testify, in his opinion the case should be dismissed. As a former prosecutor himself, he assured me that, were he still in that role, he wouldn't pursue the case if I wasn't on board.

He was concerned that the current prosecutor's office thought differently, so he said to me, "Boy, if you go to the hearing tomorrow, you'll be on their playground. No telling what might happen. I can't imagine they'll go so far as to hold you in contempt or put you in jail, but if they do that, I'll represent you for free. I'll call the press, make sure everyone knows what's going on. Legally, they can put you in jail for contempt. But people would see that as making you a victim twice, and that's unpopular."

If you go. Had he meant for me to hear that?

But first things first.

"*Jail?*" I asked, horrified. "They might put me in *jail?*" I'd only decided with certainty *yesterday* that I didn't want to testify against Larry. How had I already traveled to the point of *jail?*

"But," I stammered, "I thought no one could force a woman to testify against her husband. What about spousal privilege?"

"It's different in this case, Diana." He went on to explain to me that spousal privilege does not apply when the spouse herself or any minor child is the victim of the crime. It's an exception to the rule.

"However," he continued, "if they believe you to be the victim of a crime, it would be controversial to put you in jail, and thereby victimize you again."

If you go...

"What if I were to be out of town tomorrow?" I blurted a little desperately.

"The judge would probably dismiss the case." he replied evenly. "The prosecutor could refile, but that's unlikely because they'll know they won't have your cooperation."

Standing up, he said that he would be at the courthouse tomorrow at nine o'clock, and I knew our meeting was concluded.

I smiled tentatively as I said goodbye.

I knew I wouldn't be seeing him in court tomorrow.

* * *

I pushed back my breakfast plate and sipped some coffee as I glanced at my phone again.

"It'll be fine, Diana," DJ said for the hundredth time. Nine o'clock had come and gone. I'd received a call from the prosecutor, which I let go to voicemail. They were frustrated with me for not showing up, and left a message for me stating, "You're putting us in a bad position, Diana."

I was sorry about that, but I knew myself to be in a bad position, too. I'd received a call from the prosecutor's assistant, Vicki, the afternoon before, after my meeting with my attorney. Vicki had told me that I must be at their office thirty minutes before the hearing. I tried to talk to Vicki, saying, "Wait, I need to speak to you. I've asked Mr. Wilson to meet and talk about a plea, and he said no. But I don't want to testify."

Unfortunately, Vicki ignored me and proceeded curtly, "Just be here thirty minutes early. We'll be expecting you."

Thus, here I sat with DJ, having chosen breakfast out of town rather than an appearance in a courtroom where no one was listening to me.

I don't condone breaking the law, and in fact I was not breaking the law by failing to appear for court. If I'd been properly served a subpoena, I'd have gone. I wouldn't have had a choice. I'd been there when the judge set December 12 as the hearing date, but no one had served me with a subpoena. The truth of this was borne out when my attorney, Greg, called me at nine-fifteen as I sat with DJ in Twin Falls.

He got right to the point. "So, the judge dismissed the case. Without you they didn't have enough evidence against Larry, so all the charges were dropped. The prosecutor was frustrated, but admitted that he'd emailed you a subpoena, which was not proper service. The judge said that wouldn't count against you, and dismissed everything. He didn't even reinstate the no-contact order. You guys are free to resume your lives in whatever way you wish."

It was what I'd hoped for. My desperate little trip this morning to Twin Falls had paid off.

"The prosecutor did say," Greg continued, "that he will refile. I don't know if he really will, since he knows he can't count on you as a witness, but that was what he said today."

My happy balloon deflated some. I didn't want a repeat of the stress of today's jaunt. However, I would have to think about that only if they refiled. Not today.

The next call I received was from my very happy husband. "The judge dismissed the case! And he didn't reinstate the no-contact order. Will you go to dinner with me?"

Therefore, if anyone is in Christ,

he is a new creation; old things have passed away;

behold, all things have become new.

(II Corinthians 5:17 NKJV)

CHAPTER **FOUR**

It didn't take long for me to see for myself that all of Larry's changes were real. I agreed to go on a date with him, and then another. At first I nearly held my breath, waiting for the other shoe to drop. I wondered when Old Larry, as I termed it, would reappear. But I never got a glimpse of him. Not one. New Larry was easygoing and relaxed. He was helpful, generous, kind to everyone. It wasn't an act. Anger, bitterness, resentment, self-pity, *GONE!* Furrowed brow? Wiped smooth.

His faith in God was genuine and childlike. He'd been learning how to pray, and, whereas before he'd never prayed aloud with me, now he took my hand and burst into prayer over meals, over his legal situation, over our future when I would fret about it. He ended every prayer, big or small, with, "In Jesus' Name, Amen."

With him at all times was a book called *God's Word for Every Circumstance*, by Casey and Wendy Treat. This small but power-packed volume helped him find quick biblical insight whenever he needed it. When I admired it, he bought me one for Christmas!

I initially told him I wanted to wait for three months before I made any decision about his moving back home. He agreed to that, but it backfired when I found myself wanting more of his company, and couldn't always have it.

He was living with friends – friends who had rescued him from his isolation out at Magic. They had insisted he move in with them and not stay alone, so far out of town. At first he'd wept day in and day out, and they were everything anyone could hope for in real friends. They were kind, supportive, and welcoming. In the six weeks he'd been living there, though, they had come to depend on him as part of their family. They'd learned to count on him for lots of little odd jobs around the house.

He fixed things, moved things, ran errands. Old Larry never ran errands. Other people ran errands for *him*.

I marveled when he explained to me that, though he was very sorry, he couldn't see me one weekend because he was house-sitting. He needed to be home with the dogs. He'd committed to this before he and I had begun dating again.

It didn't take me long to know I wanted to try again with our marriage. I wasn't letting go of this guy just when he was getting good! I wanted him to come home, and I didn't want to wait three months.

His voice was joyful when he called the friends with whom he'd been living. "Guess what?" he cried, "three months just turned into two weeks! I'm going home!"

He planned to move back in over Christmas, when I would be in California again with the kids. We'd made plans while I'd been there for Joshua's birth. My son-in-law had purchased my ticket with his own saved-up miles. I told Larry I still planned to go, and again saw his good nature when he agreed that, of course, I must go. He'd use the time to move in and take care of some things around our own home.

We were in a good season at last, the first truly good season of our marriage. We talked all the time. Larry read aloud to me from some of his books. We never turned on the TV. Many of our dates were at home, where Larry, quite the chef himself, would create delicious meals. I always sat near the kitchen and chatted with him. In our euphoria, we went to Boise together and traded my old car for a new one.

I savored every moment of this newfound relationship. As planned, until I went to California shortly before Christmas, he went home to his other place every night. It was an unbelievably sweet, precious time.

* * *

It was while I was driving to the airport for my Christmas trip that an invisible arrow zoomed through the atmosphere, found my happy balloon, and popped it. Larry had called, unnerved. As promised, the prosecutor had refiled. Prelim No. 3 was set for January 23, 2013.

My stomach knotted. They knew I was unwilling to testify. They refiled anyway. To me, that could only mean one thing: They were going to try to force my testimony. As I drove, I prayed. I tried to cast my care upon the Lord, as the Bible tells us to do in 1 Peter 5:7. I wasn't very successful.

A dark and ominous mountain had just landed squarely in front of me, a seemingly insurmountable obstacle blocking the roadway of my life. I had faith that God would be with me in any circumstance. I also knew that my flesh was going to have to walk this out and that it was going to be difficult, perhaps the most difficult thing I'd ever faced.

Greg's words haunted my mind. *"I can't imagine they'll go so far as to hold you in contempt or put you in jail, but if they do that, I'll represent you for free."*

Had it come to that, after all? Contempt of court? Jail? Could they be planning anything less, knowing what they knew?

Testify or be in contempt. Prison for Larry or jail for me. I pulled the car off the road as my stomach heaved.

They track us down in each step we take;

now they surround us;

they set their eyes to cast us to the ground,

like a lion greedy and eager to tear his prey,

and as a young lion lurking in hidden places.

(Psalm 17:11-12 AMP)

CHAPTER **FIVE**

I was on a porch. I didn't recognize it. I knew I was here for my own protection, but that protection had run out. A police officer had parked in the yard and was approaching the steps that led to my position near the railing. He asked me if I was Diana, and my dry lips could find no denial. He said, "I've come to place you under arrest, and you'll be going to jail for a very long time. No telling when you'll get out." He reached out and locked handcuffs to my wrists, now bound in front of me.

My heart was pounding. I couldn't breathe. My chest, back, and left arm were gripped in intense pain. Where was everyone? Why was I all alone on this porch, with this officer arresting me, telling me I'd be in jail a long time? How could I make him understand I was ill, something was terribly wrong. He couldn't take me to jail when I couldn't breathe...

The scene blurred and I swam up from deep within my nightmare. I left the porch, the officer and the handcuffs behind, but brought the pain along with me as I came awake. I was in my darkened room, all alone in my remote cabin. My body was drenched in sweat, and I was fighting for breath. Not the hyperventilation I'd suffered after the gun incident. This was different. There wasn't enough air, somehow. At least, there wasn't enough room in my body to receive any.

Now awake, I told myself it had only been a dream. I tried again to draw a deep, steadying breath, but could not. I managed a gasp and a cough. What was wrong with me? Even though I was lying down, I felt dizzy. My heart was pounding. My left arm felt like it was being wrung out like a wet dishtowel. The pressure was unbelievable. And my chest pinned me to the bed, an invisible boulder crushing my breastbone right through to my back.

Calm down, Diana. I'd heard stories of panic attacks, and thought this could be one. Anything else I wouldn't even consider. *Settle yourself, and this will pass.*

But it didn't pass. Fresh, cold sweat broke out upon me again. Turning my head to see the clock made me nauseous. Five o'clock a.m. I knew I needed to stay put and feel better. I didn't know anyone I could call for help if I needed it. I was too far out of town, and I would have been too embarrassed to call anyone anyway. I didn't want to alarm Larry, so I decided to put off calling him as well. I would call him once the vice-like pain had eased.

Time passed slowly as I remained still, willing myself to feel better. At one point I tried to sit up, thinking a change of position would help. I immediately felt so queasy that I feared a bathroom run would be necessary, and so dizzy that a fall along the way seemed a certainty. It was no good. I had to stay flat for now.

After an hour or two my breathing came more easily and the pain was less intense. I flexed the fingers on my left hand. The pressure down my left arm, though not completely gone, was less severe.

I was able to reach for my cell phone on the night stand. I opened it up to recent calls, found Larry's name, and tapped it. He answered within a couple rings with a cheerful, "Well, good morning, baby! You're up early. Everything okay?" I managed a whimpered, "I don't know," before feeling my eyes well up, hot tears already forming.

People respond to different things differently, have you noticed? Some people are terrible in a crisis, and then respond all hands on deck when the emergency is over. Not me. I'm okay during the crisis, like when my daughter broke her front teeth, or my other daughter broke her arm. I don't go to pieces. But *later*, when the moment is over and things have calmed down, I'm at my most vulnerable. And if someone says something kind? Done deal. I'll cry every time. Totally annoying, especially when I want to put up a strong front, but there it is. I'm an after-crisis crier.

So it should come as no surprise that, now, hearing my husband's voice on the phone, asking if I was okay, sounding strong and sure and vibrant and kind, I started blubbering. It had been a difficult few months, and I was tired; I was in the middle of nowhere in the middle of winter; my dog was dead, my cat was gone. I'd had the most horrifying dream. And now I felt dreadful physically.

I tried to relate to Larry the details of my dream. I wanted him to understand why I was so frightened. "Larry, he said he was going to arrest me and put me in jail for a long time; he didn't even *know* how long!"

"It's okay, honey. No one is going to arrest you. I understand you had a bad dream, but it's just because you've got this stuff on your mind and it's making you nervous. They can't arrest you. No one is going to put you in jail. Try to calm down and feel better. Take it easy."

Take it easy. This is Larry's standard line when I'm anxious. It's never condescending, and sometimes it even works. At times those three words have helped me settle down and regain my perspective.

This time was an exception. I was, in fact, living at my cabin because I didn't want to be served a subpoena – a subpoena that would require my presence in court to testify against my husband. I was pretty sure my location wasn't a huge secret. If he felt so inclined, the Sheriff could even now drive out and hand me my summons. The fact that no one had come out, yet, had lulled me into a nice sense of security, right up until my nightmare.

Now my cozy hideaway seemed a lonely outpost, far from help or comfort of any kind. It was January and bitterly cold outside. Maybe that's why no one had ventured out here with my order to appear in court.

With his all-encompassing, "Take it easy," Larry had to hang up and get back to work. He told me to stay in bed, relax until I felt better, and he was sure everything was fine.

CHAPTER **SIX**

It's funny how things are magnified when you are alone and already edgy.

I eventually felt well enough to get out of bed and clean myself up. I'd have to wash my hair later, though. No energy for that yet. I put on some sweats and went out to the kitchen in search of coffee. I'd made it the previous evening and set the timer for 6:00 a.m. Even though it was nearly eight, it was still on and nice and hot. Favorite mug. Creamer. No one knocking on the door.

A look outside showed everything to be quiet and normal, a winter wonderland. Smooth white snow surrounded me in every direction, setting off my mid-sized maroon SUV in pretty relief. The small trailer and side trailer neighboring our cabin were silent and empty, the snow around them undisturbed. No one, except for myself, had been in the vicinity for a very long time.

The setting was picturesque, the coffee was wonderful, and my night fright was fading quickly.

Taking a look around the kitchen, I spotted my old cell phone lying there. I still carried it with me, and occasionally checked messages. There was still a chance that someone would try to reach me at that number. I'd have to turn it off soon, but it had two more months on its contract. It made sense to let it expire naturally.

I hadn't checked the voicemail on that phone for a few days, so I picked it up and connected to my voice mailbox…then nearly dropped the phone. The first message was from a Sheriff's deputy, informing me that they were looking for me to serve me my subpoena. He said that if I didn't return his call and receive my summons, I would be arrested!

The room swam. My nightmare replayed in my mind. I was going to be arrested after all! And why? Because they hadn't served me a subpoena?

No, wait. No one could do that. I stared at the phone in my hand. Other messages were playing, but I couldn't hear them. I tried to reason it through. If someone wanted to drive out here to arrest me, why couldn't they drive out here and hand me the paper? Of course they could. And would. *Right*?

I considered driving into town, finding a deputy, and asking for my subpoena. I wanted to stop the madness. But what if they already had orders to cuff me on sight?

My eyes traveled to the large picture windows that dominate the southeastern side of our cabin, my gaze falling to my shiny red car. Oh, that would never do.

I didn't know what my next step should be, but I wasn't going to sit in here with my Nissan in the driveway, broadcasting my presence. Had a deputy pulled up to my gate and approached my front door, considering my recent nightmare and phone message, I probably would have passed out cold.

I needed to move the car.

I pulled on my boots, shrugging into my coat while grabbing the key. I would park the car a few streets over on a friend's property.

When I got there I found a nice secluded spot next to their shed and backed the car in. I then walked back to my cabin and used a snow shovel to smooth out my footprints. My efforts yielded a walk that looked shoveled, but not freshly trodden upon.

The region was in the middle of a cold snap, and the temperature in the night had been below zero. When I finished smoothing away my tire tracks and footprints I happily went inside, closing and locking the door. I removed my gloves and rubbed my hands together, wondering if I should hold them under some warm water. Just then I heard a crunching of snow that signaled a vehicle coming down the road – a road that passed in front of our cabin. I froze as I made out a white SUV a few hundred feet away, coming my direction.

Our Sheriff's vehicles are white SUVs. I couldn't see the side panels to determine if this was Sheriff or citizen. I didn't move a muscle. I figured that, even from his distance, any sudden movements that I made would be visible to the driver through our wall of windows.

The SUV pulled closer but didn't slow. It bore no insignia, no markings of any kind, and it carried on right past the cabin.

CHAPTER **SEVEN**

I sprang into action. I closed all the blinds and reassured myself that the porch light was off. From without, the cabin would look uninhabited. From within, it felt like a dark cave. Depressing. Then it struck me that, though I didn't want to go *home*, I didn't have to stay *here* all day either, worrying about every passing car.

I decided to go to Twin Falls, our nearest city, about forty miles south of Magic Reservoir. I needed to forget my problems for a while, and an outing seemed just the thing.

I was still in my sweats, having pulled on boots but not street clothes in my rush to move the car. My hair was sweat-soaked after my nightmare and all that had followed. I showered, enjoying the warm water and sudsy shampoo. Finished, I blew my hair dry and got ready for the day, bundling up against the bitter cold.

Walking to where I'd stashed my Murano would put me out in the open. Risky, but there was no help for it. I peeped out through the blinds, my ears straining for the sound of a vehicle. I saw no one, and heard only snow-covered silence. I locked the door carefully behind me and set off. I'd smoothed the path to where fresh footprints wouldn't show, which of course made it slippery. Easy does it.

Our driveway at the cabin is paved, and we have a four-foot high chain-link fence around the entire perimeter of our property. I closed the gate behind, made sure it was also locked, and was able to retrieve my car without incident.

I exulted in my freedom as I drove away. I had nothing in particular to do in town, but I was heading in the opposite direction from anyone trying to serve me a subpoena. It felt wonderful!

That day out was just what the doctor ordered. I enjoyed the drive, blasting Christian music in my car and singing along at the top of my lungs. In Twin Falls, I moseyed around Walmart, picked up some vitamin-enriched water at Costco, washed the car, and even grabbed some (tummy-friendly) fast food. I'd lost 15 pounds due to all of the recent trauma, and it was lovely to feel hungry!

The trip home was just as fun. I enjoyed my music all the way to the West Magic Road turn-off. My inner Nervous Nellie piped up and reminded me that this road was small. Anyone coming from the other direction – like an officer who had just been to my front door? – would spot me in an instant. But that seemed so unlikely just then that I shushed Nellie and enjoyed the rest of my drive.

I told myself that if anyone were to come way out here, it would probably be during the day. As it was now nearly evening, I thought I could park my car, if not in the driveway, then at least closer than my friend's shed. Before I parked, however, I wanted to unload the case of water I'd bought at Costco, so I pulled up to our gate.

And saw the disturbed snow.

Someone had been here.

The berm edging up to our driveway had been driven through by what could only have been a large SUV. There were fresh tire tracks near the fence where a vehicle had clearly driven in, stopped, and reversed back out again.

A single set of footprints left the drive and led off into the snow. I placed my foot next to one of them. It was considerably larger than my own foot. Whoever had been here was a man wearing substantial boots, probably a Sheriff's deputy. The footprints circled all the way around the small trailer that sits just outside of our fence. I followed the footprints and realized this had been a reconnaissance mission. Whoever had been here had checked to see if the fence enclosed our entire property. Walking around this trailer would have given him a complete view of our yard. Having made one full circle, the prints led right back to where the vehicle's door must have been.

The gate remained locked. A glance up to the front door revealed no notices, no messages left by anyone seeking an audience with me. I was alone, but someone had been here and had looked carefully to see if they could get to the front door without hopping the fence. Spooky.

I again wondered if I should just go home, accept my summons, go to court and get this over with. My choices seemed grim. I could:

A) Go home and possibly get arrested for...what? Being hard to find? Or,

B) Stay here, hiding like some kind of outlaw.

Don't get me wrong. I had no axe to grind with law enforcement. In fact, I felt bad for the guy who had had to trek all the way out here. These officers weren't my enemy. My problems had just been compounded from bad to worse, ever since my confession to Larry.

I had tried to talk to the prosecutor's office, but they'd been unwilling to listen. I'd told them I wouldn't testify, that Larry was a changed man, that he'd never been in trouble before. I had asked for a plea agreement. But they had refiled anyway, and now they were leaving me threatening voicemails.

They felt that Larry should be tried for a felony, and they were playing hardball. I could see no upside to my stepping into their court, if you'll pardon the double entendre.

Going home, therefore, was out of the question. The trouble was, especially after my nightmare, my little hideaway no longer felt safe, either.

I wouldn't have to hang on much longer, in any case. Tomorrow Larry was due in court.

CHAPTER **EIGHT**

The next morning dawned bright, sunny, and cold. January 23, 2013. Prelim No. 3.

I planned to stay out at Magic, with my car stashed out of sight and the blinds drawn tight. By nine-thirty it would be over. They'd been unable to subpoena me, and the case would be dismissed. Again. Surely, that would be the end of it.

It was therefore Larry's difficult task to call me shortly after nine-thirty. He told me that the judge had given the prosecutor five more days to find me. This was Wednesday, and they had until Monday morning to serve me my papers or die trying.

This was an unexpected blow. I looked around quickly. I couldn't stay here! Even now a Sheriff's deputy could be zooming along the highway to search for me one more time. I didn't want to be found out here alone. The threat hanging over my head, after all, was not that I would merely be handed a summons. The current threat was that I would be hauled off in handcuffs! I quickly put the cabin in order so I could leave.

I packed my things lickety-split and retrieved my car. As a last minute and very desperate measure, I grabbed a wig from the floor of my closet. Larry and I had dressed as pirate and wench one year for a Halloween party, and I owned a wavy, waist-length, red-haired wig. I'd only worn it that one time.

My car was new, its license plates not yet installed. I hoped that a deputy on the alert for a blonde in a blue car wouldn't notice a redhead driving a red car. Sunglasses were my finishing touch. I didn't recognize myself.

Even as I dashed out the door I could hear that still, small voice within my heart, whispering to me the words of II Timothy 1:7:

> *For God has not given us a spirit of fear,*
> *but of power and of love and of a sound mind.*
> *(NKJV)*

Well, yes, I acknowledged. *But I would rather work on my fearlessness in Boise.*

It didn't occur to me, as I prepared to venture forth in disguise, that perhaps the Lord was actually emphasizing the *"sound mind"* part of that verse.

I smoothed my red tresses and locked up the cabin. I backed the car out, pulled the gate shut behind me and locked that too. I was on my way.

* * *

It's ten miles to the highway from our cabin. The entire ten miles is comprised of a lonely, winding road just wide enough for two vehicles to pass. It's not enough of a road for the County to decorate with a center stripe. So few vehicles travel that road that, when you do pass someone, it's customary to give a wave to your fellow traveler. Even UPS drivers gear down into friendly mode on this remote stretch, and they wave a greeting as they wend their way to and from the Magic bar. Most deliveries are left there, rather than asking the driver to bump along dirt roads in search of obscure residences.

My chances of escaping notice on West Magic Road were slim to none. I resolved that, should I see a Sheriff's SUV approaching in the oncoming lane, I would smile and wave as if I hadn't a care in the world. I considered what I would do if I *were* pulled over. Would I maintain my disguise and try to breeze through the stop, hoping he wouldn't ask for my license? Or would I sheepishly slide the long red tresses from my head, stash them behind the seat before he got to my window, and admit that the jig was up?

Fortunately, I didn't need to make that decision, as I did not see an official vehicle of any kind on my way out to the highway. Once I reached the mouth of West Magic Road, I had only two choices: left or right onto the highway. Left meant home and all the trouble that came with that. Right meant bigger cities and anonymity. I straightened my sunglasses, adjusted my wig, and turned right.

My head started itching under that cheap wig before I'd gotten ten miles down the highway. I didn't dare stop to deal with it. I scratched my head the best I could and drove on to the small town of Shoshone. I was still fairly close to home, but this was a different county. Even so, I wouldn't linger. I left Shoshone, drove a few miles more, then pulled off the road. I tore that awful wig from my head, vastly relieved.

While I was stopped, I used my cell phone to reserve a hotel room in Boise. Fortunately, it was the middle of the week in the middle of winter. A weekend booking in the summer would have been impossible at such short notice. Indeed, they were slow enough now that they allowed an early, 1:00 p.m. check-in.

I'd also called my brother, while on the road, and arranged to visit him the following day. I had wondered what I'd do with myself in Boise for five days, but seeing my little brother, who lived about an hour out of Idaho's biggest city, would be a great start.

At around 5:00 p.m. I tucked a book under my arm and made my way to a favorite restaurant. I loved their salmon Caesar salads. I sat in the lounge area, propped up my book, ordered my salad, and tried to forget I was alone in a restaurant. Eating alone in a restaurant was something I'd never done before. I felt like a fish out of water.

Amy had insisted, when she knew I would be on my own, "Mom, don't eat fast food. Go someplace you like, take a book, and give yourself a little treat. You need it." She was right. The servers were attentive, the food was wonderful, and my book protected me from unwanted casual conversation.

After dinner I walked across the street to choose from 21 movies playing at the Spectrum. I settled on *Argo*, about a covert operation in Iran, but I was so tired that I fell asleep right there in the theater. I missed a huge chunk right in the middle of the movie.

* * *

I did try to go and see my brother the next day, although the weather was against us. Kirk called to tell me that the roads near his house were icy, and that he and his pickup had slid right past his driveway earlier in the morning. Hoping it would thaw out some in a couple of hours, I got ready, had an extra cup of coffee to kill time, and headed out.

I was traveling on I-84, west out of Boise, when the medium-sized rain suddenly became a freezing onslaught. The sky pummeled my car with massive drops of rain, ice, and a slushy, snowy mix. To make matters worse, I was behind a big rig and his tires were throwing up a deluge against my windshield. I couldn't see a thing.

My wipers went into supersonic hyper-speed without my touching any controls. What was happening? My new car was taking over! What else might it do? I had to get off this freeway before one of my wiper blades cut loose and flew right off the car!

I slowed enough so the big rig would speed away from me, but not so much that I would create a hazard for other drivers. As soon as I was able, I merged right three lanes and found the nearest off-ramp. I came to a stop at the first light, working my fingers from their death grip on the steering wheel. That had been *gnarly!*

I pulled into a gas station so I would be well off the road, and called Kirk. I let him know that there was just no way it was safe to visit him today, and that I was going to try to make it back to Boise alive, then stay put.

This journey was clearly meant to be traveled alone.

I made it back to Boise and stopped at Barnes & Noble. I bought a cup of coffee and set off to Bible browse. I found an ESV (English Standard Version) Large Print, simulated leather Bible that I liked, so I purchased it and felt slightly better. I would take it back to my room and explore my way through it. I needed the strength and comfort I could find only in God's Word, and the novelty of a brand new Bible would help chase away my troubles for a little while.

There was no escaping the fact, however, that it was by now only Thursday, and I was stuck in town until Monday morning.

My routine never varied over the ensuing few days. Late afternoon would find me in the lounge of my favorite restaurant, book in hand and salmon Caesar before me. After that I went to the movies, and fell asleep during every single one of them. *Never* before had I fallen asleep in a movie theater. Stress was taking its toll.

CHAPTER **NINE**

So passed my time on the lam. I was hiding from the law, though I wasn't wanted for a crime. I was sought only to testify, and that, I now knew, I could never do.

Monday morning arrived at last, and I saw no reason to stay in Boise any longer. The hearing was set for 10:00 a.m. My drive would be two and a half hours, so I knew I could get moving by nine.

I hoped this would all be over soon. The prosecutor would surely let this go, knowing by now that I wouldn't help his case. Larry and I wanted to continue rebuilding our lives. We wanted peace.

I was driving on the I-84 again, this time headed home, and in better weather, when my phone rang. It was Larry. It was only 9:30, so I figured he was calling to say hello, and maybe let me know he was headed to court.

No. Nothing that pleasant.

"Baby," he began, "I'm so sorry. I need to ask you to call Greg."

Why would I need to call my attorney?

"Maybe there's something he can do," Larry continued. "I just got a call from Tommy, and he said there are police surrounding our house. He's upset, worried about the effect this will have on our neighbors. He wants us to take care of it."

Un. Be. Lievable.

Tommy was our community's property and association manager. He must be tearing his hair out at the sight of armed police surrounding one of his units. What was their plan? Were their orders to drag me to court, kicking and screaming? No, they wouldn't do that. But then a vision of my handcuffed-on-the-porch dream rose in my mind and I thought, *hmmm*. Maybe they *would* cuff me and force me to court. Or maybe somebody was just trying to scare me into opening the door and coming quietly. It didn't matter, though, because I was 150 miles away.

Promising Larry I'd do what I could, I hung up and asked my car to call my attorney. Gotta love modern technology.

I was relieved that Greg was in his office and accepted my call. I relayed the situation to him, and he assured me he would check into it. He also wanted to make it to court in time to see what transpired there.

He told me later that he went to our complex, but by the time he arrived the police were already gone. He then went to court, and, since the prosecution still hadn't found me, the judge dismissed the case. Larry was free to go.

The prosecutor, however, was livid. I learned that he approached Greg, eyes blazing, and said, "I'm going to have her arrested!" Greg just smiled and said, "You can ask." Greg didn't think the judge would give them permission to arrest me just because they couldn't serve me a subpoena. Not that it would come to that point again, in any event.

Greg informed the enraged prosecutor that he would be representing me going forward. He knew that this information would take any thought of my arrest off the table. Mr. Wilson would understand that, if I were represented by counsel, he could serve my subpoena on Greg.

When Greg told me of this conversation later, he also said, "No more running, Diana. If they refile, we're just going to have to face this."

And Mr. Wilson did exactly that, within a week. The speed of this refile took my breath away. I learned of it from my own attorney. Greg called me himself to tell me that Prelim No. 4 was set for March 13, 2013. He'd been served my subpoena, and I would have no choice but to go.

Aside from legal troubles, Larry and I were doing great, so my position was firmer than ever. I would not testify. Indeed, when I tried to imagine myself on the witness stand, my imaginary tongue would stick to the roof of my imaginary mouth. I knew I wouldn't be able to get the words out, regardless of threats. And the prosecutor remained unwilling, in spite of everything, to discuss a plea.

CHAPTER **TEN**

March 12, 2013.

Our saga had begun four and a half months earlier, with my confession. Then came Hell Month, followed by Glock Night. Temporary separation then led to redemption and restoration, which in turn led to hope and peace. But our new hope and peace were under the threat of fire hotter than anything we'd yet endured.

Throughout the weeks between the last prelim and today, Larry hadn't spoken to me about my decision not to testify. He listened when I wanted to talk it out, but he didn't offer an opinion. He had already made his position plain, that he would plead guilty, even to the felony, if I said this was all too much for me. Beyond that, his attorney told him to avoid any words at all that might influence me. It bears repeating that they couldn't risk accusations of witness tampering.

But my mind was made up, and my decision was my own. I wouldn't, couldn't testify. In so many ways Larry and I had self-combusted, to coin a phrase. Neither one of us was fully to blame, nor fully innocent. Larry's sin had him in trouble with the law. My sin, in the Old Testament, would have gotten me stoned. Only God's grace and forgiveness had saved us, and we were living now on *that* foundation, together. I wasn't going to tear it apart.

Greg had called and asked me to come into his office, and when I sat down he again came straight to the point.

"Sooooo…there are two kinds of contempt."

Gulp!

"The first one," he went on, "is strictly punitive. The judge can put you in jail for five days to punish you for refusing to testify."

Five days. I held onto my chair tightly. Five days. Could I live through five jail days to spare Larry five years? I had friends in there. Would that help? I steeled myself not to buckle under the weight of five days. I might think it would kill me, but I knew I would, in fact, live through it. I thought five days was terrible, but survivable. Maybe it wouldn't be the end of the world.

"The other kind of contempt," Greg went on, "is the kind where the judge orders you to remain in jail until you are cured. That means you stay locked up until you change your mind and say you'll testify. I also need to let you know that there have been cases, not in our county, but in the country, where people have been kept incarcerated for a very long time for refusing to testify in court. Well over a year, and in one well-known case, nearly two years."

Five days looked okay! Let's go back to that one!

But Greg was still speaking.

"Of course, we hope that the judge won't charge you with either of those. I never would have thought it would come to this, but right now I really don't know what they may do. Left to me when I was the prosecutor, this would have gone away a long time ago. If you weren't a willing witness, I'd have dropped it and let you take your chances. But they might be afraid that if they drop the charges, and you end up dead next week, they'll be blamed."

I could actually understand the reasoning there, but I couldn't see where locking me up was any kind of answer.

"This doesn't seem to be about watching out for me, Greg. I am not feeling super protected here."

"Yeah," he agreed, "I hear you. But for now, let's talk about you. In light of what I've told you, about unlikely but possible contempt charges, is it still your wish to refuse to testify?"

"It is," I replied, praying quickly for some courage. "Believe me, if there was another way, I'd take it. If Larry were a career criminal, it would be different. But I can't let one bad night destroy his life, and at his age, I'm afraid five years in prison might even *take* his life."

"Okay then. That's decided. If the judge puts you in jail, I'll go public. I'll start with Channel 7. As I said, the law allows it, but putting a woman in your situation in jail is really controversial. Publicity is our best bet. Let's hope it doesn't come to that." And as was his habit, he stood up to signal an end to our meeting.

This time when he said, "I'll see you in court in the morning," I agreed and replied, "I'll be there."

* * *

March 13, 2013.

We've come full circle, and have arrived back at the beginning of my tale.

That fateful Wednesday morning arrived far too soon, and a glance out the window showed the promise of a beautiful day. So often in March, the weather still felt like winter, but today's forecast held warmth and sunshine.

Larry made me my favorite breakfast of scrambled egg whites and gluten free toast. I read my Bible, prayed, and committed this day to God.

I set my one prescription bottle on our dining room table. I took the unopened box, containing my paperback copy of Joyce Meyer's *Everyday Life Bible,* and placed it carefully next to the small bottle of pills. I'd left the box sealed. There was no other way they would accept it at the jail.

I slipped into a light jacket and looked around our home. I didn't know if I would next see it in an hour or six months. My hands shook as I reached for my handbag.

Time to go.

*"For the mountains may move
and the hills disappear,
but even then my faithful love
for you will remain.
My covenant of blessing will
never be broken,"
says the Lord, who has mercy on you.*
(Isaiah 54:10 NLT)

CHAPTER **ELEVEN**

COUNTY JAIL, DAY ONE: SHORTLY BEFORE 10:00 P.M.

I shivered in my cell and thought warm thoughts of home. This morning, getting ready to go to court, seemed so long ago. Time crept by slowly in jail, and my one day here already felt like a week. I had another day to get through tomorrow, one interminable minute at a time.

I held my Bible lovingly. Buying that Bible had been the best possible thing I could have done for myself. I was so thankful for it. So thankful Grizz had allowed me to have it.

Yawwwwn. I was so tired.

"Bunk up for bed count." I nearly jumped out of my skin as the announcement came over the public address system. Did that mean it was nearly 10:00 p.m.? I hoped so. All I wanted was to fall asleep and make some of my hours go faster. The way my eyes were stinging, I was sure I'd be able to fall asleep – even if I had to use only my arm for a pillow.

I wondered if there was something I was supposed to do. Probably not. I was already on my bunk. I was alone in a cell, all of which was on camera. There was no way they could misplace me.

I moved my Bible, book, and writing things to the tote where it sat in My Personal Arctic Circle. I removed my glasses and set them on top of my Bible. I then sat on my bunk and waited for them to turn the lights off. It seemed I waited forever. I didn't want to lie down until I had a hope of falling asleep. When, at last, the lights went out, my cell took on a fairly bright glow. There was still a lot of light coming in from the booking area, but at least it was darker than before.

I took the blanket I'd been wrapped in and spread it on top of the bed. I then peeled back the top sheet and both blankets and tried to squeeze between the sheets, wishing I were shorter. This bed might not be quite as difficult for a tiny person.

The bunk was narrow, not very long, and, again, ice-cold metal. Even with two foam pads, my pallet was rock hard. I lay down, bent my right arm up to support my head, and drew what I hoped would be a relaxing breath.

After a few minutes, however, my back began to ache and my arm went numb. Rolling over disrupted my entire set of carefully made bedding. I rearranged it, but I eventually realized that, even with both blankets on the bed, I was cold. I'd left my clothes on, and my socks, but even so I was chilled through. I took the top blanket and folded it in half to double it up. Since it was then too short to tuck in or drape over the side, I knew I'd have to lie very still to keep it in place. I had no hope, however, of lying still. I moved every few minutes to alleviate some new pressure point.

And so it went. I tried everything I could think of throughout the night to find, if not comfort, then at least a position that didn't *hurt*. I thought of my inmate friends, how they always seemed well rested and, for the most part, in good shape. I decided they were either just incredibly *young*, or they'd adapted. Or both. I, on the other hand, wasn't young. My body wasn't used to all of these hard, cold surfaces, and it protested with every position change.

Throughout the night, the central phone rang frequently, amplified and blaring throughout booking. I'm sure that was necessary, so that guards could hear it no matter where they were, but since my cell was near booking, it startled me every time.

Guards chatted amiably near the booking desk, and though I was incased in my box, their voices carried clearly. I heard every laugh, every comment, everything. One particularly cheerful guard whistled the night away as he made his rounds. There was no quiet to be found.

Sleepless time dragged on, and though I'd been looking forward to night, now all I wanted was morning, so I could sit up and stop this sham.

It was probably around midnight when the leg cramps started. I writhed in agony through each one, massaging my calves where the muscles were sucked in and concave. Just as I'd feel one start to ease up, the same thing began in my feet. The tops of my feet sank down into themselves, leaving my foot bones high and dry, and making my toes curl unnaturally. I grabbed desperately at my feet and tried to uncurl my toes with my fingers.

When I wasn't stretching or massaging my legs and feet, I tried in every way possible to make use of my sweatshirt. I thought if I could just get more comfortable, the charley horses would go away. I took my sweatshirt off and wadded it up to use it as a pillow. Ugh. Too lumpy. A blindfold, perhaps? Too heavy. A complete head wrap that would shield my eyes from the light and my ears from all the noise? Believe it or not, too hot. I rolled it up and pretended it was a stuffed animal I could hold onto and relax with, enough to sleep. I folded it in half, stretched out just the two arms, then twisted them together and put them under my neck to gain some support. Nothing worked.

By the time the lights came on at 6:00 a.m., I was exhausted and frustrated. I hadn't slept at all.

The God of all comfort

Who gives songs in the night.

(2 Corinthians 1:4) (Job 35:10)

I'm always here with you
Ever your strong rescue
even in darkness you
can always find My light.

And when you feel alone
You are not on your own
You're never far from home
You're always in My sight.

CHAPTER **TWELVE**

COUNTY JAIL, DAY TWO: 6:00 A.M.

I was learning to more readily recognize the songs the Lord would feed into my mind, as I left sleep behind and rose to each new day. I called them my wake-up songs, but as I hadn't slept and therefore could not wake up, this would have to be my morning song, instead.

The moment the lights came on in my small cell, the popular contemporary Christian song, *Here With You*, had dropped cleanly into my head. I could hear the lead singer's voice as he reminded us of the nearness of the Lord. As I struggled back into actually *wearing* my sweatshirt, I promised God I would remember later and thank Him properly. I knew He was speaking to me at a level I couldn't appreciate yet this morning. I knew the message was touching and I did manage a small smile. I just couldn't absorb it properly. I realized He was saying He was with me, but I couldn't actually *feel* the Lord's presence.

What I felt was sore from head to toe. My leg and foot cramps had tormented me relentlessly throughout the remainder of the night. Several times I'd stood up, hoping that bearing my weight and flexing my feet would ease the cramping in the backs of my calves. All I had really accomplished was a renewed round of foot spasms, as my feet objected to the cold cement floor.

The residual tenderness from the muscle cramps joined the aches in every joint in my body. Shoulders hurt, hips hurt, back ached. Worst of all was a pernicious headache that I hoped breakfast and lots of water would tamp down. I couldn't afford to have that intensify. I rolled my shoulders and tried some careful stretches to see if my stiff neck would relax. Nothing I'd tried with my sweatshirt had provided the support my neck craved.

My eyes were burning, and I was woozy from lack of sleep. I felt like I was suffering from a hangover and a jarring car accident, all at once.

Coffee would help. Just the thought cheered me a little. A sip of coffee, even black, would surely help me to feel human again. I'm not usually hungry at 6:00 in the morning, but I found myself eager for the meal to arrive, just so I could have some coffee. Forget the food. I wanted a hot drink.

And sure enough, not five minutes later my cell door opened and the guard asked, "Wanna eat?" I stepped over to the doorway to take my tray, then waited for them to ask for my cup so they could pour some coffee into it.

Are you smiling yet? You are, if you have ever been an inmate.

Coffee, in most county jails, is a luxury. Buy your own from the commissary, if you can afford it; guard it zealously against theft; and be assured that no one's just going to give you any.

But naive as my hopes may have been, they had still been hopes. I was lost as the door slammed shut and I stood in the center of my overly bright cell, breakfast tray in hand, same miserable surroundings as yesterday. I tried to come to grips with the fact that this horrible experience had just been made worse. Nothing hot to drink. Not an ounce of comfort anywhere. Just this glaring, chilly cell.

I set my tray down in My Personal Arctic Circle and seated myself next to it, too unhappy to even take note of the frozen nature of my perch.

I looked at the breakfast tray and realized I couldn't eat any of it if I wanted to feel well. Hmmm. Let's rephrase. I couldn't eat any of it if I didn't want to feel worse than I already did. My stomach was the only thing NOT bothering me at the moment, and I didn't want to change that.

The meal consisted of scrambled eggs – powdered eggs containing milk products. Then there was oatmeal, coffee cake, and a piece of bread. No, no and extra no. I nibbled a few bites of the eggs, an equally few bites of oatmeal, and gave up. I just couldn't risk it. Instead I forced down several of my little cups of water and then placed my tray in the slot.

What was I going to do with myself, now? It must have been all of 6:20 in the morning, and the day stretched out mercilessly before me. I wouldn't go back to court until three-thirty.

Maybe some hygiene would be in order. I dug through my tote and found the baggie with all the goodies. I squeezed some of the clear substance labeled Toothpaste onto my tiny toothbrush. Kind of a chore reaching your back teeth when your toothbrush is mostly bristles and has almost no handle, but I managed it. I had soap. I was very cognizant of the eye-in-the-sky in the upper corner of my cell, so I left my sweatshirt on and attempted a sink bath. By the time I was finished, if I wasn't feeling *better*, at least I was feeling more awake.

I peered into an item above the sink that was slyly passing itself off as a mirror. It was made of some kind of burnished, unbreakable substance, and you could see a blurry and distorted reflection of yourself in it, if you held very still.

Uh-oh. I put my glasses on and tried to get a better look. Yep. My suspicions were confirmed. One of my eyebrows was gone! I had studiously avoided washing my upper face the night before, thinking I could hold onto some semblance of browage for my court appearance. But with one eyebrow completely gone, there was nothing for it but to rub the other one off as well.

As with many women, I'd tried and failed in the tweezing and shaping of my eyebrows. After enduring a lifetime of my tortuous efforts, they had finally refused to grow back. I didn't have any eyebrows of my own. I'd tried the permanent makeup route, aka eyebrow tattoos. Regrettably, the ink hadn't stuck properly. I'd been left with odd, thin, asymmetrical lines on my face. I got by with corrective pencils, and finally decided to wear my hair with bangs. I figured that way I could take at least one of my brows right out of the equation.

I had no makeup, obviously, so I tugged my bangs over one thinly tattooed, crooked brow, and decided not to worry about it. What else could I do?

I then picked up the micro-comb and set about combing out my long hair. It took a while, but I wasn't going anywhere. All the time in the world.

I made up my bed. I couldn't bear the site of any untidiness in my cramped quarters.

And that was it. Morning ablutions, County Jail style, completed.

Well, I certainly had time for a good quiet time with the Lord. I laid out my book, my Bible, my notebook and pen, then settled into my writing position. I was achy, cold, and hungry. Also, if I'm honest, I was just plain frightened. I wanted to vent some against the people who'd put me here, even if that only meant finding scriptures that would help me do so.

Warming to the topic, I thought about the one in Luke 9:54, when James and John, speaking of some Samaritans, indignantly asked Jesus, "Lord, should we call down fire from heaven to burn them up?"

But, no. Jesus had rebuked them for that. Foolish disciples. Bad idea, both for the disciples at the time and for me now.

What then? What should I read? I had no concordance. Closing my eyes, I tried to think.

Then *wow!* My spirit heard the whisper even as a red neon sign lit up the inside of my mind. The words said and read, "Isaiah 61." I hadn't spent much time in the book of Isaiah over the years, apart from my yearly reading plan. I couldn't remember if Isaiah even *had* sixty-one chapters. It seemed to me there were sixty. I must be imagining things.

I picked up my Bible and found that there is, indeed, a Chapter 61. At that moment, the Lord Almighty, the One Great God, Creator of the entire universe, zeroed in on me in that desperate little cell. His Holy Spirit grabbed hold of me and changed everything forever, as I read, starting in verse 1:

> *The Spirit of the Lord God is upon me,*
> *because the Lord has anointed and qualified me*
> *to preach the Gospel of good tidings to the meek,*
> *the poor, and afflicted; He has sent me to bind*
> *up and heal the brokenhearted, to proclaim liberty*
> *to the [physical and spiritual] captives and*
> *the opening of the prison and of the eyes to those who*
> *are bound.*

Verse 6 leapt out at me as well:

> *But you shall be called the priests of the Lord;*
> *people will speak of you as the ministers of our God.*
> *You shall eat the wealth of the nations, and the glory*
> *[once that of your captors] shall be yours.*
> (AMP)

Cold? Hungry? Scared? NO WAY! The Lord had just spoken to me, and I was in no doubt about that. I knew that, in Luke 4, Jesus read these same words, and that they are, taken literally, a prophecy about Him. But what stood out to me were the words, "anointed AND QUALIFIED!" Qualified for what? "To proclaim liberty to the [physical and spiritual] captives and the opening of the prison and of the eyes to those who are bound."

In an instant God turned my attention from my own circumstances, and He gave me two promises.

First, a promise that although this experience in jail might *disqualify* me in the eyes of the authorities, it *qualified* me in the eyes of the Lord. I realized I could look at this as a training ground. Training in understanding, in compassion; training in the area of first-hand and experiential knowledge of arrest, booking, a solitary cell. I knew, as I'd never known before, what it felt like to quake under the authority of our legal system, to tremble before a judge as he decided my fate.

My inmate friends knew these things well. I was now certain that the Lord wanted me to know them, too. I was comforted by the assurance that God was watching over me. He knew right where I was, and He had a plan to work this and all things together for good.

Second, the words *priests* and *ministers.* Plural. I'd prayed for years that Larry and I would be in ministry together. Now here was this verse, spoken at this time, promising just that.

At this moment I remembered the song the Spirit had dropped into my head first thing this morning. *Here With You.* I had by now arrived at a place where I could marvel and thank Him for being here with me, as He most surely was.

I would need to keep reminding myself of this, throughout that long, long day.

CHAPTER **THIRTEEN**

COUNTY JAIL, DAY TWO: AFTER LUNCH

Lunch had come and gone. I'd been startled when the cell door had suddenly jerked open. A guard had held the door for an inmate worker as he pulled my lunch from the trolley. They'd handed me my tray and shut the door, opening the slot beneath the window so I could set my empty tray there later.

Lunch had consisted of a small salad entirely made up of iceberg lettuce, a sandwich that held a slice of the same mystery meat that had been floating in the bean dish the night before, another piece of coffee cake, and a large cookie. There was also quite a lot of lettuce sitting next to the sandwich. It was up to me to construct it.

Looking at my starchy, gluten-filled meal, I wanted a do-over of my initial intake. I had said no to food allergies, because I felt embarrassed and didn't want to make waves. I regretted it. They ask those questions for a reason.

I looked at my sandwich. I didn't want to add a stomachache to the headache I already had. The trouble was that I had eaten next to nothing for breakfast. I was getting pretty hungry. Maybe I should tear up my sandwich's mystery slice, put it with the lettuce and eat it that way. That didn't seem very appetizing or, to be truthful, very filling. I pondered the bread again. Two thin slices of processed wheat bread. Dare I risk it?

Two and a half months ago I'd been in California visiting my daughter Amy over Christmas. While I was there, I ventured to a wonderful breakfast place with Amy and the boys, happy that this restaurant offered as much vanilla coffee creamer as you wanted. We got Caden his apple juice and placed our order. The danger came when the server asked me what kind of toast I'd like with my veggie omelet. I'd thrown caution to the wind and thought recklessly, *I'm on vacation*! I promptly answered, "Sourdough!"

Four hours later, back in Amy's apartment while the boys napped, I was nearly doubled over in pain. I couldn't even stand up straight. As my eyes watered and my belly spasmed, I kept muttering aloud, "I can't understand what this is all about. What on earth is up with my stomach?"

Amy was loading the morning's photos onto her computer. She was arranging them and choosing the best to post online. Always observant and quick-witted, Amy barely looked up from her laptop as she reminded me of my self-inflicted injury. "Yeah, so," she began, clicking away with her mouse, "I seem to remember something about *sourdough toast* this morning!!"

We then both dissolved into fits of laughter that toppled me right off my feet and down to my knees. Whipping my glasses off, I wiped tears away. If my eyes had to be watery, better to have tears of laughter than of pain.

With that memory fresh in my mind, I knew what I was in for if I ate that bread. But as I said, in the last twenty-eight hours I'd only nibbled a few careful bites. My stomach was growling, my lunch-size salad was small, and my sandwich was right in front of me. I'd been provided a packet of mayo. I added that and some of the lettuce to my bread and mystery meat, promising my digestive system I would only eat half.

With tremendous effort, I nearly made it. I scarfed down two-thirds of it before I stopped myself. I set the remaining portion to the side and, still hungry, stabbed disconsolately at the remaining lettuce with my spork. My large cookie beckoned to me invitingly, but I knew better. I had to face a judge in a few hours. I didn't want to make myself sick beforehand.

I wondered if I'd be back from court in time for dinner. If not, it was going to be an even longer night than the one I'd already lived through.

When I decided I was being inordinately tempted by my remaining flour-filled lunch items, I got up and put the lunch tray in the food flap. Before too long, someone came by and took it away. They left the food flap open, though, so I could see out, just a tiny bit. I could hear voices, clangings and footsteps. I didn't want anyone to come along and close the slot. Having it open made me feel less isolated, less alone.

Remember, my cell door had no bars in it. It was a heavy steel door that sported a thick glass window in its upper portion, but that window was a tease as much as anything. There was a screen on the outside of it, one of those accordion-type screens that sits at the bottom of the sill. It could be raised to any level and stay put. The guards would raise that screen either partially or fully whenever they deemed it necessary. I never knew the reason, and I seldom caught them at it. I would look up occasionally and see that the curtain was completely obscuring my small window, when a moment before it had been at half-mast.

The screen was in its full upright position, blocking all view, at the time I was enjoying my open food flap. *Please leave it open,* I thought. *I can't stand it in here.*

I sat there staring at that open slot, refusing to lose a precious moment of out-of-my-cell air, until someone did indeed slam it shut. Immediately my chest tightened and my throat closed up. I had to consciously tell myself to draw breath. My head, already throbbing with the headache that started the day, now boomed along with each heartbeat. *Whong, whong, whong* went my brain. My vision blurred, I felt lightheaded and dizzy.

The slot was closed. The screen was closed. I couldn't see anyone, yet I knew I was being watched. I hoped the unseen glances into my cell were minimal. I mean, I really had to be a fairly boring show, as inmates go.

I drew in a few shallow breaths, then tried some deeper ones. My hands had been unwittingly clenched together in my lap. I forced myself to relax my grip and set each hand beside me on My Personal Arctic Circle's icy bench. I waited until each hand was chilled right through, and then I pressed them to my face. Another breath. I refroze my hands and repeated the exercise until my vision cleared and my breathing eased.

I needed a change, something to take my mind off my solitary enclosure. I stood up and walked back and forth in my cell. Well, I stepped and turned. A step and a half was the total distance I could actually pace before bumping into the door on the one end and the Arctic Circle on the other. I quickly realized I wasn't going to be able to walk off my intense bout of cabin fever.

Lunges, then. I proceeded to perform fifty lunges with each leg, then I devoted myself to squats. A bunch of them. Good. My efforts were raising my heart rate in the *right* way. Next I sat back on the cold bench and gripped the smooth edge of it with my hands, bending my knees directly in front of me, feet flat on the floor. I lifted myself off the bench and lowered my rear toward the floor, and then lifted myself back up in a triceps press. I did as many of those as I could, which was probably only twenty. It was fun while it lasted, but I finally yielded to my hands' painful response to the concrete.

My exercises had probably consumed fifteen minutes, but at least for the moment I wasn't cold. I felt a little less like a slug who'd been sitting on a metal shelf for nearly two days.

CHAPTER **FOURTEEN**

COUNTY JAIL, DAY TWO: MAYBE 12:30 P.M.

I didn't know what else to do with myself. The walls began closing in again. I wanted *out!* I had to get *out, Out, OUT* of here!

I stood in the center of my cell and contemplated more lunges just to distract myself, but my nighttime leg spasms were already threatening to return. More leg work might be pushing things. Slightly warmer from my exertions, I sat down on my bunk without my extra blanket-slash-shawl. I reluctantly drew my writing desk back onto my lap.

There was nothing for it. I could either read, write, or freak out. I pictured myself screaming and banging desperately on my cell door, kicking at it with the rubber toes of my flat, orange canvas shoes. The thought made me smile a bit. That just wasn't me. And if I did lose it like that, I'd no doubt be thrown into more restraints. Then I'd spontaneously combust for sure.

I took up my pen and wrote the following:

> *So lunch means noon, and it's probably half an hour since they brought it. That means in three hours, I'll be back in court, and since he promised to send me straight back if I still won't speak, then back I'll come. Lord, I commit myself into Your hands. You know what You're doing. Help me, help me, Lord, to know what to say.*

Help me, help me, Lord, not to panic when they say
they're returning me to this place.

I spent most of my time writing Scripture, and I needed a post-lunch pick-me-up. Perhaps I was harkening back to my crazy flight from Magic, because, once again, II Timothy came to mind:

For God has not given us a spirit of fear,
but of power and of love and of a sound mind.

I went further and added the next part:

Therefore do not be ashamed of the testimony of our
Lord, nor of me His prisoner,
but share with me in the sufferings for the gospel
according to the power of God..

(II Timothy 1:7-8 NKJV)

And also:

Greater love has no one than this,
than to lay down one's life for his friends.

(John 15:13 NKJV)

II Timothy 2:7 reminded me not to give in to fear. Verse 8 brought Paul's imprisonment to mind. How harsh that must have been! Just for him to mention, at the end of Colossians, "Remember my chains," filled me with compassion for him. Not only imprisoned, but beaten, and left in chains day in, day out. I couldn't even imagine it!

As to John 15:13, I knew I wasn't in the position of having to lay down my life for someone, yet I felt a kinship with this verse all the same. Jail wasn't death, but it was pretty darned awful.

I remembered something Joyce Meyer had said regarding Matthew 5:4, "Blessed are those who mourn, for they shall be comforted." She reminded us that God's comfort goes beyond any kind of ordinary comfort. Well, I certainly needed comfort now. I thought about her advice to ask God for His comfort.

Okay! I'll do it! I set my Bible and my journal aside and sat on the edge of the bunk. I closed my eyes and began to sing. That started something! I sang song after song, each one lifting my spirit more than the last. If there's one thing that can be said for a small cell like mine, the acoustics are incredible. I'm not a strong singer, but in this cell I felt like I could give Aretha Franklin a run for her money!

No one came to shut me up, so I sang until I wore myself out. Quiet at last, I sat on the edge of the bed, eyes closed. As I began to pray, the Lord's peace fell upon me like a soft, warm, and very real cocoon. I was enveloped in the Lord's love and assurance. I identified with Joyce Meyer's comments about God's comfort being far beyond any kind of ordinary comfort. In those moments, anxiety and discomfort vanished.

As I prayed, I first thanked Him for being with me in my tiny cell, and for His nearness that had touched me as I began to pray. Then, as a daughter might hold onto her father after a nightmare, and even describe the nightmare to him, I reported to God all that had been building within me over these past days. I spoke of my fear when I'd been put in handcuffs and driven to the jail. I told the Lord I didn't think I could stand being sent back here after court today; that I was afraid I would break into little pieces if that happened. I quoted to Him some words of King David in Psalm 70:5:

> *But as for me, I am poor and needy.*
> *Come quickly to me, O God.*
> *You are my help and my deliverer;*
> *Lord, do not delay.*

(NIV)

I shuddered as I verbalized my fear of the judge and his power over my life, his authority to decide what I would eat and where I would sleep, whether I would remain incarcerated, and for how long. I told Him I didn't want bitterness to creep into my heart. I knew if resentment took hold within me that it would eat me alive. I recognized that anger, terror, despair and a sense of *unfairness* hammered at the walls of my soul and demanded entrance.

I needed God's help to deliver me, not only from the hands of men, but from the temptation to dive headlong into fury on the one hand, and self-pity on the other. I knew how important it was to come through this with the right heart attitude. I promised to work on that with His guidance, but I repeated that, right now, I needed His comfort as never before.

I prayed as David did in Psalm 25:16-17:

> *Turn to me and be gracious to me,*
> *for I am lonely and afflicted.*
> *Relieve the troubles of my heart and*
> *free me from my anguish.*

(NIV)

I then shifted topics and went back through my conversation with Captain Harris the evening before. The Captain had listened patiently to me as I explained that I couldn't testify, that Larry had changed and he was really trying. I told the captain that our marriage was stronger than ever, and that I couldn't let one terrible evening destroy Larry's life and mine with it. Captain Harris understood, and he was gracious when he informed me that my privileges must be suspended. I could no longer bring church services to the ladies in his care. It was policy.

In absolute honesty, I was able to hand this matter over to the Lord very quickly. The fact of the jail ministry was so miraculous to me in the first place, that I knew it would be His to handle moving forward. Then there was God's promise from this morning. I truly had zero concern, which is not to say I wasn't sad at the prospect of leaving the ladies. I just knew that if I couldn't come, God would raise up someone else to join Patty and meet with the women here.

"But Lord," I added, "If it's Your will that I be allowed to come back some day, then I know nothing will get in Your way."

I then moved on to the tough night I'd just endured. I explained that my body was hurting, and I asked Him to pour His beneficial sleep onto me this evening if they brought me back.

I asked Him for words to say in court as I resumed the witness stand. I would return to face a prosecutor who was bent on forcing me to testify, and a judge from whom I now expected no mercy.

The thought of court was so daunting that I decided to stir up my faith by reading Psalm 18:28-30 to God:

> *You light a lamp for me.*
> *The Lord, my God, lights up my darkness.*
> *In your strength I can crush an army:*
> *with my God I can scale any wall.*
> *God's way is perfect.*
> *All the Lord's promises prove true.*
> *He is a shield to all who look to Him for protection.*

(NLT)

As I prayed and read Scripture to the Lord, I felt a surge of strength pass through me, so that, for a moment, I wasn't afraid. I'd been zapped with Holy Ghost jumper cables, and I sat there for some time, just reveling in it. And though the surge passed, and my surroundings brought back to mind my grim reality, I knew with a rock-solid certainty that God was *all over* this business. He knew exactly where I was sitting.

I opened my eyes and drew in a deep breath. I had prayed until I was spent. I had poured out my heart to my Father, and when I was finished, I felt both encouraged and drained. My spiritual high gave way to the physical low that was bound to reappear. It had been so good to exercise, to sing, and to pray. Now, as I heard a guard in booking tell another guard that it was two o'clock, I realized how exhausted I was from the cold, the lack of sleep, so little food, and all of my bodily aches and pains.

I picked up my Bible, and the words were blurry. I couldn't finish a sentence. My head hurt terribly, and my eyes stung. My cell was obscenely bright, making rest seem out of the question. I saw no point in lying down on my metal bunk, but I couldn't help myself. I took my tiny towel, folded it up so I could place it over my eyes. Maybe it would block out some of the glare. I hugged my blanket to myself and tipped over onto my rock hard bed. I curled up in a fetal position as weariness swept over me. Maybe I could doze, just a little.

So at last the king gave orders for Daniel
to be arrested and thrown into the den of lions.
The king said to him, "May your God, whom you
serve so faithfully, rescue you."
(Daniel 6:16 NLT)

CHAPTER **FIFTEEN**

COUNTY JAIL, DAY TWO: NEARLY 3:00 P.M.

I lay on my bunk for twenty, possibly thirty minutes. At first, waves of weariness washed over me and my brain clouded pleasantly. I was finally at the edge of falling asleep when the public-address-volume telephone rang again in booking. It startled me as it did every single time. I didn't move, hoping I could recapture my drowsiness, but I was by now alert enough to notice that my bed was uncomfortable, increasing the aches in my bones. I gave up, sat up, and put my tiny towel back in my tote.

Drawing my 'writing desk' onto my lap, I wrote the following:

> Psalm 61:1:
> *God, You are my Rock; earnestly will I seek You; my inner self thirsts for You, my flesh longs and is faint for You, in a dry and weary land where no water is.*
> *I am nervous, Lord. And I know that no matter what happens I have to come back here. I need to get back to preparing myself for at least a few more days...*

I wanted to go home desperately. I knew I would probably be returned to jail. Yesterday my attorney had said he'd come and see me. I'd been hoping all day that he would arrive and bring news. He hadn't come, and so I knew either he was busy or there was no news.

There was still no question of my testifying. If I thought this was bad, I couldn't imagine what it would be like for Larry if he went to prison for *years*. He was my husband, my other half. He and I were *one*, at last. I wouldn't send him there if I could help it.

I knew that he could still be in a lot of trouble anyway. The State could read my statement and play the 911 call for the Court. If they did that, Larry was on his own. The judge might well find there was enough evidence to bind him over for trial in district court.

But they looked to be hanging their entire case on my testimony. The officer who had testified in court yesterday hadn't seen anything. He could only testify to what he had heard secondhand on the night of the arrest. There was also a question of proper handling of the Miranda warning. They didn't have enough. They needed me. The prosecutor had said as much to my attorney, when he admitted, "I have no case without her."

Well, then, they had no case. Desperate as my situation was, I knew I couldn't testify. I was terrified that I would be returned to jail after court, but I couldn't be the hammer that nailed my own husband's coffin shut. I'd read an article online about a woman in a domestic case (in a different state) who refused to testify against her husband. The judge put her in jail. After a few days she couldn't stand it anymore and she testified. Her husband went to prison.

That wasn't going to happen with me. I didn't feel like a mighty warrior, but all I had to do was *not* say anything. I could do that. Surely I could do that. Best to set my mind on staying here a while. I wouldn't allow myself thoughts of going home tonight.

So, back to practical matters. Today was Thursday. I couldn't order commissary (extra stuff you can buy for yourself) until next Tuesday, and my order wouldn't be delivered for two days after that. Next Thursday, one week from today, was the soonest

I could hope to have shampoo, conditioner, Chapstick and deodorant. *Have mercy!*

I wondered if my face would break out as my hair got filthy. My tote held the generic shampoo, but without conditioner I'd never get my hair combed back out. I was pretty sure it was against the rules for any other inmate to let me use her products. I would have to wait until I could order and receive hair care products.

I picked up my pen and resumed with my journal, rambling now:

> *Okay, I put the pen down and tried to read, but it's no good. I am antsy. I shouldn't be. I know I am coming back no matter what. They told me that last night. It takes time for people to get released. And I could well be staying. Last night was rough, but tonight I'll be more tired since I didn't sleep last night. I plan to turn the mattress around so I'll be facing away from the bright lights of the booking area.*

Or maybe, just maybe, I'd be moved to one of the blocks and would no longer be alone.

CHAPTER **SIXTEEN**

COUNTY JAIL, DAY TWO: 3:15 P.M.

With a *swish* of air my cell door banged open, and there stood Deputy Hansen. "Time to go," he said. He stood aside and waited for me to scramble into my flat orange shoes and exit the cell.

It felt strange to go somewhere without gathering up my things first. At home, when I needed to go out, I would find my cell phone, coat, sunglasses; I would check my purse to make sure I had a digestion-friendly protein bar with me; I'd double check that my regular glasses were in my bag and that there was water in the dog bowl; I would check that the front door was locked and then turn off all the lights.

But now I just stood up and walked out. I wouldn't call it a liberating experience, though, as the deputy was only calling me out so he could shackle me up. Face the wall. Place your hands in front of you on the wall. He wrapped a chain around my waist. From that chain another longer chain dangled from my belly to my feet. Attached to that long chain were two ankle cuffs. He then told me to bend my knee and lift my right foot up behind me so he could secure that ankle cuff. He did likewise with my left ankle. The result was that, not only were my ankles cuffed together, they were chained to my waist.

He then instructed me to lower my right arm. He proceeded to lock my wrist into a handcuff dangling from the waist chain. He followed suit with my left arm. I was well and truly trussed.

I'd better not cry, I thought. I wouldn't be able to reach my face to wipe my eyes.

The interesting point came just as he was lowering my right arm to secure it to my waist chain.

"So," asked Deputy Hansen, "who was the guy in the Bible who they threw into the lions' den?"

"You mean Daniel?" I asked.

"Yeah, Daniel," he agreed, his face inscrutable. Clicking the final cuff into place, he added, "That's who you are, and you're heading back into the lions' den right now."

I was blown away! I wouldn't complain about being compared to Daniel!

I was still trying to absorb this small conversation when he turned me around and gave me instructions on how to walk. "You'll want to take very tiny steps, or you'll fall. Watch yourself." He let me take a few practice steps while he held my elbow.

Satisfied that I was getting the hang of it, he reached for his walkie-talkie and spoke to it. The unseen power that was Control unlocked the door into the back bay. Stepping through that door, I discovered that my same bailiff, with his same no-leg-room cruiser, awaited my arrival.

I believe I have adequately described the sheer impossibility of getting my five-foot-nine-inch frame into the back seat of that car, so I won't belabor the point. I will, however, ask you to imagine the scenario now just a little differently. On my ride to the jail I wore only handcuffs. For this trip, I was chained hand and foot. I couldn't use my hands to support me, and my feet could only move inches from each other at a time.

Having my hands cuffed to my waist instead of behind my back was a vast improvement when it came to sitting down, but my feet were stuck together. This challenged my iffy balance. I was grateful when the bailiff held my arm and covered my head while I eased down into the car. Left to my own devices I'd probably have either bonked my head or taken a tumble. Once seated, I had to lean backwards in order to bring both chained feet into the car at once. I felt awkward and embarrassed, but the bailiff didn't try to hurry me. Once my feet were in, I hunched my knees to my chin and swung my whole self around so my knees faced the center of the car, as previously described. I was getting better at that part.

The bailiff belted me in once more and shut the door.

* * *

My ride back to the courthouse felt surreal. It was a beautiful, sunny day. There were cars and people everywhere, out and about, free as birds. I was chained hand and foot, sitting in the back of a Sheriff's cruiser and trying to ignore a sense of doom. I reminded myself, again, that the Lord works all things together for good, and even in this horrible mess, He had a plan. He'd made me a promise just today, right in my jail cell. Even as authorities, indeed, jail policy itself, informed me I wouldn't be allowed to minister to prisoners, the Lord said to me that He was anointing and qualifying me to do just that!

I was very concerned that I would have to remain in jail, but I wasn't worried about God's plans for me. Afraid of my immediate circumstances, I wasn't afraid of His will. I believe that was God's grace in action, giving me His peace in the midst of my own terror.

I can perhaps illustrate that concept briefly by recalling a near accident when Amy was two and she and I were traveling together on an airplane. As the plane came in for a landing, it hit a wind shear. It felt like the plane had hit a steel wall. The entire aircraft jolted and tilted sharply to the left. We were quite near the ground, and all of the passengers gasped collectively. We were certain the wing was going to hit the runway and spin us into a fiery crash.

In that split second, Amy turned her wide blue eyes to me, seeking reassurance. My heart skipped a beat as I grasped our peril, but I was instantly at peace. "We're fine, honey," I said. Within myself, I knew we were sure to die, and it wasn't what I would have chosen for her. I hoped the impact would take us away before any fire could reach us, but it was out of my hands. However it happened, in a moment we'd be with Jesus.

Obviously, our heroic pilot regained control of the aircraft and landed safely, to the wild applause of all his passengers.

I relate that story simply to emphasize how it is possible to be terrified because of your situation, yet be at peace in God's hands at the same time.

My aching head pondered these things as the cruiser carried me back to court. I was afraid of being brought back before the prosecutor and the judge. I was afraid of being sent back to jail. I tried to stir my faith, reminding myself over and over that that would only happen if God allowed it. I called to mind the words of Deputy Hansen, hoping they were prophetic when he compared me to Daniel. After all, Daniel, having spent one long night alone, probably cold and hungry, with nowhere soft to sleep (sound familiar?), was released unharmed the next day. At the command of the Lord, the lions didn't touch him, and no one could touch me, either, without God either stopping it or helping me through it.

As we drove along we passed a young man riding happily on his Moped, enjoying the late afternoon warmth on his face. I knew him. He and his young family attended our church regularly. He passed by, completely unaware that he knew the squashed and fettered woman in the Sheriff's cruiser; a woman headed to the courthouse to face, once again, her own lions.

* * *

Back at the courthouse the bailiff helped me to struggle out of the car. When I was at last on my feet, I baby-stepped my way across the sidewalk and then to the stairs. I had trouble climbing the steps because of my ankle chains and my poor balance. For the past few months, and for some unknown reason, (stress? age?), I often felt like I was about to fall, even in normal walking. I was always careful, therefore, to use handrails when I used any stairs. Now, however, even if there had been handrails, I couldn't have reached them.

My ankle chains had just enough length to allow me to get a decent toehold on a step, then edge forward to be sure of my footing. I could then lift up my other foot onto the same step. The bailiff stood nearby, watching my every move, ready to steady me if I tripped.

It's just as well I had to concentrate on my feet and couldn't look around. The courthouse is in the center of town. Anybody driving by could have recognized me. People across the street might have stopped to stare at the prisoner being taken to court in chains. As I carefully negotiated one step at a time, I felt clumsy, unbalanced, vulnerable, and shamed.

Inmates must be secured, there is no question. I am pointing no fingers, and I understand the precautions. I was not being mistreated. I discovered, however, in a way I never could have learned otherwise, that being chained up like that will scar your very soul. I felt like less of a human being at that moment than I ever had before.

I am in the midst of lions;
I am forced to dwell among ravenous beasts –
men whose teeth are spears and arrows,
whose tongues are sharp swords.
(Psalm 57:4 NIV)

BUT.........

Those who live in the shelter of the Most High
will find rest in the shadow of the Almighty.
This I declare about the Lord:
He alone is my refuge, my place of safety;
He is my God, and I trust Him.
(Psalm 91:1-2 NLT)

CHAPTER **SEVENTEEN**

COURT, DAY TWO: 3:30 P.M.

We left the outside world behind and I found myself back in the same jury room. I'd seen my pastor's pickup parked outside. I felt helpless, mortified that he would see me in chains when I entered the courtroom. I could almost hear a devilish voice whispering slyly into one of my ears, *Your pastor will think you're getting what you deserve, first for your sin, and then for hurting Larry with your confession.*

Into my other ear, however, an angelic voice seemed to say, *Hush, now. Pastor Mark thinks no such thing. He is here because he cares about you both.*

I mentally called on the name of Jesus and told the devil to scram. Things were difficult enough without listening to his lies.

I looked about the room, unsure if I was to take a seat or remain standing. I didn't know how long it would be before I'd be taken into the courtroom. The bailiff, however, approached me and – wonderful! – said he was going to remove my shackles. I'd been to court many times to lend moral support to inmate friends, and they'd all remained in their shackles when they came into court. I always hated seeing them that way. I knew, therefore, that it was a deviation from protocol to remove my chains. Curious, I asked the bailiff why my shackles were coming off when that wasn't the norm.

"You're a little different," was the only explanation he gave me.

Whatever the reason, what a blessed relief to have them gone. I felt a bit better, knowing I could walk normally, without fear of falling. Now the only things identifying me as an inmate were my oversized sweatshirt with the words "County Jail" stamped on the back, orange shoes, and my mussed, eyebrowless appearance. Under the sweatshirt I was still in my own black stretch pants and turtleneck.

After the final chain fell away, the bailiff opened the door into the courtroom and told me to have a seat in the jury box. He took his normal station near the clerk's desk.

Almost the moment I sat down, I saw my attorney, Greg, enter from the courthouse lobby door. He walked right through the courtroom, empty except for the bailiff and me, and told me that the judge wanted all of the attorneys to meet with him in chambers before we resumed the hearing.

"This is good for you," said Greg, "that the judge wants to see us privately first. They may ask me if you are still determined to stay silent and not testify. I'm going to tell them you're strong." He looked more closely at me. "Right?"

I nodded. It was all I could manage. I wasn't going to change my mind, but "strong" wasn't a word I'd have used to describe myself. My head was killing me and I felt weak and rubbery. I so wanted to just go *home,* and not back to jail.

But Greg was satisfied with my head nod.

"Okay," he said, "I have to go in now. I'll see you shortly."

And he was gone.

No sooner had he left than Larry walked into the courtroom. He saw me and immediately asked the bailiff, "Can I talk to her?" The bailiff nodded, so Larry walked right through to the jury box and reached for my hands.

"Hey, baby. How are you doing? Did you get any sleep?"

I was so happy to see him! Tears stung my eyes, but I managed to hold them back. Seeing tears from me now would rip his heart to pieces.

"No," I managed, "I didn't sleep at all. It was so cold, and I'm not used to so many hard surfaces."

"I know," he empathized. He went on to explain that his attorney had been busy on my behalf. "Drew has been trying nonstop to reach a deal with the prosecutor, so I can plead guilty and get you out of there."

"Not to a felony," I said stubbornly.

"He knows, honey," was all Larry said.

At that moment, Drew entered the courtroom himself and motioned for Larry to come and speak with him. Larry squeezed my hands and left to confer outside the courtroom. Even as he was leaving, Pastor Mark entered, located me with his eyes, and came to speak with me.

"Hey, Diana."

"Hi, Mark. Thanks for coming." I felt a little bashful in my jail sweatshirt. I hoped I didn't smell bad.

"Nothing was going to keep me away today," he said. Then he surprised me with, "Hey, did they give you another blanket?"

"No," I answered glumly. "It's against the rules to give an inmate more than two."

At this he fixed his gaze on some far corner of the courtroom, his mouth grim. I'd forgotten that one of the last things we discussed during his visit was that I would ask for another blanket. He, clearly, remembered.

A shuffling in the courtroom indicated that people were taking their places. Apparently the conference in chambers hadn't yielded a resolution. It was time to begin. Pastor Mark left me in the jury box and went to find a seat in the audience section.

"All rise," from the bailiff. We all stood as the judge entered and took his seat behind his bench. I trembled as he ordered me to stand once again before the clerk and be sworn in.

A note about the clerk. I knew ahead of time, well before

yesterday, that I couldn't afford to be sworn to tell the truth. I had no intention of *telling* anything.

Yesterday, therefore, when the clerk had attempted to swear me in with, "Do you swear to tell the truth, the whole truth, and nothing but the truth?" I'd replied with, "I swear that anything I say will be the truth."

Judge Jordan's head had snapped up. "Wait a minute! Wait a minute!" he growled. "You don't get to do that. You will stand there and take the oath as it's given."

Stranded in the middle of the courtroom before we even began, I'd said, "But, your Honor, the prosecutor knows I won't be testifying. I can't swear to tell anything at all."

Long story short, the judge had insisted that I take the oath. I hadn't been ready to get into a fight with him about it. I didn't want to go to jail before I could even refuse to testify!

I'd stuck my right hand in the air and hoped for I knew not what. I knew I couldn't swear to talk.

But then the delightfully marvelous clerk had had mercy on me and changed the language subtly!

"Do you swear that anything you say will be the truth, the whole truth, and nothing but the truth?" she'd asked.

Did anyone notice but me?

"I *do*!!"

And with that, I took the stand, respectfully refused to testify, and we have seen all that followed.

So that was yesterday, but the clerk hadn't forgotten. I stepped before her now and raised my right hand again. Was that compassion I saw in her eyes?

For the second day in a row she showed me incredible mercy by repeating the oath with her own subtle changes.

"Do you swear that anything you say will be the truth, the whole truth, and nothing but the truth?" she asked again.

"I do," I answered promptly, warmed a little on the inside. There was nothing funny here, and these proceedings were no joke, but I was so very *touched* at this unexpected kindness that I almost smiled. Almost.

Then back to the witness stand I went.

* * *

"Ms. Kilpatrick (I had not yet taken Larry's last name), are you telling me that you are going to defy my direct order to answer Mr. Wilson's questions?"

"With respect, your Honor, I cannot testify."

"You realize I can keep you incarcerated until you testify, and yet you still refuse?"

Struck dumb with panic, I looked at my attorney. It was irregular for an attorney to approach a witness without permission, but the circumstances were bizarre. The judge didn't stop Greg when he came over to me and whispered into my ear, "You can say or not say anything you want. If you want to answer questions, you can do that."

"I don't want to," I whispered back.

"Then you don't have to," he murmured, and he made his way back to his seat.

I looked at Prosecutor Wilson. He had one job to do: To convict and imprison Larry. Every question he asked me would be working towards that end. I couldn't answer his questions.

I don't know if I was brave or desperate when I took one more shot at explaining my situation to the judge.

"Your Honor, I respect the Court. I do. I am in an unthinkable situation. If I couldn't testify yesterday, then today there are even more reasons that I cannot. I am a volunteer at the jail, and I've been bringing church services to the ladies there. Last night I was informed I will no longer be allowed to do that. That hurts the women in our jail, and I'm afraid the damage is done.

"In addition, my job requires my life to be above reproach regarding the law, and so now my job is in jeopardy. If this continues, I will lose it for sure. It is therefore imperative that my husband not lose his business as well. I didn't testify yesterday because I love my husband and I don't believe he should go to prison. That reason holds true today, and the additional things I've just explained make it more impossible for me to testify than ever."

"So you are determined, then, to refuse to answer this man's questions?" he queried forcefully.

I quaked as I responded, "I can't testify, your Honor."

The courtroom was deathly silent. I held my breath.

"Ms. Kilpatrick," Judge Jordan then intoned, "I have given this a lot of thought. Once again, I've considered lesser ways to convince you that you must testify. I've considered suspending your court reporter's license."

WHAT????

"I've also considered fining you a thousand dollars a day until you consent to speak."

The blood literally drained from my face and I was instantly dizzy, nauseous. I searched for the arm of the chair and held on, hoping I wouldn't faint.

As the room swam before me, I heard his voice rumbling on. To me, each word sealed my earlier sense of doom into place. I barely caught up with him when he said at last, "But I think the only thing that will persuade you of the gravity of your situation is to return you to jail. Tomorrow being Friday, court will not be in session. I hereby remand you to the Sheriff's custody until Monday afternoon at 3:30 p.m., at which time I hope you'll have changed your mind. This court is adjourned."

Boom went the gavel. I was going back to jail.

Four more days. Five if you counted what was left of today.

You know those tower rides that take you straight up, really high, pause for a few seconds, and then let you *fall?*

My insides felt like *that.*

I was falling through a sickening hole, but I had nothing buckling me in, and this ride had no end in sight.

* * *

I didn't notice the courtroom emptying out. By the time I realized the bailiff was standing next to me, I saw that we were alone. He didn't order me over to the door to cuff me this time. He'd brought me here in shackles, but the chains were still in the jury room. He told me to return to the jury box and wait for him to come for me.

I wondered idly where everyone had gone in such a hurry, but I didn't put a lot of effort into my musings. I was staring into space, my mind grappling with the certainty that I had to return to my cell.

"Oh, doggone it!"

Who was that?

I focused my eyes and sought the source of the voice I'd heard. There, on the far side of the room, was the kindly clerk. She sounded frustrated. Because there wasn't anyone around to object, I spoke to her.

"What's wrong?" I asked.

She looked up at me, slightly harried. "Oh, the printer is jammed and there's nothing I can seem to do with it. I need to get the judge's order printed, but it won't let me."

Immediately, without plan or warning, I saw in my mind's eye a very happy angel, sitting on an invisible chair above the printer, wings relaxed on either side of him. To my absolute delight, the vision in my head advanced as the angel gleefully stuck his finger into the printer's inner workings!

AND THEN I KNEW!!! *I WAS GOING HOME!!!*

I had no doubt at all. I'd been waiting to see what God would do, and *He was doing it!* It seemed His plan didn't involve more time in jail for me, after all!

I had lots of courage now, and called out to the clerk, "Stop trying to fix it! They're negotiating in the hall!" *How did I know that?*

She was startled. "They are?"

"Yes!" I was exultant, quite certain.

In a flash she ran through the courtroom and out into the hallway. A moment later, she zoomed back through, this time past her own station and into the judge's chambers. So I was right! And she wanted to catch the judge before he left!

I was going home!

A minute later Greg entered the courtroom and took a seat next to me in the jury box, a smile on his face.

"This is over," he said. "You'll be home for dinner."

I know, I know, I know! I was already quietly celebrating.

"What happened?" I asked a little giddily.

"The prosecutor accepted the plea deal that Larry's attorney has been asking for all along," he explained. "Just in time, too, because I was on my way home to call CNN. I didn't do it last night. I didn't want to anger the judge in case he was just testing your resolve. But after he decided to send you back, I planned to go national with it."

How had we gotten from Channel 7 to CNN? He registered my look of surprise, and said, "That wouldn't have been a good thing for you, for your life to become a big news story, but it came very close to that."

I nodded, thinking of the implications. I shuddered to think of the story's headlines, but that would have been better than months behind bars.

As we waited for the other parties to re-enter the courtroom, Greg chatted with me some. He spoke more freely, now that I was in safer waters.

"I expect you had a pretty rough night."

"Yeah," I agreed. "I didn't think they'd make me stay alone."

"You were in a cell *alone?*" he asked incredulously.

"Yes." I didn't elaborate. I'd hated being alone in my cell, but I knew I had needed to be alone in my cell so I could hear what the Lord had to say to me today. I didn't know if Greg would understand, though, so I held that part close.

He was shaking his head, and after a few seconds he said, without malice, "I've always thought that judges who have the power to put people in jail ought to spend a weekend there themselves, so they know what they're consigning people to."

I grinned. Grinning was easier now. I wondered if any judges had ever actually done that. It didn't seem likely.

* * *

All the parties resumed their places in the courtroom. Larry looked nervous. I remained in the jury box, not yet released from custody.

"All rise." We stood, and Judge Jordan flowed back into the courtroom and took his seat at his bench.

What followed involved a considerable amount of procedure, which I will spare you. Drew and Prosecutor Wilson made small speeches, and ultimately agreed that they had reached a plea, and that Larry wished to plead guilty to domestic assault, a misdemeanor. Part of the agreement stressed that Larry would be sentenced to no more than thirty days in jail.

The difficult part came when the judge required Larry to actually plead guilty and explain his crime in detail. His voice shook and cracked several times. He cleared his throat a lot, as he was prone to do when nerves betook him. But he was determined, and he got through it.

The judge was satisfied for the moment and set a date for sentencing.

At last, the part I was waiting for:

"As all parties have come to an agreement regarding a plea in this case, I hereby render Ms. Kilpatrick's contempt of court moot, and order that she be released from the Sheriff's custody. This court is adjourned."

Boom went the gavel.

I was free.

* * *

Well, what do you know! The printer worked just fine now. It finally printed out the original order sending me back to jail, the order that had been stuck, but it was followed promptly by the order releasing me instead. The bailiff scooped up the paperwork, as I chatted with Larry and Pastor Mark. Larry asked me what I wanted for dinner.

"Steak," I said immediately. They both laughed, and Larry told me he'd pick it up while I got processed out, and he'd be at the jail soon to get me.

Back in the jury room, the bailiff told me he would bind the shackles loosely. Protocol required that I wear them, but everything was different now. Since they weren't tight, I wasn't quite as miserable in them.

Quite the pro now at getting into the pint-sized back seat of the Sheriff's cruiser, I needed no assistance. I was lighter than air. I was going home! I kept picturing the vision of the angel, and couldn't keep the smile off my face. The Lord was with me! I believed with my whole heart that the Holy Spirit had revealed to me a for-real angel who was having fun while helping me out.

On the ride back to the jail, I received an unexpected surprise from the bailiff. He was a quiet man, and he kept his thoughts to himself as he carried out his duties. But now I was no longer a prisoner, and he could speak.

Looking at me in his rearview mirror, he said, "I want you to know I really admire you. I respect both the love you have for your husband, and the way you've carried yourself throughout this thing. I think most women would have said, 'Just go hang the man.' They wouldn't have done what you did." His eyes returned to the road as he finished quietly with, "I thought you should know."

I really couldn't absorb such kindness. Again and again, I was learning that a lot of people were paying attention to my drama, and not all of their opinions were bad. In fact, except for the judge, I hadn't heard *anyone* say a negative thing.

I had to hand this one over to the Lord. We've seen my weakness, my fear, and my misery throughout these traumatic events. If anyone saw anything good in me during my ordeal, I knew categorically that what they saw was the strength and grace of Jesus Christ. Staring out the window with news eyes, I thanked God that His power is made perfect in weakness.

* * *

I walked into booking, still in my shackles. Sergeant Green gave me a sad look, silently saying he was sorry I was back.

"No!" I cried happily. "I'm being released!"

Then he was all smiles, and as soon as my chains were off, he led me to my cell to clear it out. I couldn't keep my notebook, so I carefully tore out all of the pages containing my jail journal and tucked them into my Bible. I wanted to keep that Bible. It was precious to me. Inmates weren't usually allowed to take books with them when they were released, but Sergeant Green, after a moment's hesitation, said I could keep it. He then left to attend to some other business, so I stripped down the bed and took off my sweatshirt. I put everything into my tote, which now sat in Someone Else's Personal Arctic Circle.

I signed for my belongings at the desk, gratefully slipping into my green sweater shell. I slid my wedding ring back onto my finger, where it belonged, and replaced my watch and earrings.

At last, with my release papers clutched in one hand and my Bible in the other, I followed a deputy through the corridors to the exit I was most accustomed to – through the *front* of the jail.

As I was about to leave, though, Sergeant Green came running down the hallway, calling my name.

"Diana, hang on a second. Listen, I can't promise anything, but don't give up on coming in for church services. We're going to have a special meeting to discuss it. Don't plan to come this Sunday, but just don't give up. Okay?"

My spirit lit up even more!

Anointed and qualified to preach the Gospel of good tidings to the meek, the poor, and afflicted; He has sent me to bind up and heal the brokenhearted, to proclaim liberty to the physical and spiritual captives, and the opening of the prison and of the eyes to those who are bound.

God made me two promises while I was in jail. He was keeping the first one before I even left the building. I was sure I already knew what the outcome of the special meeting would be.

And we know that in all things

God works for the good

of those who love him,

who have been called

according to his purpose.

(Romans 8:28 NIV)

CHAPTER **EIGHTEEN**

I awoke the next morning to pre-dawn darkness. I'd been dreaming that I was still in jail. I ran my hands along soft sheets and reached up to feel a lovely pillow beneath my head, assuring myself that it was only a dream, and that I was really home.

I could hear the sound of water in the bathroom. Larry was up and getting ready to go to work. I lay still a bit longer, remembering all that had happened after I walked out of the jail's interior, late yesterday afternoon.

Larry had put money on my books at the jail so that, should my stay be prolonged, I'd be able to make commissary purchases. When I was released and walked out into the lobby, I found that Larry was already there, chatting with the jail clerk (not to be confused with the judge's clerk who'd helped me out in court). This woman, a cheerful lady named Peggy, was in full throttle when I emerged.

"We couldn't believe it!" she was saying to Larry. "We were all searching online to see if it was legal to put her in jail. And you know what? We couldn't find a single instance in the history of the county where this kind of thing has happened before!"

Peggy spotted me and included me in the conversation. "Women *never* testify against their husbands. *Never!* And none of them were ever put in jail! We couldn't figure it out!"

She stopped to hand Larry a check which refunded the money he'd put on my books, and then continued, looking right at me. "And *you*," she exclaimed, "you were so quiet!"

They'd noticed me?

"So many women cry, and will even become hysterical when they are put in those cells. But you didn't make a sound!"

She'd obviously missed my singing, but point taken. I hadn't made any unhappy noises. I was more thankful than ever that I hadn't kicked the door and screamed. Unbeknownst to me, people *were* paying attention. I was so glad that I, as a Christian, as a leader of jail church services, had behaved myself!

A few minutes later I walked out of the county jail a free woman. I was tired, I was hungry, and I was deliriously happy that this *thing,* this unavoidable mountain in my road, was behind me. The Lord didn't remove it, and He didn't let me step around it. I was clearly meant to scale it, but not alone. In my darkest moments, the Spirit brought songs to me, gave me promises, encouraged me through the words of others, and, I believe, sent an angel to jam a printer.

When Larry and I got to his truck, the first thing I noticed was my cell phone dangling from his charger. He had it fired up and ready for me. Smiling hugely, I reached for the phone and called Amy. She already knew of my release, because of course Larry had sent text messages to my family. She picked up immediately.

After some celebratory preamble, I mentioned that the jail's clerk told us that, in the history of our county, she could find no record of another crime victim being locked up for refusing to testify. If true, then I was the first.

"Of *course!* Of *course it would be you!*" Amy cried a little hysterically. "The *one woman!* The *one woman* who might actually *get* something out of it, might learn something valuable from it! Of *course* it was you!"

Poor Amy was so relieved that I was out, so happy, and at the same time she was battling tears and massive emotions. Yesterday, Larry had sent her a dreaded text that said only, "They took your mom to jail."

As a high school Spanish teacher, she wasn't technically allowed to use her cell phone during class. But Amy knew we were
in court, knew the stakes were high, and so she'd kept her phone
close at hand and saw the text immediately. The news that I'd
been hauled off to jail struck her so hard, she told me, that she
had to flee from the classroom where she was teaching, run to
the teacher's break room, where she completely lost it. She said
when she did manage to get back to class, her students each had
to come up and read their assignment to the class while she,
their teacher, looked on with unchecked tears streaming down
her face.

When I got home, I called my younger daughter, Bethany,
and I learned that she'd been unable to sleep a wink the night
before. All she could do was toss and turn and think about where
her mom was.

I couldn't believe the pain my ordeal had put my family
through. How terrible! I was so thankful it hadn't lasted any
longer, now for their sakes as much as for my own.

* * *

I'd been home about two hours. So far I'd spoken to both
of my daughters, and also another young woman, Megan, with
whom I had a weekly telephone appointment. Megan was in
prison, and every Thursday at 7:00 p.m. she called me. Normally,
I listened to all Megan was learning and working through in her
prison program, but tonight it was her turn to listen to me.

When I told her I'd just come home from jail myself, and told
her the reasons why, she cried, "Oh, I hurt for you! My heart is
hurting for you!"

Here was a young woman in prison herself, a woman with
three small children and lots of pain and problems in her own
life, and *she* hurt for *me?*

She was sad that I'd been kept alone, and told me if I'd been
in one of the blocks, the other ladies could have shown me how

to be more comfortable. She was so sweet and caring. Megan touched my heart in that phone call. At last, some very real, hot tears not only stung my eyes, but finally rolled down my cheeks. I'm an after-crisis crier, remember. I'd tried to hold it together over these last days, but kindness blasted right through my not-so-stiff upper lip and opened the floodgate.

I was trying to mop myself up enough to eat the steak Larry had grilled for me, when the phone rang yet again. This time it was Sergeant Green calling with news for me. The board had already convened their special meeting regarding my status, even though it was evening, and they unanimously decided *not* to revoke my privileges to enter the jail as a volunteer!

"You can still come and hold church services! You can even come this Sunday if you want to!" His voice was clearly happy with the outcome, and I could tell he was pleased to have good news to give me.

It was a day of miracles, from the moment the lights came on and *Here With You* dropped into my head, to my zap from Holy Ghost jumper cables in my cell, to a reversal in the courtroom, and now to a complete restoration of jail privileges.

It certainly wasn't an easy day, but it was a day that had God's fingerprints all over it.

PART **FIVE**

THE BEGINNING

Do not be anxious about anything,

but in every situation,

by prayer and petition, with thanksgiving,

present your requests to God.

(Philippians 4:6 NIV)

CHAPTER **ONE**

Larry was scheduled to be sentenced five weeks after my own release. He had a number of different assignments to complete, including counseling, a psychological evaluation, ongoing AA meetings, et cetera.

I, on the other hand, had my own dilemmas to face.

First, I had to face my fear of returning to the confines of the jail for church services. I broke into a cold sweat every time I even thought about it. Patty and I had a rotating schedule in place, so that we each got every third Sunday off. The Sunday after my incarceration was my normal Sunday off, so I had over a week to prepare myself.

Throughout that week, I murmured Joyce Meyer's oft-quoted and highly appropriate advice, telling myself to, "Do it afraid." God hadn't walked me through everything so I would turn around and grow cold feet. I knew He'd called me into jail ministry. I hoped that one day He would allow me to go into prisons, too. I wasn't going to let a little fear get in the way of that.

The second thing I found myself wrestling with was some after-shock, if you will. I struggled with recurring dreams about being sent back to jail. I cried when I had to put the leash on our dog Sienna. The chain reminded me of my shackles, and I battled my emotions every time she needed to go out.

The hardest part for me was the day of actual sentencing for Larry. Pastor Mark, along with several members of our church family, came along for moral support. The audience section was also jam-packed with high-school students who had a Court Observation Day. Larry was the last person on the docket, and we'd seen the judge hand down harsh sentence after harsh sentence all day long. We'd heard defendant after defendant make the same case and provide the same arguments for leniency that Larry planned to make.

"I've been to AA. I've been to church. I've found Jesus. I've changed."

We heard it so often I feared the judge would be immune to declarations of transformation. In Larry's case, the change was real. *So* real. Surely my own unwillingness to testify demonstrated that. But would Judge Jordan believe it?

He didn't. He threw the book at Larry and said if it were up to him, he'd give Larry even more than the thirty days allowed under the plea. But the judge knew that if he did that, Larry could withdraw the plea agreement, and we'd be right back to another prelim, with yours truly on the witness stand. Apparently no one wanted that.

Judge Jordan sentenced Larry to thirty days in jail, with credit for two days served. The evening and the morning Larry spent in jail after the gun incident counted as two days. The judge did give him approval for work release. This meant that, though he must spend every night and every Sunday in jail, he would be allowed to go to work for nine hours a day the other six days of the week.

The judge even, at the last moment, took what he termed "a leap of faith," and gave Larry a withheld judgment. That meant that no crime would go onto Larry's permanent record if he kept out of trouble successfully for two years.

Those were good things, absolutely. But though the judge allowed all the other defendants to turn themselves in to the jail at a pre-determined date, it seemed he was still irritated with us. He ordered Larry taken into custody immediately, right there in front of our church members and all the kids.

* * *

Maybe we should have seen it coming, but Drew, Larry's attorney, had been sure the judge would only give him a couple of weekends in jail. In no way were we prepared for the harsh sentence Larry was handed, and I experienced the heartbreak and loss known to every person who finds a loved one led away, unexpectedly, in handcuffs.

Larry managed to call me that night and tell me what time he'd be released in the morning to go to work. The next morning, I brought Larry's truck, along with Sienna and a travel mug of hot coffee, and met Larry in the jail's parking lot. He climbed into the truck, fell into my arms, and wept. Huge, heaving sobs wracked his frame.

Finally, a very concerned Sienna nosed her way between us so she could lick his face, and he was able to smile, the crisis over.

And it really was over. From that point on, Larry endured his sentence with amazing cheerfulness and resilience. On that first morning I drove him to work. His employee would then drive me home, and then return the truck to the lab. Henceforward, Larry would use it to commute.

He had to turn himself back in at 4:00 p.m., and so I met him across the street from the jail's entrance. He parked his truck, gave Sienna back to me, and walked inside. Our pattern was established.

Each morning I brought coffee and Sienna to his truck. He gave me a kiss, thanked me for the coffee, and took himself to work. We never chatted. He had to go straight to work or risk losing his work-release privileges. If he lost those, he'd lose his business.

Larry was a model inmate. He stayed out of trouble, did as he was told, and went to bed early. I couldn't believe it when he told me he was actually able to sleep at night, since he's taller and larger than I am. How could he sleep on those narrow bunks? But his body demanded it, and he said he slept well on most nights.

He was always up early. He showered, and was either reading his Bible or cleaning the block when the time came for him to leave for the day. They actually had to tell him at one point to quit cleaning, as the other inmates were expected to help with that!

Since Larry had a thirty-day sentence, he was entitled to apply for early release, or what inmates call "good time." That meant that, if he was rewarded for good behavior, he could shave five days off his time. When he first began his sentence, he was told he couldn't apply yet, because they didn't know if his time would be "good" or not. He had to be good for at least two weeks before they would consider his application.

After two weeks, he finally applied, and then he was told that he'd waited too long! They couldn't process the application in the week and half left before his early out should start!

That was disheartening, but we decided there was nothing to be lost by trying, so he turned it in anyway. We heard nothing for a week. Larry made some careful inquiries and learned that each and every guard had to sign off on his application. That took quite some time, due in large part to varying schedules and shifts. All the sergeants had to sign it. Captain Harris had to sign it. At the time of Larry's inquiry, the guards had signed it, but it was sitting in one sergeant's inbox, and he was away!

Then the improbable became the impossible. We learned that not only must the staff at the jail sign the paper, but the prosecutor *and the judge* must also sign it.

By now it was Wednesday, and Larry had served twenty-two days of his sentence. Tomorrow would be twenty-three days, and that, plus his two days' credit for time served, gave him twenty-five days. He wouldn't have to serve the final five days of his thirty-day sentence if his good time came through. With good time, he could be out tomorrow.

That looked unlikely, though. Nobody thought there was enough time for the sergeants, the captain, the prosecutor and the judge to decide in favor of Larry's good time and sign his paper.

One friend at church, who had been at Larry's sentencing and heard the judge's harsh tone, warned me not to get my hopes up.

"Diana," he said, "I heard the way the judge spoke to Larry. He wanted to give Larry *more* time than the plea allowed. There is no way he's going to sign off on a reduction in Larry's sentence."

We were hearing a great big NO everywhere we turned. On this, the day before he hoped to get out, Larry finally called Captain Harris personally and asked him what his chances were. Captain Harris said he did have the document in his possession and that he had signed it. He cautioned Larry, though, that that didn't always mean early release. It was up to the prosecutor and the judge, and they would have to see it, sign it, and return it to the jail by tomorrow. It looked hopeless.

* * *

Thursday morning dawned, and I was up early, preparing to take Larry's dog and coffee to the jail for what I had hoped would be the last time. I had a job in Twin Falls, but it would only take a portion of the day. After I saw Larry briefly, I returned home and took up a prayer project.

As I'd done in my jail cell, I used Scripture to help me pray.

I read Philippians 4:6, which in the Amplified it says you needn't fret or have anxiety, but you can, *with thanksgiving*, make specific requests to the Lord.

I started there. I spent a considerable amount of time giving thanks. I thanked the Lord for everything I could think of. We had our health, after all. We had our jobs. We had each other!!! We were saved and headed to heaven! We had our family and our home and our church. We lived in a free country and could worship God as we chose. I gave thanks that the prosecutor had agreed to Larry's plea rather than making me stay in jail. Since we were nearing the end of Larry's sentence, I gave thanks again for the withheld judgment. If Larry stayed out of trouble for two years, the Court could dismiss his case outright, and he'd have no record!

You get the idea. I had so much to be thankful for, and I spent time expressing it.

Now for the next part.

As I knelt before my coffee table, I opened my Bible to Matthew 7 and read verse 7 aloud to the Lord several times.

> *Keep on asking and it will be given you;*
> *keep on seeking and you will find;*
> *keep on knocking [reverently] and*
> *[the door] will be opened to you.*
>
> (Matthew 7:7 AMP)

I love the Amplified. It makes things so clear. Keep on! Don't ask once and quit. Ask in faith, and ask often!

I read James 4:3 to God:

> *When you ask, you do not receive,*
> *because you ask with wrong motives,*
> *that you may spend what you get on your pleasures.*
>
> (AMP)

Right! I must check my motives. Did my request line up with God's character? Was I being greedy? Selfish?

Yes, no, and no. God is good, and I saw no problem with asking Him to have mercy on Larry by springing him five days early. I didn't feel greedy. I didn't feel selfish. I was asking on Larry's behalf, after all.

I then turned to Psalm 66 and read verse 18 to Him. I wanted to cover all the bases!

If I regard iniquity in my heart,
the Lord will not hear me.

(AMP)

I had to be quiet and wait on this one. I knew that if I was serious about praying and believing for Larry's early release, I couldn't pray with a dirty heart. I asked the Lord to convict me if there was unknown sin in my heart that I should deal with.

Judge Jordan's face popped immediately into my mind, and I cringed. I knew I needed to forgive him. I knew that the judge had not acted illegally when he locked me up. Whether or not he *should* have done so is probably not for me to say. I'd been trying hard to keep bitterness at bay, but I think we can agree that the judge's decision to send me to jail had caused me considerable trauma. I was still working through the after effects of it.

So I asked the Lord how I should forgive a person who, technically, hadn't done anything wrong. And I asked Him further, saying, "If I say I forgive him, how can I mean it? Even the thought of the judge's *voice* alarms me."

Pray for him.

Such a simple instruction. Could that really work? Would praying for the judge change even the unexpressed, hidden hurt in my heart?

Well, I was on a prayer mission, with a definite goal, so I knew I must be obedient in everything. I wanted my prayer to hug close the Bible in every aspect. I set myself to pray for Judge Jordan. I prayed for the Lord to bless him, to lead him to salvation if he didn't have it yet; I prayed that he would have a wonderfully smooth day, and that even his wife would say something special to him; I prayed for the staff at the courthouse to be kind and helpful; I prayed for his inner peace and also that he would have great wisdom in handling his docket that day.

I prayed and prayed. And you know what? It did help. I found my heart less tremulous as I fixed Judge Jordan's face in my mind's eye. I found I couldn't pray sincerely for blessings and retain even unacknowledged bitterness in my heart.

So then I was back to the promises Jesus spoke, reading Matthew 7, verse 8:

> For everyone who keeps on asking receives;
> and he who keeps on seeking finds;
> and to him who keeps on knocking,
> [the door] will be opened.

(Matthew 7:8 AMP)

I had done all I knew to do. My motives were pure. My heart was clean. I was thankful for so, so much. Now it was time to keep on asking.

* * *

On the drive to Twin Falls, I reminded myself, every ten minutes or so, to ask again. This was the day we needed an answer, so I dedicated the whole day to my prayer. I did have to work, but at breaks I lifted my request again before God's throne. On the drive home, same thing. Frequently I said aloud, "I'm back, Lord! I will keep my request before You until either You answer me with a yes, or Larry goes back in. Then I'll know Your answer was no. Until then, I'm praying!"

I did everything I could that day to demonstrate active faith. Larry and I share an electric toothbrush, and we switch the heads when it's our turn to use the base unit. My toothbrush head had been on the holder for 23 days now. This morning, however, I took it off and put Larry's on, in faith that tomorrow morning he'd be here to use it.

When I got back into town from Twin Falls, I stopped at the store and bought some fresh food so Larry would have a nice meal this evening "when" he got out.

Arriving back home at three in the afternoon, I parked my car on my side of the garage. I'd been taking my half out of the middle for three and a half weeks, but "when" Larry came home he'd need to be able to pull his truck in.

I went upstairs and voiced some more prayers to the Lord. Then it was a matter of waiting. I called Larry. He'd heard nothing. At 3:45 he was driving south from work, and said I should just meet him and get the dog. Clearly, his request for good time wasn't coming through.

I dawdled around the living room and kitchen all the same, not wanting to leave. I'd been praying all day that Larry would come home to me today, that I wouldn't have pick up Sienna and watch him disappear inside.

This Sunday was his birthday, and Sunday was the one day inmates were not allowed out on work release. If he didn't get his good time, he'd be inside the jail all day on his birthday. Not the end of the world, I know, but that had been a huge motivation for my by-the-Book prayer project.

I had to be at the jail by 3:55 or Larry would have to leave Sienna in the truck and go in anyway, trusting that I'd be there soon to get her. It's a five-minute drive to the jail. I looked at my watch. 3:49. Okay. That was it, then. I had to go. I turned to pick up my car keys just as my phone rang. It was Larry.

"I'M OUT!!!!" he cried. "Grizz just called me! Looks like the judge signed the order! I can't believe it! I'm out! Haha!" He was joyful, and I started dancing around the house. What a celebration! I would have such a wonderful story to tell him when he got home!

We hung up so he could go inside and get processed out. I skipped around, thanking the Lord, and then I fell to my knees.

"You did this, Lord," I proclaimed, looking up. "I don't believe for a minute that Larry would have been released early except that You heard me. You intervened, You touched the judge's heart, and You sped Larry's application along. Thank You,

Lord! Help me, Lord, to always keep my heart clean, so that I'll be ready to pray like I prayed today, in season and out, at a moment's notice."

Larry was coming home! I laughed as I added one obvious, but very fun fact aloud to God, "I won't even have to move my car!"

I, even I, am He Who blots out

your transgressions for My own sake,

and I will not remember your sins.

(Isaiah 43:25 NKJV)

CHAPTER **TWO**

Five nights later Larry returned with me to our final night of the School of Ministry. He'd missed six weeks when we were separated, and he'd just missed three more Monday nights, but Pastor Mark told him if he did make-up work by watching a series of teaching videos, he could graduate with the rest of us.

It was a relaxed evening, and the biggest thing on the agenda was prayer for each student. Pastor Mark and his co-leader prayed over each student in turn, and when they came to Larry and me, they prayed for us not individually, but as a couple.

It was nearly the end of May, and over the last months we'd been through a lot together. When I say "we," I include our schoolmates. Larry and I weren't the only ones who had walked through personal difficulties during the two-year period of our Bible school. We'd all shared together, we'd cried at times, and we'd deepened the sense of family that we first experienced when we played our songs for each other.

Over the course of our reconciliation and renewed relationship, Larry and I had agreed that we should renew our marriage vows, once everything had settled down. As our pastor's prayer for us concluded, that night at our Bible school, Larry looked me in the eye, holding my hand tightly in his, and asked, "Will you marry me?"

My sin was forgiven and gone. Larry's sin was forgiven and gone. Legal pressures and consequences were behind us. It was time to begin brand new lives together on the rock solid foundation of Jesus.

My beloved spoke and said to me,

Arise, my darling, my beautiful one,

and come with me.

See! The winter is past;

The rains are over and gone.

(Song of Songs 2:10-11 NIV)

CHAPTER **THREE**

I wanted to wear purple. It was my favorite color, and since this was a renewal, and not a wedding, I figured I could wear what I wanted.

I found a calf-length, deep purple dress with a flowing skirt that I thought was perfect. Since our renewal was to be held in February, I also wore a thin ivory-colored cardigan as part of my ensemble, and finished the outfit with some stylish, camel-colored boots.

I made an appointment with my friend Juliette, who had offered a room to me when I was at my most desperate. She was not only my friend, but also my hairstylist, so on the morning of my wedding she arranged my hair in an elaborate updo that fitted the occasion to a tee. She then ran home to change clothes so she could attend our renewal herself.

We invited our entire church, as well as our other friends and neighbors.

We planned the ceremony down to the last detail. We chose flowers and music, and, with the help of some dear friends, made the church ready.

As a surprise for Larry, I created a video using pictures taken throughout our 15-plus years together. I set it to the music of Keith Green's beautiful song, *When I Hear the Praises Start*, and whenever I watched it myself I couldn't hold back the tears.

I chose other meaningful songs to be played during different parts of the ceremony. Amy wrote a song for us, but she lived in California, had two very young sons, and we all knew that getting her to Idaho would be impossible. I didn't press her about it. Since traveling to Idaho couldn't happen, she went to great pains to make a video of her song so that everyone could watch it, part way through the service, via the internet.

I wasn't allowed to hear her song ahead of time. I knew only the title, *This is the Beginning*. I couldn't wait to see the video and hear the whole song!

As the time for our renewal finally arrived, Larry and I stood in the church's foyer to greet our guests. This was no formal wedding where I, as the bride, needed to remain hidden while everyone was seated. This was a celebration! We wanted to thank everyone for coming. And our friends did come! Friends, neighbors, and our church family filled the sanctuary.

When everyone was seated, Larry and I stood in the back while my music/picture video played. The song was so lovely, the pictures so "us," that Larry barely held himself together. When it finished playing, we marched forward, waving to everyone, and took our seats.

The ceremony went as planned at first, but a major snag hit right before Amy's video was meant to play. We were all supposed to see her on the big screen, playing the song she'd written. That was when Pastor Mark, who was supposed to introduce the video, said there'd been a change in plan.

I was horrified! I'd worked so hard to make sure the ceremony would be flawless! I'd printed the exact order of things and handed it out to all of our helpers. Why would someone, without consulting me, change anything at all? And Amy's video was the pivotal point in the ceremony! She'd gone to such effort to make sure we had it!

My eyes drilled into Pastor Mark's face, but he wasn't looking at me. Was he avoiding my gaze? What was *up?*

My mind snapped back into place so I could hear what Pastor Mark's next words would be. They'd better be good!

They were.

"We won't be playing the video Amy made for us at this time. Instead, we'd like to invite her to come on up here and sing for us in person."

Now Pastor Mark looked at me, eyes twinkling as he grinned broadly. I whipped my head around to the rear of the sanctuary, and there stood my own daughter! Amy, who was up to her ears in work and motherhood, and who, I thought, couldn't come. Amy, who had called me the night before, supposedly still in California and battling with her two-year old at bedtime. Amy, who had just pulled off the biggest surprise of my life!

She beamed as she walked up the aisle and took a seat on a stool that was perfectly placed on the platform. Now I could see that some orchestration had gone on here, probably while I was getting my hair done! I noted that Amy was holding my own guitar! When had she arrived? Happy tears formed in my eyes and were threatening my makeup when Larry leaned over to me and said, "You can go hug her."

He was right! By standing on formality, I'd remained sitting on my chair! But we were just among friends here, so I jumped up and rushed into my daughter's open arms. Then, wiping my eyes carefully, I returned to my seat. Amy proceeded to knock our socks off with a beautiful, hope-filled song about how we'd made Jesus our foundation, and were writing our happy ending with the promise of our hearts.

It was a perfect day. My daughter Bethany truly couldn't make it, but she'd called, and I could feel her love and presence through the miles, too.

After the ceremony we all adjourned to our townhome community's clubhouse. We had provided lots of yummy food for everyone, with a gorgeous cake as the centerpiece. On top of the cake were a tiny bride and groom, high-fiving each other. On each of their upraised wrists there dangled a miniature set of handcuffs. We couldn't resist.

Six days later, as he'd promised, Larry and I flew to Maui for the honeymoon we'd never had.

We were truly a couple at last. We were in love with the Lord and with each other. We'd come through fire together. We'd seen our weakness and God's strength. We were healed and at peace, confident in the Lord, ready for the next chapter.

The words of Amy's song express it best:

> *Now our story is one of forgiveness and grace*
> *For those who would seek*
> *A testimony of God's mercy and strength*
> *When His children are weak.*
> *But God has a plan for our lives on this earth,*
> *Now together we stand,*
> *Finally knowing what this love is worth.*
>
> *And this is the beginning!*
> *This is where it starts.*
> *We can write our happy ending*
> *With the promise of our hearts.*
> *We made Jesus our foundation,*
> *Knowing we are not enough.*
> *Before God and all creation,*
> *We renew our vow of love.*

To which I say, "Amen!"

Let the redeemed of the Lord tell their story...

(Psalm 107:2 NIV)

EPILOGUE

Two years have passed since my incarceration, which was followed closely by Larry's own time behind bars. God has continued to teach us, build us up, and draw us closer to each other and to Himself.

One year ago, in late May of 2014, God once again demonstrated His tenderness, His knowledge of my inner workings, just as I began to write the first chapters of this book.

We'd traveled to California to see our family one year, almost to the day, after Larry's release from jail. While we were there, I visited my sister Dana and got to meet the newest member of her family, a tiny Chihuahua named Bella. I fell in love. I nearly stashed Bella in my purse when Dana wasn't looking. That little dog pointed to an area of my heart that remained bruised a year and half after I'd lost my own little dog, Jazzy.

Later that night, as I was trying to sleep, I found myself weeping, wondering how Dana could be so fortunate to have such a lovely little friend, while I still had empty dog beds in my office and bedroom at home. I realized that the time had come for me to find a friend, too, and finally let Jazzy go.

The next day we began our long drive home to Idaho, and the feeling grew stronger and stronger in me through the freeways of California and the deserts of Nevada. We finally stopped for the night in Jackpot, Nevada, thinking it best to divvy up the long drive. At dinner that night, I knew I couldn't keep it in any longer.

"Honey," I was tentative. We were doing so well, but I wasn't sure of the reaction I was going to get. "I think I'm ready to get another little dog. I think it's time."

Old Larry would have said, "No way. We have Sienna. We don't need another yappy little dog in our house."

New Larry said, "Really! What kind of dog do you have in mind?"

"I want a Chihuahua," I said softly.

"Do you!" Larry exclaimed, also softly. His eyes were kind. I expect he'd seen this day coming, though my own heart hadn't yet considered replacing Jazzy.

"I think that's an awesome choice," New Larry continued. "Where will you look?"

Would I *ever* get used to this kind, considerate, *nice* husband I now had?

"I'll try to find a young one who needs a home before I start looking for a puppy."

"Okay," he agreed. "Whatever you want to do, I'm with you."

And that was it. The next morning, while Larry was still asleep, I got out my iPad, did some research, and found the doggie that was clearly waiting just for me. She was ten months old, just three and a half pounds. She had a tiny face and huge ears and beautiful black eyes. She was black except for a white marking that covered her chest and crept halfway around her neck. She had a little white lightning streak running down her forehead.

Best of all, she was living in a home in Twin Falls, with lots of other little dogs in the care of Adopt-A-Pet. She'd never been in a kennel or dog pound of any kind, and Twin Falls was right on our way home!

We filled out the application online and stopped to see her only a few hours after my early-morning internet sleuthing. We loved her immediately, and she us. By evening we were able to bring her home. We named her Sophie, and the last vestiges of pain, after so much loss, were healed.

I like to say that God loves all of His creatures, and that I believe He was a heavenly matchmaker in bringing Sophie and me together.

Now, a year later, we are Dad, Mom, and two fur-kids. A very happy family.

* * *

I did re-enter the jail, "doing it afraid" at first, but now all of that is gone and I enter that facility with delight on Sundays.

At first I was hesitant to mention my own experiences to the inmates we met with. Eventually, however, I shared my story with them, detailing the sin, despair, and brokenness Larry and I had experienced. I also shared God's absolute redemption, His healing of our hearts, our marriage, and our walk with Him.

Now, as people leave the jail and new people arrive, I tell my story to each new group. I find it to be the most effective icebreaker in the world, as each inmate learns that the "church ladies" are not perfect, either; that, indeed, God had to rescue us and restore us, just as He is willing to do for them.

I have told my tale to the sad, the withdrawn, and the hard-hearted, and I have seen the Holy Spirit use it to break through and give them hope. I have never heard a single inmate say, "Your experience was short, so it doesn't count. You can't really understand us." On the contrary, they all say, "You *get* it! You know where we live, where we sleep, what we eat! You know what it's like to be before a judge, knowing your life is in his hands. You understand!"

At last I am ready to consider Joseph, who I'd been unwilling to think about while I was in jail. He walked through such extreme difficulties, but he stayed faithful to God. Though he'd been sold into slavery and thrown into prison, Joseph was able to say to his brothers, in Genesis 50:20:

> *But as for you, you meant evil against me;*
> *but God meant it for good,*
> *in order to bring it about as it is this day,*
> *to save many people alive.*

(Genesis 50:20 NKJV)

The Lord has planted within my heart a love for the incarcerated. The prisoner. And I believe it was, indeed, He Who allowed me to know first-hand what their lives are like behind bars. What a wonder it is that I was able to experience the fear, the powerlessness, the chains, the hard surfaces, even the food, and yet emerge without a record, and with my privileges to enter the jail intact. Who but God could orchestrate such an education?

Additionally, God has kept His second promise to me, the promise that Larry and I would be known as ministers of the Lord, plural. As of this writing, Larry has completed his training with Prison Fellowship Ministries. It was no easy thing for him to get clearance to go into the jail, but as two years have passed since his own incarceration, they agreed to speak with him about it. They saw the new man, my shiny New Larry, and they cleared him.

Larry and two teammates are now entering the jail for men's services every Sunday, immediately following the services we conduct with the ladies. Our own women's team has grown by two as well, so where there were two in jail ministry from our church, now there are seven.

God's goodness knows no bounds, and as Amy so aptly sang:

THIS IS THE BEGINNING.

* * *

AFTERWORD

On January 1, 2014, I knew that the time had come to write this book. Ten months had passed since my incarceration, and I was finally healing from the fear and trauma of the year before. I knew I needed to write my story down before more time had gone by, and while my memories were still fresh. I was aware of a gentle nudging from the Lord, setting my heart in the direction of getting my tale told.

I bought creative writing software. I bought books about writing books. I even wrote the first chapter. The rest of the book, however, took a year and a half to complete. I waded with some trepidation back through difficult memories. I avoided writing the most difficult chapters. Again and again, when I was tempted to give up, the Lord would send me fresh encouragement to keep at it, to get it done.

And so I carried on, plowing through memories both glorious and painful, and saw the manuscript through to completion. I received my first book contract on the very day that Larry's withheld judgment came through. Two years of exemplary living, and the judge signed the order. He now has no criminal record at all.

And so again, I can see the fingerprints of God.

Can you?

Blessings,

Diana Weinberger

THANK **YOU!**

Thank you for joining me in telling the story. If you liked the book and have a minute to spare, I would appreciate a short comment on the page or site where you bought the book.

Reviews from readers like you make a huge difference to helping new readers find stories similar to *When Mountains Don't Move.*

- Amazon
- Barnes & Noble
- Goodreads
- iBooks

Thank you!

Diana

ABOUT THE **AUTHOR**

Diana Weinberger has led a varied, adventurous life, from her days with YWAM and Mercy Ships, to her never-dull career as a court reporter and work in prison ministry. Formerly avid bikers, she and her husband Larry now enjoy the beauty of a lake house in Southern Idaho with their devoted dogs, Sophie and Sienna.

Follow Diana at:

Website: DianaWeinberger.com
Facebook: @dianaweinbergerbooks

Made in the USA
Lexington, KY
27 February 2018